IMPRISONED
IN
INDIA

IMPRISONED IN INDIA

CORRUPTION AND EXTORTION IN THE WORLD'S LARGEST DEMOCRACY

JAMES TOOLEY

Biteback Publishing

First published in Great Britain in 2016 by
Biteback Publishing Ltd
Westminster Tower
3 Albert Embankment
London SE1 7SP

Copyright © James Tooley 2016

ISBN 978-1-78590-101-0

10 9 8 7 6 5 4 3 2 1

A CIP catalogue record for this book is available from the British Library.

To Lisa and Nick Dunn

CONTENTS

CHAPTER 1

A REST IN HYDERABAD

ON 2 MARCH 2014, I returned to Hyderabad, India –
my first visit for two years. In the interim, I'd been working in
some of the world's most difficult places: South Sudan, Sierra
Leone, Liberia and northern Nigeria, as well as Ghana. It was
great to be back in India, where I knew I could rest in comfort
and security.

In a review of my book, *The Beautiful Tree*, I'd been described
as 'a 21st-century Indiana Jones', who travelled to 'the remot-
est regions on Earth researching something many regard as
mythical'. I liked that image of myself: intrepid, adventurous.
And the 'mythical' thing I was tracking? Private schools serving the poor. I called it 'grassroots privatisation' of education,

by the people, for the people. These schools were everywhere in the slums and villages of Africa, South Asia and Latin America. But because they were an initiative of the poor, nothing to do with international agencies or governments, they'd remained entirely unnoticed. My research changed that. Now, many people wanted to talk about them.

I'd first found these low-cost private schools in the slums of Hyderabad in 2000; I was back in this metropolis in south-central India because my friend Andrew Coulson of the Cato Institute was making a documentary for American television about educational entrepreneurship. He wanted to interview me where I'd first discovered these low-cost private schools, for an episode about school choice among the poor.

Hyderabad had prospered a lot in the fourteen years I'd been going there. India in general had grown wealthier; Hyderabad in particular had become a hub for high-tech industries. It boasted a new international airport and fancy highways. What had been slums where I'd first found these schools had often become presentable lower-middle-class neighbourhoods.

Coming back to India after a two-year absence felt like a holiday. It was a respite from the kinds of places I normally travel to, a chance to be somewhere safe and welcoming. It was also a relief being among like-minded people: my work is controversial and politically charged – it highlights how corruption and incompetence prevent governments from providing quality education for the poor. Government officials, not surprisingly, are often unsympathetic, and international aid organisations antagonistic. But this week in Hyderabad I could relax among old friends.

Andrew Coulson had booked me into a very swish hotel, the Park Hyatt in Banjara Hills, one of the most luxurious in Hyderabad. I normally stay in very simple places, but I can tolerate opulence if others are paying. I was joined by Sara and my niece, Alissa, who had been staying with Sara's family in east India as part of her gap year between school and university.

Sara's real name is Saraswati, after the goddess of knowledge, music and nature. She lets me shorten it to Sara. She has dark eyes, flowing dark hair, is beautiful, glamorous and vivacious. Somewhat surprisingly, to most people who see us together and especially to myself, she's my girlfriend. For the few years I've known her, she's been living in India running her family's schools, while I've been a professor in England. Long-distance relationships like this are hard to sustain. So it was particularly special for us to be together in Hyderabad, where we had first started seeing each other back in 2009 when I was more or less living there. Revisiting old haunts brought us close together. And in the evenings we had dinner and drinks with old friends, people such as Ayham from Lebanon, who bore the exciting news that he knew George Clooney's bride-to-be, Amal; Sara and Alissa were sure he could arrange an invitation for them to their wedding.

When everyone had gone to bed, Sara, Alissa and I stayed up talking and laughing into the night. We were surrounded by friends and family, in comfort, doing something meaningful to boot; it was, Sara and I agreed, our happiest time together.

We finished filming the documentary on Thursday 6 March. Alissa was leaving that evening for Thailand for the next leg of her gap year. Sara had booked a long weekend in Goa for us, flying early Friday morning. I seldom take holidays because I tend to feel guilty about having time off when there is so much work to be done, but I went along with it, for the sake of a peaceful existence. In any case, it was only a short break, I reassured myself, before I continued on to lecture in Delhi, then Dubai (sharing the platform with former president Bill Clinton), then on to Ghana and Sierra Leone to trouble-shoot in the schools I was running, before heading back to Newcastle University and then on to America. Business as usual. By the time Thursday arrived, however, I was feeling uncharacteristically relaxed and rather looking forward to our break.

Around 5 p.m. on Thursday evening, after we'd bid good-bye to Alissa, I got a call from Mohammed, who runs schools in the Muslim Old City. Someone from CID – the Criminal Investigation Department – had been to visit, and he had told her where I was staying. She was on her way to see me.

'Nothing to worry about, she's kind,' he said. 'She just wants to clarify a few issues.'

'Which issues?' I asked.

'About the Educare Trust.'

'Really?' I wondered why that had come up again.

Reluctantly, I went down to wait for her. Five-star hotels compete on how cold they can make it with their air conditioning, so I took my jacket with me, with my passport in one inside pocket, and notebook and pen in the other. People are often late in Hyderabad, so I also took my copy of Jad Adams's recent biography *Gandhi: Naked Ambition* to read while I waited.

I have a fascination with Gandhi. I like his ideas and the vigour with which he pursued them, but I don't like him as a person. He was too fastidious and prickly, unable to make even minor compromises to rub along with people. I was aware of the quip that 'it cost his friends a great deal of money to keep him in poverty' and felt irritated by him being so sanctimonious. But a new book was out about him, and I had to read it.

The CID arrived at 7 p.m., a policewoman in charge accompanied by her male assistant. She showed me her identification card: 'Mrs [name], Deputy Superintendent, Criminal Investigation Department'. We shall call her 'Mrs T. Mantra'. She was in her mid-forties and wore a sari of a dirty green colour ('the colour of algae', Sara said later). Her thin hair was tied into a ponytail and she was wearing a pair of old-fashioned, gold-rimmed spectacles. She wore a single gold bangle on each arm. Sara remarked later that Mrs Mantra had not been covering herself in a proper manner: the '*pallu*' of a sari should be pinned quite high on the shoulder, but she had it low, so it fell off her shoulder, 'exposing too much', as Sara put it. I can't say I noticed.

What I did notice, however, was her smile. Her huge smile was sweet and friendly.

Mantra treated her junior colleague in the way many official Indians treat their inferiors: with exasperation and impatience. I never got his name that night, nor during the whole period

I knew him. He was tall and dark, with a very kind, wearied face; his life had made him sympathetic to the world. His shirt, a formal half-sleeve, was untucked over his formal black trousers. He carried a cotton bag – the sort that villagers carry, a *theli* – which held assorted items used throughout the evening.

We sat together in the elegant hotel lobby, on luxurious leather chairs so deep that we had to lean well forward to hear each other. A fashion show was being prepared in the banqueting rooms; glamorous models accompanied by older women chaperones walked briskly past, flirtily catching the eyes of men seated in the comfy chairs, or at least that's how it appeared to the men.

Mantra explained why she had come. The Educare Trust, which I had set up in 2002, may have received some foreign currency without the proper approvals under the FCRA, the Foreign Contribution (Regulation) Act. Yes, I knew this may have been a problem. Two years ago, when I had last been in Hyderabad, someone from CID had asked me to visit Police Headquarters where I'd given a thorough statement. I'd found a lawyer, Vashnu, on the recommendation of one of the junior managers at the Taj Banjara, a business hotel in a nearby part of town. His advice was that the problem, if indeed there was a problem, was not serious; it was nothing to do with me anyway, as I was not running the trust day-to-day. The solution was simple: we should close the trust down (its work in any case had ceased) and that would be the end of it. With my statement given and the trust closed, I had assumed I would hear no more of the matter.

I told her all of this. 'Yes,' she said, smiling sweetly. 'But the officer you saw has retired. I've taken over his cases, but all his files are lost. Just make a statement again so I can close the case.' I explained that when I had made the earlier statement I had access to some trust documents, found in one of the schools. By now I'd forgotten such details and wasn't sure whether I'd be able to find any of the documents again.

'Don't worry,' she said. 'Make a statement from memory. We just need *something* to close the case.' Taking down my statement took a long time. She had brought sheets of legal-size paper and a pen, but spent considerable time getting her junior to rummage around in his cotton sack to find pins, and then to pin two sheets of paper together, with carbon paper between them, which he had to run around and find (presumably from their vehicle). She then laboriously wrote out what I was saying, but made many mistakes, which I had to correct, misunderstanding what I'd said, or sometimes even writing something completely different. She seemed very keen on being distracted too, looking around her, taking in the surroundings, not focusing on the task at hand.

She asked me about my work. I told her I was a professor at Newcastle University. Taking down the statement clearly bored her, and this seemed as good a subject as any to be diverted by: 'A good university?' she asked. Proudly, I told her it was a very good university, part of the Russell Group of elite research-based British universities. She seemed impressed, and she began to rummage around in her bag to find a photograph of her son. She had two sons, she told me. The older one was at one of the elite management schools in India doing an MBA, but her younger son was floundering in an indifferent school.

'He needs to go to a British university,' she said.

'That would be great,' I replied.

'A good British university will properly recognise his talents,' she said.

'I hope he finds one,' I said.

'One like yours,' she said.

'It's a very good university,' I agreed. 'Anyway,' (trying to get her back on task, aware that Sara and Andrew had just gone upstairs to dinner) 'I'm professor there, but my work focuses on researching the education of low-income families, in countries like' – and I listed the countries. She turned back to her pinned-together pages and laboriously wrote them all down.

'Are you married?' She asked, apropos of nothing.

'No,' I said.

'Then you can marry me,' she said matter-of-factly.

Flustered, I flunked my reply, making it seem that I was too interested in her personal life: 'You're *Mrs* Mantra, it says on your identity card, so how could I marry you?'

'I'm a widow,' she said, 'with two sons who need a father.'

I was lost for words, but she saved me: 'Don't worry, I joke. In India, once we're widowed we're finished.'

She was smiling all the time, and this smile that had beguiled Mohammed began to worry me.

It took two hours to finish my statement. Finally, she asked me for a copy of my passport, but I suggested that my driving licence was easier to find, and she said, 'OK'. My passport had been in my inside pocket all along, but I was not going to hand over even a copy of my passport to her! I was not that trusting.

As she was getting ready to leave, she said that I should come in to the police station the next day, in case details needed following up. I was reluctant to tell her too much – I've learnt never to be totally trusting of the police. In Ghana, a small boy had gone missing from one of our schools; after searching for twenty-four hours, we took the mother to the police station, and there he was, sitting forlornly in the officers' room. The police apparently had abducted him in order to get a bribe from the foreigner involved with the local schools. But that was Africa, this is India, 'Incredible India': a shining example to other emerging economies. I should be able to tell her the truth: 'I'm taking the weekend off. Can I come on Tuesday?'

'Yes, of course, Tuesday is fine,' she said packing up her papers, sharply criticising her sidekick for putting the papers in the bag in the wrong order, which turned out to be the right order, once he'd taken the papers out and shown her, although this didn't stop him getting criticised again.

It was after 9 p.m. I rushed upstairs to the restaurant and a terrific farewell dinner with my wonderful friends, entertained by a jazz duo. I was in bed by 11.30 p.m., to fall into a deep sleep.

At 1 a.m., the hotel room phone rang. 'The lady you spoke to this evening wants to have words with you again,' said the hotel duty manager.

I felt afraid immediately. How was I going to cope with this?

Clearly she had come to close the sexual deal that, it dawned on me, she had been hinting at all evening, what with all her talk of marriage and sons who need a father. Sara had difficulty waking up.

'What's wrong?' she said eventually.

'Mrs Mantra. She's back. I think she wants to sleep with me.'

Sara chuckled. 'Well, you'll have to shake her off.'

'She's not arresting me, is she?'

'No, don't be stupid. This is India, not...' and she made some disparaging remark about the kind of African country I work in.

Sara said she would watch from the window that overlooked the inner courtyard of the hotel. I tossed on my clothes and grabbed my jacket, but left my passport behind. 'Look after this,' I said. 'Just in case.'

'Don't be silly,' she responded. 'Just shake her off, but be kind about it. Unless you want something else!' Sara was flirting with me.

I took the lift downstairs. There was that wonderfully calm feel to the place; a grand hotel at night, winding down at the end of a long day; a couple of receptionists sleepily tidied up the day's accounts, and a sweeper slowly made her way around the lobby. Mrs Mantra was there, at the head of a group of six men in a triangle behind her. Her smile was still broad. One of the men approached from behind her, unsmiling, and said, 'Mr James Nicholas, we are arresting you.'

'They're arresting me,' I told Sara over the phone. Suddenly she was all action. I saw her dart away from her bedroom window, and in an instant she was down by my side.

The hotel duty manager, a diminutive man in his early thirties, asked for the arrest warrant. The police didn't have one. He conferred with someone by phone, then told the police that they couldn't arrest me without one. No one took any notice of him. Sara got angry with Mrs Mantra, telling her that she couldn't do this at one o'clock in the morning, without a warrant, and that she should come back tomorrow.

In the end, however much we remonstrated, I realised I had to go; the burlier of the policemen were getting ready to bundle me into their vehicle. I calmed Sara: 'It will be fine, I'll go and see her "higher-uppers".' (Me using such an Indian expression would normally make her chuckle. It had no effect this time.) 'We'll get the lawyer who closed the trust for us – Vashnu – to sort it all out for us. You remember him; have we got his number?'

Because I'd done nothing wrong, once I met with Mrs Mantra's superiors in the calmness of the police station, all would be easily resolved. 'Don't worry,' I reassured Sara. 'I've done nothing wrong.'

They had two police vehicles, dirty grey 4x4 Mahindra Scorpios; I got in one as indicated, sitting wedged between two of the burly men, Mrs Mantra in front. Sara was not allowed to come with us, but the quick-thinking duty manager got a limousine ready and Sara set out behind. Nights in Hyderabad at that time of year are cool; I was glad of my jacket, which I huddled into.

We drove through the Hyderabad streets, deserted apart from roving packs of howling dogs and the occasional meandering cow grazing on scattered rubbish; on some raised pavements, homeless families slept. I didn't know where I was going at the time, although the way was to become very familiar to me: to Lakdikapul, where the police and CID are headquartered. We turned into the driveway of an unimposing building and Mrs Mantra told Sara she couldn't come any further. Sara pleaded, but the decision was final. I tried to calm her.

'You can phone our lawyer as soon as you wake up.'

'How can I sleep?' she protested.

'You must,' I said. 'One of us needs to be fresh tomorrow.' Seeing she was not convinced, I said, 'Don't worry, it's going to be fine. I've done nothing wrong.'

We stood around in the cool air until Sara's car had gone; then they bundled me back into their vehicle and drove me a mile or so down the road. It made me a little nervous that Sara didn't know where I was and that apparently they had stopped at this unknown building in order to throw her off the scent. We arrived at CID headquarters, a huge but austere concrete building with armed guards at the gates, who waved us through.

They led me up the sweeping broad outside stairway to the staff library on the first floor. In the middle of the room was a long table, with a Formica fake-wooden top, the day's newspapers haphazardly strewn around.

No one told me what to do, so I sat on one of the blue office chairs at the far end of the table. Mrs Mantra went off, leaving three policemen with me. One was the man with the kindly but worn face who had been with her in the hotel. The three sat around the middle of the table, and for the rest of the night they discussed politics, sometimes shouting, sometimes laughing. They spoke only in Telugu, the state language of Andhra Pradesh, of which Hyderabad is the capital, so I couldn't understand any detail, but I picked up enough words like 'Modi', 'BJP', 'Rahul Gandhi' and 'Congress' to know that they were talking about national politics. India's election was two months away.

Not knowing what I was supposed to be doing, finding it odd that I should just sit there while they talked, I huddled into my jacket. Sara phoned a couple of times to tell me she was trying to get hold of our lawyer, without success. At one point I went over to look at the library books. There was an English general reading section, full of books that could keep me occupied. I went to pick up William Dalrymple's latest, *Return of a King*, about the British in Afghanistan. The oldest of the policemen barked at me, 'Leave it! It's *government* property!'

Whatever I was supposed to be doing, it was not reading books. I retired to my chair, my back to the window, facing them. I tried to sleep, burying my head in my folded arms on the desk. 'Wake up!' the oldest of the policeman barked at me. Neither reading nor sleeping was allowed.

I needed to pee a couple of times during the night. The kindly man was assigned the duty of accompanying me. Each time I apologised for inconveniencing him, but he smiled reassuringly and held my arm as we walked down the corridor to a filthy toilet, where he stood outside the door, waiting to accompany me back to the library.

As a peacock announced the morning from a tree in the garden, the senior policeman who had shouted at me went outside, to return with three neem twigs, which he gave to his colleagues. They scrubbed their teeth with these natural toothbrushes, and used them to scrape their tongues too. Someone then came in with chai – milky, sugary tea. They didn't offer me any. I was thirsty, hungry, tired.

Just after 8 a.m., Sara phoned to say she had finally managed to get hold of our lawyer, Vashnu. He had said that I couldn't have been arrested, I must just have been taken in for questioning. 'I haven't been questioned,' I told her. 'And last night they said they were arresting me.' Anyway, he was coming in at 10 a.m. and Vashnu had said that everything would be easily sorted out.

After about 9 a.m., other policemen and women came to work in the library. Some used the computers along one of the walls, others browsed manuals in the legal section. I felt very conspicuous; they each looked at me curiously. At 10 a.m., Sara arrived with Vashnu and his junior, Prandakur, whom I met for the first time. They strode into the room briskly; they looked as though they had come to take charge.

Vashnu was in his mid-forties, of medium height, clean-shaven, with a slight belly held in by a thick leather belt. His face was broad, with a big nose, a tiny chin and a larger double chin underneath. He was always dressed immaculately, that day in a crisp white shirt with starched black trousers and well-polished black leather shoes. Prandakur was ten or more years younger than Vashnu. He was very tall, perhaps 6ft 2in. That day he wore casual clothes, long jeans and a T-shirt. He was clean-shaven too, and brimming with the confidence of youth.

But take charge they could not. They asked the policemen what was going on, but were told sharply to wait for Mrs Mantra. I tried to talk to my lawyers, but they barely acknowledged me. Instead, they talked among themselves and occasionally to Sara. I began to feel diminished in their eyes too.

At 10.30 a.m., Mrs Mantra arrived. She had changed her clothes, and was wearing a grey ('dirty grey,' said Sara later) Punjabi dress, with an off-white blouse. She too ignored me completely as she swept into the library. She looked surprised to see Vashnu and Prandakur, but they sidled up to her and explained who they were; soon they were talking pleasantly enough together in Telugu.

I sat in the library all day. Mrs Mantra spent most of her time sitting in one of the computer booths, not on the computer but writing slowly in long-hand on sheets of foolscap paper, which she then got one of the junior office boys to type onto the computer. What was she writing? Whatever it was, it wasn't from notes, only from memory. I observed Vashnu getting uneasy as he caught sight of a few words. He had sent Prandakur to get a copy of the Foreign Contribution (Regulation) Act. Surely, I thought, they must know all about this Act, as he had advised me on what to do two years ago in regard to foreign currency received by the trust. When he returned, they stood together and flicked through it, as if for the first time, but they did not share any of their observations with me or Sara. When they were both otherwise occupied, Sara picked it up and found there was a maximum of five years' imprisonment for FCRA offences. But that's only for the most serious offences, she told me, nothing like the minor infringements (if any) of the Educare Trust.

After a while it became obvious that Mrs Mantra was deliberately trying to slow things down. Vashnu informed Sara that the court closed for the weekend at 5 p.m. and so I would have to get there well before that to ensure I got bail. And if I didn't? Then I would have to go to the magistrate's home after court hours, in which case there could be no bail and so prison for the weekend before I could come before the judge on Monday morning. Obviously that could not happen; that scenario was absolutely beyond anything I deserved or could cope with. I had been to the Hyderabadi prison before, helping with literacy classes for the inmates when I first came to Hyderabad over a decade ago. I vividly remember seeing how the inmates lay on the floor with no space between each, like slaves on a slave ship. Most vividly I recalled some prisoners kept in cages outside, like dogs, presumably as some sort of punishment. It was inconceivable that I could be sent somewhere like that. 'Don't worry,' Sara said. 'We'll get you to court on time.'

But noon came and went, 1 p.m., 1.30, and still Mantra was sitting there, writing laboriously, the officer juniors single-finger typing, equally slowly. Vashnu found out that I hadn't eaten or drunk anything, and so Sara went out to get street food, but I didn't feel like it. I'm always a bit careful about what I eat in India, having suffered bad tummies in the past. I reminded her I had a long week ahead of me; talks in Delhi then Dubai – best not risk getting sick. I did have some water, though, from the small bottle she brought me.

At 2 p.m., Mrs Mantra said to Vashnu – no one was talking to me by this stage – that they were going to seize my passport. I saw him blanch. He probed why they needed to do that, went back and forth in Telugu with Mrs Mantra and Prandakur, but in the end told Sara that she had to go and get it for me. When she was away, Vashnu for the first time responded to my questioning about how long it would take to get the passport back: 'A week,' he said. I felt hopeless, trapped.

'I can't wait a week. I've got to fly to the Emirates, to West Africa, to America.'

He motioned for me to be quiet, making a characteristic sign that I would see so often from him; an impatient sucking of his tongue to signify disapproval. 'Not like that,' he said, dismissing my concerns. 'Let's get bail first.'

Vashnu signalled that we had to get a receipt for my passport when Sara returned. But Mantra couldn't find a receipt book.

She sent various juniors scurrying around to assorted offices, but each came back empty-handed. Eventually we had to settle for a handwritten receipt; she painstakingly wrote a full page long-hand and signed it equally laboriously.

By 3 p.m., Vashnu was getting visibly agitated. Finally, the office junior printed out a corrected copy of the statement they had been working on all day. It was brought across to me. 'His arrest papers. Make him sign,' Mantra said to Vashnu.

Vashnu said to Sara, 'He has to sign it.'

Of course that meant that I hadn't been arrested after all during the night, so what had I been doing there, held against my will? I never sign anything without reading it first. Reading this document, I felt very worried. There was stuff about the Educare Trust and the FCRA offence, that ₹35 lakhs[1] (equal to about £35,000) was received without the correct permissions. But the report continued: 'The objective in establishing the trust was for the upliftment of downtrodden or poor children', but, instead, I 'diverted the foreign money', which I 'lavishly spent' for my 'aristocratic habits'. 'After fraudulently and dishonestly spending the amount as his whims and fancies dictate, he cheated the government of India,' it said. I felt scared. I had only ever brought my own funds into India to give to the poor; I had never cheated anyone, let alone the government of India.

'It's not true,' I said to Vashnu.

---

1   In the Indian number system, a *lakh* is 100,000 and a *crore* is 100 lakh, i.e. 10,000,000. ₹ is the symbol for rupee.

'Sign it,' he said.

'None of it's true,' I protested.

He shrugged. 'They're arresting you. You have to sign.'

I signed, but added in parenthesis 'Without prejudice' – a legal-sounding phrase the meaning of which I was not entirely sure – 'I categorically deny any of the charges above.'

There was more conferring between Mantra and my lawyers in Telugu. Sara (who couldn't speak Telugu either) eventually understood that, before I was to go to court, Mantra was insisting I go for a medical. It's just timewasting, Sara protested, so that I'm prevented from getting to court before it closes.

'Not at all,' Mantra said. 'We have to be a bit careful for a man of his age.'

'I'm fine,' I told her, but she wouldn't even acknowledge me, let alone talk to me. Her smile had completely gone. She said she would order a police vehicle to take me to the government hospital. Sara and Vashnu pleaded with her to let me go in Sara's hired taxi, as ordering a police car would take far too long. The clock was ticking. I absolutely had to get to court well before 5 p.m.

Eventually, Mantra agreed that I could go in Sara's car; Sara can be very persuasive at times. I sat in the back, wedged between two CID officers, while Sara and Prandakur crowded onto the front seat next to the driver.

Old City Hyderabad traffic is not designed for those in a hurry. It was chock-a-block this time of day, with autorickshaws and two-wheelers clogging every space between the cars, trucks and buses. Nevertheless, the driver manoeuvred manfully through the traffic as quickly as he could. We found the government hospital after a couple of false starts, dived out of the car and into the reception area. To get into the hospital you generally have to show ID to the two policemen posted at the entrance. I didn't need to, however; the CID showed theirs and I was waved through. I was becoming a non-person.

We rushed down filthy, dark corridors, where people lay along the edges, crying in agony, moaning in pain, family members gathered around not knowing what to do, helpless. There were lots of used medical swabs strewn along the corridor. Opposite the reception area where we had to wait, there was a courtyard. Meant to bring in fresh air and light, the door leading out to it was twisted and broken, and the courtyard was used as a rubbish dump, piled high with used plastic bottles, and medical waste.

As we arrived, Prandakur took his cotton handkerchief from his pocket and covered his nose. 'The smell is unbearable,' he said to Sara. I'm not sure I even noticed, so keen was I to get to court. Seeing that I was looking anxiously at my watch, Sara reassured me, 'A couple of quick checks, they'll sign your papers and then we'll rush you over to court.'

'It's already nearly four, how is it possible?' I asked.

'You're always too pessimistic,' said Sara. 'Of course we can make it.'

But there was a problem. The junior doctor who first took my blood pressure showed me the reading: 190/100 mmHg, a level that signifies danger. 'It's high because he's stressed,' said Sara, 'but he'll be fine as soon as he gets to court.' The young doctor was sympathetic, so he said, 'Let's get another opinion.' We raced down other dark, dirty corridors lined with sick people and their families. The next doctor confirmed the analysis, and so referred me to a third and then finally a fourth doctor. It was now 4 p.m.

This doctor got me to lie down. He was kindly. 'You must relax,' he said. 'You must try to be calm.' I heard him say I will have to be admitted to the hospital. 'He's at risk of a stroke or a heart attack,' the doctor said, sotto voce, but I picked it up. Sara pleaded, and they agreed to give me a couple of minutes, to see if my blood pressure would come down of its own accord. A nurse gave me a tablet, which I swallowed without the water offered. I had to be careful about what I drank. I closed my eyes. There was so much noise and activity around; this was the admission ward of a huge metropolitan government hospital. I was desperately trying to be calm, and I knew what I had to do. In my mind, I went to my home, Daisy Cottage, a remote stone cottage set in the heather moors of Northumberland, the wildest, least populated county of England. I imagined my favourite time of the year, late June; the patio doors open, the curtains gently billowing in the wind, the sun breaking through a partly cloudy sky, the calming contours of the Simonside Hills in the background and the house martins and swallows twittering idly in the mild warmth of the English summer. In my mind, I was there.

It worked, to an extent. My blood pressure came down a bit.

Sara pleaded with the doctor in charge, a petite woman in her fifties with a bright, colourful sari underneath her white medical coat, 'His blood pressure is usually normal.'

I added, 'I've been up for fourteen hours, without food and drink, they've interrogated me all night, kept me awake,' and so on. She said rules were rules and that I had now been admitted to the hospital. It was 4.30 p.m. Vashnu phoned Sara and told her that it was preferable that I was ill now, because it was too late for bail and hospital is preferable to prison. Mrs Mantra apparently started phoning the ward, saying that she had sent me there, so she can have me back, that I was absconding from prison, pretending to be ill. But the hospital refused to budge.

I spent Friday night in the government hospital, in the accident and emergency ward. There was no space between the beds; I lay on mine, no sheets or blankets or pillows, between a poor young woman who was having a terrible asthma attack, gasping for breath, crying for relief, and an older woman coughing and vomiting and sighing all night. There were many air-conditioning units positioned around the room, but none worked. There were some fans that rattled noisily, moving hot air around. It was claustrophobically hot, the air thick with sickness and grief. Mosquitos were everywhere. Without anything to cover me, I was at their mercy.

I needed to relieve myself, and was accompanied again by the kindly CID man, down one long corridor. The toilets were the filthiest I had ever seen; it was unclear where the latrines began and the floor ended – people urinated and defecated seemingly wherever they wanted. The kindly CID man peered in and shuddered and, when we were back in the ward, asked the doctors if I could use their facilities, the door to which happened to be near my bed. At first, the doctors were all men, and they allowed me. When some female doctors came on duty, however, they refused me access. They would have no truck with this dirty prisoner invading the sanctity of their private facilities.

The police commandeered the central area in the ward, where the doctors had previously sat and written up their notes. All night, between three and six CID men sat there, making everyone feel that I was a dangerous criminal. I heard doctors and patients alike calling me 'prisoner'. As the night wore on, it was clear the medical staff were becoming thoroughly sick of me.

Then Mrs Mantra arrived and sat there in the middle with her back to me; her horrible profile I will remember for ever. Her stocky, pear shape, her legs squatting solidly either side of her chair, feet flat on the ground, her back stooped as she bent forward to write slowly by long-hand on dual pieces of paper pinned together. What on earth was she writing this time? Three of the CID men had been up for as long as me; I began to feel sorry for them, for at least I could lie down. The kindly man had to get his blood pressure checked too, and was asked to lie down on the bed next to me when the asthmatic girl was removed. Later, a groaning young man arrived covered in festering sores, and the kindly officer was ousted from his temporary respite.

Amazingly, I fell into a deep sleep, so great was my tiredness.

Later I was told that I had two visitors that night while I slept: one was Mrs Mantra's youngest son, the unsung prodigy who she wanted to go to a good British university. The other was the court crier, someone I would get to know well over the coming days; on the instructions of the judge he had come to check if I was ill or play-acting.

When the morning round took place, my blood pressure had returned to normal, and I was clearly looking perkier. The doctor in charge, the petite woman still with a colourful sari underneath her medical coat, had a long conversation with Mrs Mantra before coming over to me with her junior doctors and relating to them precisely what I'd told her the day before – that my blood pressure had been high only because of the stress I was under, and that usually I was fit and healthy. If she'd believed that when I'd told her, of course, I could have gone straight to court and sorted everything out quickly. But what did this mean now? Surely it couldn't mean prison?

One of the CID men – the guy who had shouted at me for trying to read a book in the library – had grown friendlier as the night wore on. He had asked for Sara's phone number; when she arrived, she carried biryanis for breakfast for him and his men, on his instructions. They hungrily tucked in, mashing the rice and sauce together in their right hands and scooping it into their mouths.

She came with an Egg McMuffin for me, the last meal I would have for some time. Vashnu had phoned, she said, and

I must appear as ill as I could, as hospital was still the preferred option. She had brought me a sheet from the hotel, because there were none on the hospital beds, and my bed was filthy with blood and other more dubious-looking stains. I wrapped myself in the sheet, able to shield myself from the mosquitos at last, shut my eyes tightly, and tried to look as ill as I could.

CHAPTER 2

IN THE MARGINS

TRYING TO LOOK ILL didn't convince anyone, least of all Mrs Mantra and her new friend, the senior hospital registrar.

At 2 p.m. on Saturday I was on the move again. Sara told me, quietly, that Mrs Mantra had told my lawyers that if she was paid ₹5 lakhs (£5,000) she would say 'no objection' to the judge and so he would let me go free until the court hearing on Monday. The lawyers had consulted Sara and negotiated back and forth, until eventually Mantra agreed to one-tenth of that: ₹50,000 (£500). 'But don't you worry about it,' Sara said, sensing my disgust. 'We'll sort it out later. It's nothing to do with you.' Sara also told me that Mrs Mantra had said the judge would most likely let me free until court on Monday, but worst case scenario and he didn't, then I would spend the weekend in the CID library again – definitely preferable to both hospital and prison.

Again we bundled into Sara's hired taxi, Sara in front, me wedged between Mrs Mantra and the older, chubby-faced CID man who had shouted at me in the library, but with whom I now seemed to have a rapport. He had told Sara that Mrs Mantra shouldn't be behaving like this, she was overstepping the mark. We drove to the judge's apartment block in a some-what leafy suburb off one of Hyderabad's congested, noisy main artery roads; his flat was on the first floor.

My lawyers, Vashnu and Prandakur, who had arrived by separate vehicles, ran past as they donned their lawyers' clothes (always kept in the back of their cars, for any such eventual-ity) – black, flowing academic gowns and white shirts with stiff white wing-collars, with white bands hanging down. They told Sara to tell me to look very ill. They climbed the stairs first, followed by the chubby-faced CID man, then me, then Mrs Mantra. Sara was told not to come. The judge had been enjoying an afternoon siesta on his balcony, sitting in a pale blue plastic chair opposite his neat row of potted plants, when we disturbed him. He was wearing a sarong and a stripy, collared T-shirt and looked unassuming, the sort of guy who surely wouldn't come between me and my freedom.

He already had papers concerning my case, presumably deliv-ered by the CID earlier. All the discussion was in Telugu, but I guessed that the lawyers presented arguments for my release.

Mrs Mantra said nothing. (I thought she was supposed to say 'no objection'?) The magistrate listened to my lawyers' pleas, then wrote something on my papers. Vashnu and Prandakur then starting getting angry, gesticulating wildly at him, which seemed an odd approach to take with a judge who held my future in his hands. In response, he wrote something extra on my papers.

We filed downstairs to the car in silence. As we milled around downstairs, I asked what was happening. My lawyers ignored me and glared at Mrs Mantra, then got into their vehicles and drove off.

We got back into Sara's hired car. Mrs Mantra and Sara were arguing, partly in English, partly in Hindi; I picked up enough to see that they were discussing why she hadn't said 'no objection' to allow my release, and what size bribe she had or had not agreed to.

No one said what was happening, but I guessed where we were going.

It was a 45-minute drive to Cherlapally Central Jail. As we neared the gate, Mrs Mantra, her huge wide smile turned back on again, told me that I was not allowed to take *anything* inside, but not to worry, there would be a nice meal served soon, and everything else was provided, so I'd be just fine.

We drove through the prison gates, down a lengthy driveway through rather beautiful grounds, with trees and shrubs, and birds singing at the end of the day. I put on my jacket, which had my notebook and biography of Gandhi wedged in one pocket and several pens in the inner pockets; I made my way to the imposing wooden prison doors.

We asked one of the jailers standing by the door when Sara could come to visit. There were no visiting hours until Monday. I could not hold back my tears then. It was 5.30 p.m. on Saturday. How could I make it until then, *in an Indian prison*, for God's sake, without seeing anyone, without any contact with the outside world? Sara started to cry too, her eyes welling up, which made it worse, because now I had to worry about her too.

'I've done nothing,' I blubbered. 'I've done nothing wrong.'

The kindly CID officer, the one who had been there with Mrs Mantra from the beginning, miraculously appeared beside me at the gates, apparently having driven all the way on his two-wheeler, of his own volition. He had been with me almost non-stop for the forty hours I'd been in police custody. Seeing my tears, he rubbed my back gently. He didn't speak English and I had no Telugu, but his stroking, his caring, sad smile, told me I was not alone. I didn't even know his name. Later, I discovered that he had told Sara that they could put some money into my 'account' so I could make phone calls and buy extras inside. But Sara only had ₹300 (£3) on her. He took this and added ₹1,000 (£10) from his own pocket, so at least I had something to use inside.

I gave myself up to what had to happen. I hurriedly kissed Sara on the cheek and was ushered inside.

First the admissions room, where an unfriendly young man in his twenties, with a withered right arm, took down my details: name, father's name, address and crime (not *alleged* crime, I noticed, but I was in no position to discuss semantics). Then back to the main entrance lobby, where the kindly CID man was waiting. Seeing my watch, he signalled for me to hand it back to Sara outside, through the circular peep-hole in the massive prison doors. He called Sara to receive it. Just after Sara grabbed my watch, one of the prison guards roughly pushed me back, so that I stumbled and fell onto the hard floor. This was the first indication that things might not be fine inside.

I was brought in to sit in front of Mr Karan, the Deputy Superintendent (DSP) of the prison, in his large office to the side of the entry hall. He was a rather plump, avuncular fellow in his mid to late thirties. He was clean-shaven and dark-skinned, wearing the khaki uniform of the prison jailers and sporting a big, chunky golden watch and gold rings on two or more fingers on each hand. He was wearing sunglasses when I entered, which he took off during the interview. On his desk was displayed a large photograph of what I guessed was his young daughter. Next to her was his very large, very latest Samsung smartphone.

Mrs Mantra was sitting by him. Responding to my disquiet, he told me that there was nothing to worry about. 'You are in very good hands with Mr Karan,' said Mrs Mantra. Two cups of tea were brought in. On happier occasions – like when a professor from an eminent British university had visited to deliver literacy classes for prisoners – there would have been three cups of tea. But I was now stripped of any rank. I was not someone to share a cup of tea with any more.

I was escorted to a covered area, where I was searched by two hostile prison guards. My belt was taken away from me, as were my notebook and pens, but not my jacket and Gandhi biography. That's it. I was given my prison identity card. I discovered later that this was colour-coded, and regretfully I had not noticed what colour it was. It was taken away from me on entry to the admissions block, so this little bit of information that could have been comforting, or not, remained unknown to me.

The admissions block was called 'Mansara'. To get there I had to go through well-appointed gardens, with mature trees and neat paths and driveways. Through a security checkpoint, where I had to show my card and say my prison number, which was there on the (which colour?) card, and announce my name, my father's name, 'where from?', and my crime.

The prison guards each carried a five-foot-long lathi: a thick, transparent plastic, threatening-looking baton. Having satisfied the guard's checks, I was let in and led to the building's entrance steps, where several prison guards, all with lathis, were lounging; one greeted me, said that he remembered me from last year and asked what I had done now. I said, no it was my first time. He pooh-poohed this. He knew me very well, he said, and would make sure they kept a close eye on me this time. My opinion on whether I had or had not been to prison before didn't matter any more.

Two guards with lathis took me down a corridor, turned right, left, right again. I didn't take much in, just the bars on the

cells, the musty smell and the distant echoes of people shouting. They stood me in front of cell 13 and opened the barred
door. The cell was a room about 9 feet square. On the far wall
was a big, barred window at shoulder height, facing out on to
a space between two buildings, strewn with rubbish. The walls
were covered with the spit of men down the ages – the red spit
they eject when chewing pan. The floor was rough concrete,
and set in the high ceiling was a fan going at a lively clip. At
the top of one wall was a long white fluorescent tube light from
which hung cobwebs replete with long-dead flies.

There was no furniture. The cell was completely bare apart
from a torn piece of dirty cardboard in one corner, and three
piles of shit in the middle, with shit apparently smeared over
much of the floor. It was small shit, like a child's, I reasoned,
which made it more worrying. I pointed it out to my jailers,
who shrugged at my concern and said it would be cleaned 'after
some time', an Indian expression that always annoys me outside,
but there I accepted without blush. (It was not cleaned until the
morning.) Meanwhile, I brushed it away from the corner that
was not visible from the barred cell door with the cardboard,
and there I made a pillow of my jacket. The door was bolted
behind me. I was worried about needing to urinate at night,
but it was pointed out that there was an 'en suite' facility; by
the window there was a separate, tiny room without a door; it
was surprisingly clean, given the state of the cell, with a hole in
the ground of the rough floor, a tap that didn't leak and a small,
not too dirty bucket next to it.

Then I was on my own.

It struck me as odd how much we know about what to do in such circumstances, from watching films about prison. They tell you that it is possible to cope. There is no point in feeling sorry for yourself or repeating that you'd done nothing wrong, that it was all unfair. You had to pull yourself together, that was your only option.

The first thing to do, I recalled, was to carefully investigate your surroundings. I paced the cell, and measured it at nearly three paces by three paces. I observed the number '786' scrawled in large numbers on the wall above where I'd placed my jacket. Was that the number of days that someone had spent there? No; I recalled from my visits to the Muslim Old City that one of the schools the Educare Trust had helped was '786 High School'. Wasn't it a Muslim sacred number, the number you get if you add up the numerical values of the opening phrase of the Qur'an?

I didn't investigate any further the shit on the floor.

That was my cell. I stood at the barred door and looked across the six-foot-wide corridor to the two larger cells opposite, with a dozen or more people in each. The Indian inmates crowded around their doors to see the foreign arrival. One young man spoke good English.

'What time do they serve food?' I asked.

'Food was two hours ago,' he said. 'Nothing until cup of tea at 6 a.m.'

'Where can I get drinking water?' I asked.

'You get water after 6 a.m.,' he said.

'When do they bring blankets?' I asked. I was feeling a bit chilly.

'You bring your own blankets,' he said.

I had to cope. I instantly put out of my mind any possible downside of all I had just learnt. Instead, I pointed to the fan:

'Can I turn it down? I'm rather cold,' I said.

'It's either on or off, there's no speed control,' he said. 'Best keep it on, or the mosquitos will eat you alive.'

Helpfully, one of his companions demonstrated from his side how to switch off the fan in case I changed my mind. You stuck your arm out through the bars in the door and bent it backwards to get to the fan switch further along the wall out-side. I tried to do it from my side, but mistakenly I switched off my light instead. Suddenly they were rather nervous; this was a serious mistake – I must put it back on quickly. To universal relief, I managed to do so.

'When is lights out?' I asked, finally. He shook his head. There was no lights out.

I paced back into my cell. I didn't feel anything. I had to cope, I had to survive.

After a few minutes, the prisoner who spoke good English called across the corridor from his cell. The prisoners had got together a package of a banana, an orange, some grapes, a half loaf of bread, some jam, a blanket and a big bottle of water. I will never forget that moment. They didn't have to do any-thing for me; who was I to them? They could have simply ignored my problems; they themselves had few comforts, nothing much to spare. Instead, they responded with this deep generosity and kindness, helping me in my hour of need.

Something stirred in me that moment, which carried me through the whole experience.

We tried to see how we could get the food and blanket across the corridor, but it was not possible, we were too far apart. It was risky, potentially antagonising the jailers, but the young man who spoke English well said that the duty jailer that night was OK, and we should call him. He came and helpfully transferred the objects across the corridor to my cell, squeezing them in between the bars.

Their kindness overwhelmed me. Now I had a blanket, which I spread out on the floor in my corner, with my jacket for a pillow. I had food – I ate some bread and the bananas and orange, but left the grapes as I had to protect my stomach from washed food. I realised the water they had given me was in an unsealed bottle, so was not pure water; I drank it as sparingly as possible, for I could not get sick: I had much to do the next week out in the world when I was free again.

I lay down on the blanket, calmed my mind with thoughts of Daisy Cottage and tried to sleep a little. It was so uncomfortable, the ground so hard, my body a rather different shape from the cold concrete. There were only a few mosquitos around (although plenty in the toilet), so at some point in the night I decided I would turn the fan off, because it was just too cold. I pushed my arm precariously through the bars, aware that it set a beautiful target to hit with a lathi should a jailer feel so inclined. Without the fan, the mosquitos quickly swarmed around me, eating me alive as the others had warned. I figured the cold was the least bad option.

I pulled out my Gandhi book. He was in South Africa. At the end of 1907, Gandhi appeared in court and was asked to leave the country – if only they'd asked me to do the same! On his refusal he was sentenced to two months' imprisonment. In prison he was accompanied by his own secretary and cook, and allowed to bring his typewriter. He had a bed and mattress and a chair. Perhaps the Indians could learn from how the British treated their Indian prisoners, I mused. All I had was my Gandhi biography; he had Ruskin, Tolstoy and Plato, the Bhagavad Gita, Koran and Bible for company. In prison, Gandhi 'was in his element ... firm in his resolution of passing his term in jail in perfect happiness and peace'. I wondered whether I could find any such solace.

I knew what I was most afraid of. The rape scene in *The Shawshank Redemption* is hard to forget. Pacing my cell I knew I had to be ready for whatever would happen. I saw nothing of the jailers, but knew that I could be visited in the night. Would the jailers come at any time and beat me or rape me? Or get other prisoners to do the same? I tried to imagine how it might happen, so that if the worst case scenario should unfold, I would at least be prepared.

I lay down again, cold from the ground, cold from the air. But unbelievably, again, I slept for a while. But then cats started to howl; the worst, loudest, most aggressive tomcat howling I had ever heard, building up to a screeching crescendo – and then I felt someone touching my arm. I jumped up. The cat – not someone – recoiled away, screeching out of the cell, and another darted away with him, interrupted in her toilet.

So it was not child shit, but cat shit. This cell was not often used – I realised later that it was where foreigners like me were put for their first couple of nights – so the cats had taken it over as their latrine. It made me feel a bit better knowing that the shit I'd been lying in was from cats, not a child.

It started to grow light. Somewhere close by, within the prison compound, the Muslim call to prayer began. It was the most haunting, wistful, terrifying call to prayer I had ever heard. It too will stay with me for ever. And then, it must have been 6 a.m., the jailers came. One by one I heard the clanging of metal bolts as doors were opened the length of the corridor. At first I didn't know what to do. But then the young man from the cell opposite came across and opened my door wide. 'Come outside,' he said. 'You're free until the afternoon to go anywhere around here.' That was a wonderful realisation. I thought I'd be locked up in this dank, dirty cell all day. I stepped out to see what the day had to offer. First, said my companion, there's chai, served outside.

||||||||||||||||||

His name was Aditya, the young man with good English. He was twenty-one, with frizzy black hair and a shadow of a beard.

He was lean, athletic in build, and wore a white T-shirt, with 'Only two things unite men: fear and self-interest' in bold black letters.

'You don't have a cup,' he said. 'Take mine.' He handed me his dirty, chipped enamel cup.

'What will you use?' I protested. He shrugged, and took me down the corridor, outside, past where the prison guards were sitting, down the steps and into the grounds. The morning was still cool, the sun not yet up above the mature trees bordering the prison walls.

There was a metal tea urn placed precariously on a tree stump, and a group of men around it. The guy serving tea had a lively, charismatic air about him; there was something about his eyes, so piercing; he was someone you immediately felt drawn to. His name, I learnt later, was Jitesh. Whereas we were all in civvies, he was in a uniform of off-white matching shirt and trousers, with blue borders. He saw me coming, and quickly summoned me to the front of the queue. 'Chai?' he smiled. He filled up my dirty metal cup; I was almost scalded as I held it. I sipped at the piping hot, milky, sugary tea, worrying about my health from this filthy mug.

After tea, Aditya led me back inside, as it was still cold outside. In his cell he introduced me to some of his friends, sitting on their folded blankets along the cell walls. The oldest of the group was Harish, a plump man of about forty with a jolly round face and mischievous grin. Then there was Aditya's younger brother, and an old school friend.

'What's your case?' Harish asked me.

'A trust, foreign currency,' I said.

He nodded, 'How much?'

'35 lakhs,' (£35,000) I said.

'It's OK,' he laughed, waving his right hand as if to say not to worry. Later I realised that no one believed me; it was far too small an amount to be in prison for.

'Your case?' I asked.

'Drugs,' said Aditya. They were there for manufacturing narcotics – they explained this meant fake pharmaceuticals, not recreational drugs.

'How long have you been here?' I asked. It's a question that had been worrying me all night.

Harish said, 'Ninety-seven days'; Aditya said, '101 and not out'; they laughed at his cricketing analogy. His brother said 'Ninety-nine days'.

That hit me hard. I knew I wouldn't be in for that long; my court case would be on Monday and then I'd be out. But the pain wasn't for me: it was hard hearing that *they* had been in for so long.

'All waiting for bail?' I asked. 'It takes time,' said Aditya.

Harish butted in, 'Out tomorrow.'

'Oh good,' I said, and they all smiled. Harish then had an idea: 'You England, yes?' I nodded. '*Accha*,' he said. 'When go your country, you our agent? *Theek hai*? [All right?]'

Aditya scolded him for always thinking about business. But he made me feel relaxed enough to ask them my second burning question: 'Is it safe here, do I need to fear anything, anybody?'

They said there's nothing to fear, understanding exactly what I was getting at. Then one handsome young man walked in, and they joked that he *is* a rapist. Aditya saw that I looked a bit worried and repeated, 'Don't worry, nothing like that will happen here.'

Aditya told me the young man's case: he'd been seeing a woman for a year or more, having sex, yes. But then his uncle had arranged his marriage, with someone else. The first woman then accused him of rape. 'That doesn't sound fair,' I said. Aditya said, matter-of-factly, that it would all be sorted out.

No one appeared sorry for themselves; everyone was just getting on with their lives the best they could, sitting around scheming, planning, chatting, joking. Aditya later told me that he'd been very good at school, hence his high standard of English, but then his father had died when he was in Class X, and so he had to go out to work to help support his family, including helping his younger brother through school, and that's how he ended up meeting with Harish and his lot. But it was not told to elicit sympathy. He was not feeling sorry for himself, just factually answering my probing questions.

Harish said there *was* one thing I needed to know, and got Aditya to tell me:

'On Monday, they'll move you from here. It happened to us. First we are here in the admissions block, then they move us to the other normal blocks, where there are seventy people per cell, with only two toilets, and people are fighting and everyone is sick.' He saw my fearful expression, and said, 'Don't worry, after few days, Karan, the Deputy Superintendent, called us. For ₹50,000 each (£500), we were moved back here. Our families paid a bribe to Karan. You'll be moved on Monday, but you can come back quickly.'

'Here, business class,' joked Harish. 'There, economy, cattle-class, no good!' We all laughed. I thought: I will be out on Monday, so I should be all right whatever happens.

'Are there any rules I have to be careful to obey?' I asked.

'Two things you must avoid at all costs,' Aditya said. 'Drugs and money. Both have serious punishments.'

Immediately I was worried. In the night I'd found that when the jailers had searched me, they'd not found some money that had been in one of my pockets. I told Aditya, and it was his turn to look worried. 'They left it on you deliberately, so that they can punish you. It happened to one of us. Let me have it. I will get rid of it straight away,' he said.

I went back to my cell and secretly handed it over to him. But then I worried: why am I so trusting? Perhaps *he's* the one who's going to report me and get me punished? For a couple of hours these doubts were at the back of my mind. But nothing went wrong. Aditya had genuinely wanted to help me.

Meanwhile, a team of prisoners in the white with blue border uniforms were coming around cleaning. It was explained to me that the uniform denotes a convicted prisoner; we who are awaiting bail are all in civvies. If prisoners are well behaved, they are allowed to work. One of the jobs was cleaning our cells. The guy cleaning mine was thorough and careful, liberally applying disinfectant; when he'd finished there was no evidence of any excrement. My blanket – I had no other possessions apart from what I was wearing – was rolled up and put outside the door while he worked.

As the sun was coming up, prisoners spontaneously started to march around the compound. A group of three started it up, briskly striding out together, making their way around the admissions block. Others joined in, some slower, some faster, but almost everyone marching, a morning routine to keep a grip on one's life.

Slowly, people drifted away, and the routine then seemed to be to retire to the far wall of the compound, behind where the convicted prisoners had their smoking bonfire, burning fallen branches. People sat along the wall – there were no seats or indeed any furniture anywhere in the prison, apart from in the officers' rooms. So people sat around the prison compound on the ground, on any sawn-off tree trunks, or on manhole covers. Pieces of cardboard were at a premium; if you found one of these vacant, it made for a most comfortable seat for a while.

My friends, the drugs team, sat together with their backs to the 30ft-high prison wall topped with barbed wire. Sitting at its base felt closer to freedom, I guessed. Harish, their leader, beckoned for me to join them. There was someone he wanted me to meet.

Sitting along the wall with them, slightly to one side, was Deepak. Unlike the drugs group, who admitted they'd done something wrong, Deepak was one of those who said he was innocent. It was people like him who especially started to tug at my heart. He was a quiet, intelligent young man, who looked down at the ground a lot rather than into the faces of those he was talking to. He was light-skinned, short-haired and clean-shaven, and sported trendy bright-blue spectacles. He spoke English well, with a distinctive manner, precisely clipping the ends of his words. He told me he was thirty-one, with a law degree and MBA. Before he'd been incarcerated, he had been lecturing in business and law at one of the top universities in Hyderabad.

I asked about his case. He had met this girl, not fallen in love or anything, just met her at one of the chai stalls that line the road to the university. She had told him her story. Her father was a drunkard and her mother had pushed her into prostitution. Would he help her get out? Of course he would. It's exactly how I would have responded too. He offered to pay her accommodation in a hostel for one month, as long as during that period she found a way of supporting herself. She agreed. At the end of the month, she demanded more money, and he reminded her of their agreement. She then reported him to the police for abduction and rape.

His lawyer was a woman, and he believed she would be able to show clearly that the woman was lying, because he had never touched her, never had sex or anything, and DNA tests would prove that. I was worried for him. How could they prove that? He dismissed my concerns: 'I will be OK,' he said.

This was his twenty-ninth day in prison. He said he would be out in a week. The university had dismissed him from his lectureship, but his family was standing by him. When he got out, he would change his career 'per force,' he said. He would do a software engineering course, something he'd been interested in for a long time, so it would be no hardship to change. Meanwhile, he would take a job in a call centre. 'They pay well, and they won't enquire about my background.' He was not bitter, he just wanted to get out and rebuild his life.

He told me there were different-coloured identity cards for prisoners; white signified a straightforward case – you could be out in a day; green was 'normal', which meant up to thirty days before you could apply for bail. Pink signified 'high risk', which meant ninety days before any chance of bail. His was a pink card. But anyway, you kept trying for bail whatever your card; he had already tried twice, although he had been refused each time.

I was desperate to know the colour of my card. 'They will give it back on Monday,' he said. 'You must carry it, otherwise you are in trouble.'

Of course I knew it must be white, a straightforward case. I tried to envisage the card in my mind's eye. Yes, it must have been white, it was just an ordinary card; if it had been coloured I would surely have noticed.

Deepak said I mustn't worry, he would find it for me. He added, 'Let me help you for anything you need.'

The things I really wanted were a pen and paper. I had so many thoughts going around in my head, I was seeing so many new things, it would be terrible not to be able to record them. Soap too. I hadn't washed since Thursday. He said he would see what he could do about soap, a pen and paper.

We got up from the wall and walked some more around the compound – the sun was well above the buildings, and it was pleasantly warm after the cold of the night. He took his leave.

I walked around some more. I talked to everyone. Unlike the jailers who were clearly trained not to discriminate, so treated me like (i.e. as badly as) anyone else, the prisoners were all curious as to what this white man was doing among them. 'What's your case?' was the common introduction.

A group of three men, smartly dressed in jackets and ties, walked briskly around – they were the group who began their walk earliest and maintained it for longest. I joined them.

'What's your case?' one asked me. When I told him I was in for a foreign currency offence amounting to ₹35 lakhs (£35,000), he scolded me, saying 'you can tell the truth!'

Another pointed to a middle-aged man seated on one of the manhole covers: he was in for ₹350 crores (£35 million), one thousand times more than me. My meagre amount was far too petty to have landed me in prison, I was coming to realise. But this reaffirmed my sense that it was only the weekend and my hospitalisation that had got in the way of my freedom. As soon as Mrs Mantra's superiors were around to investigate the case, the simple mistake would be uncovered.

I asked about their cases.

'We're here for ACA,' one told me. 'We've been in thirty days.'

'ACA?' I asked.

'Anti-corruption Act. We're petty bureaucrats. Everyone is doing some bribes, as you must know. There was an inquiry in our departments; we were the fall guys.'

'We're scape goats,' another offered, emphasising each syllable. 'On the same morning, someone came in and offered very small bribe, thousand rupees, nothing. We took it in the envelope, and policeman came and arrested us.'

'Same policeman who collected bribes every week to distribute to his higher-uppers,' added one.

Realising they'd been in for a month, I asked if they'd paid the bribe to stay in the admissions block. 'Yes. It's ₹50,000 bribe to Karan to stay here. You'll have to pay once you've been here a day or two. Don't get sent to the other blocks. You'll be more comfortable here.'

There was absolutely no irony to them that they were in prison for bribery and yet now paying bribes to the prison authorities. There was nothing odd about bribes being expected in prison; they are expected in every aspect of Indian life.

'Lunch' (it turns out the two meals of the day are both called lunch) arrived at 9.30 a.m. Some of the convicted prisoners – I could now identify them with their white and blue-lined uniforms – came into the compound carrying a huge dirty metal container of coarse grain rice, and metal buckets of sloppy curry. Aditya found me and handed me an enamel plate. I protested, 'It's yours, don't worry about me.'

'Take it,' he said, pushing it on me, as if it was the most natural thing in the world to be sharing all his possessions with me.

You stood in line with your plate, and one of the convicted prisoners took a big wodge of rice in one hand – a fistful of rice – and chucked it on your plate; his neighbour took a big enamel cupful of the thin gruel, with a few vegetables swimming around, and slopped it on to your rice.

I queued up and took some, more out of politeness to Aditya than anything. But I could not eat anything. It looked and smelled revolting; I was too worried about getting sick. The other men all stood around in small groups and scooped up rice and gravy and mashed it all together with their right-hand fingers until their plates were clean. I moved away from the group, not wanting anyone to see me being fastidious.

Deepak was not waiting for the food. He had some special arrangement where he got Indian breads delivered. Apparently, he'd paid an extra bribe to the Deputy Superintendent, Mr Guatam, for this, on top of his ₹50,000, which he confirmed he had also paid to stay in the admissions block. He said he would go back to his room to wait for these, but I must come and share some with him.

I was sitting with him when they were duly delivered at 9.50 a.m., lumps of burnt rotis wrapped in dirty torn newspaper. Deepak offered me one, saying I must eat; he had heard

I didn't partake of the curry outside. I took one; it had the texture of cardboard, with no flavour apart from being smoky. I struggled to eat even a mouthful.

Deepak was staying in room 1, which seemed to be the centre of the admissions block. It was a larger room than the others, perhaps 30 feet square, accommodating about twenty people. By the time I was visiting him for breads, all but one of the inmates had their blankets neatly rolled along on the edge of the room, leaving most of the floor space empty. Someone was still lying there, resting; an older man, whose son, Deepak said, was the one fussing over him.

There was a small hanging clock, so you could see the time. Room 1 seemed to be the communal day room for the whole compound. 'Move here, if you are lonely in your room,' Deepak said. 'When you pay your bribe, this is the best place for you to stay.' I wondered whether I could bear the noise of all the Indian men snoring at night and energetically clearing their throats in the morning.

Newspapers had arrived, which they eagerly scooped up, but they were all in Telugu so I left him and the others reading, and went for a further walk around the compound. I talked to whoever I could, and when I grew tired, I sat under a tree, on a spare manhole cover. It was mid-morning; the long day stretched out ahead of me. All of Sunday, then Monday and my court case, and then I'd be out of there. I could make it.

The person sitting on the adjacent manhole cover was looking unusually sad, staring into the distance. Both of us sat for a while on our neighbouring drains, before I asked him his case. He spoke good English, was clearly educated. His name was Adit. He had been convicted in a court outside Hyderabad of murdering his brother-in-law, and was now on appeal to the Hyderabad High Court. He had been in prison for over a year, convicted for life. 'I didn't kill him, it was a stitch-up.' I tried to console him, feeling his pain. But that was not all.

'As I was being brought here to Hyderabad, the CID told me they had pinned another unsolved murder on me. I'm not a murderer,' he said. 'I have done nothing wrong.' But now, even if he was acquitted of murdering his brother-in-law, he would have to return to trial for this other murder.

'When you're in prison, they can multiply your crimes, just as they want to,' he said. 'There's nothing you can do about it.' We sat in silence for a while as I contemplated the enormity of what he had told me.

||||||||||||||||||

On Sunday morning, Dr Varma – 'Prisoner Reformist Preacher' it said on his business card – came to the compound at around 10.30 a.m. to preach a Christian message. He was a rotund middle-aged man with a kindly smile and big bushy eyebrows. He came with a rather prim woman dressed in a pale blue kurta and a headscarf.

As I walked around the compound, someone ran up to tell me that the preacher had arrived; Deepak had put the word around that I should be informed. Dr Varma invited me onto the veranda where he was giving his sermon, where a group of thirty or so prisoners had gathered. He was hectoring his audience in Telugu in precisely the way I didn't want to be hectored, while his female companion looked disapprovingly down at us all. I guessed he was hectoring us about our guilt, having heard sermons somewhat similar in tone in my time as a boy going to church twice every Sunday. All have sinned, and fallen short of the glory of God. But we can be forgiven. And here's how. Jesus came to earth to wash away our sins. Give your life to Him and you can be made whole again. I could tell he was saying these things by his actions and expressions. I sat for a while, but I was being bitten too badly by the mosquitos so I had to give up.

I walked around the compound some more, talking to everyone I could, desperate for human contact. I met people who described themselves as 'political prisoners'. One white-haired, speckle-bearded man in his sixties had been there for twenty-four months, he told me; his case had now gone to the Supreme Court in New Delhi. He carried an English-language newspaper, *The Hindu*.

'I didn't know India had political prisoners,' I said.

'We're brought in on trumped-up charges about something else – in my case, a land dispute. But it's only because we're active in politics, opposed to those in power, that they arrest us and keep us here for so long. It's impossible for us to get bail.'

Another of these self-identified political prisoners, a frail old man in his seventies, was tottering around the edge of the compound, picking the fallen flowers from underneath the big trees on the border, putting them carefully into a plastic bag. 'For *Prasad*,' he told me; that is, for blessings in the Temple.

Everyone was friendly, apart from the jailers. As I walked past where they were sitting at the entrance, one shouted at me angrily, pulling at his shirt. I looked at my shirt, not knowing what the problem was. One of the other prisoners saved me: 'Shirt out,' he said. In prison, it turns out you're not allowed to have your shirt tucked in. It's all a bit like being at school, where your shirt *has* to be tucked in. I remedied the situation and continued walking. Having your shirt out made you even fairer game for the mosquitos.

Deepak had sent someone to find me, to tell me the preacher was leaving. I rushed to find the preacher – I had had an idea, and needed to meet him again! He was there, near the exit, with a group of five men. I joined the group. We all held hands and he prayed for us in English, saying that God knew our hearts and what we had, or had not, done (but, by his tone, clearly convinced about what we *had* done), and that he knew our families were missing their fathers, wondering where Daddy was; tears were streaming down the cheeks of the men – some were the ACA guys, others were like me, saying they were innocent. Then we all hugged.

They drifted off and I was left with Dr Varma. 'Is there anything I can do for you?' he asked. 'Please don't hesitate to ask.' I had been eyeing his shirt pocket ever since the sermon.

It contained a pen. I was bursting to write my thoughts and observations, because I knew I would forget them if I didn't write them down soon. But it felt rude to just ask him.

'Let me know if there's anything I can do, brother,' he repeated. So I asked him, 'Are you going out of the prison now?'

'Yes,' he said.

'So you can get another pen when you are out?' I asked.

'Yes,' he said, curious.

'So can I have your pen?' I asked.

He passed it across to me. 'God bless you, brother,' he said. And so I had something to write with – a wonderful luxury. And for paper? I had my Gandhi book. There was a blank page at the back, and I could write in the margins of every page. Gandhi's biography became my prison diary.

I found Deepak and we walked some more. He told me that I was the first person he had spoken to about his case since he had been in. I observed that people turned to him, to talk to him. 'Yes,' he said, 'but I haven't told anyone about my case. But somehow I wanted to tell you.' I felt comforted when he said this. I told him I had a pen and paper. He smiled.

'I kept a diary when I first got here too,' he said. 'But the only way to survive is to make everything normal and mundane.' And no one wants to write a diary about unremarkable things. So he had stopped after five days.

The lively young prisoner with sparkling eyes who had served chai first thing in the morning was sitting in the compound, with another man in very shabby civvies. They were both smoking rolled-up cigarettes. Deepak introduced me to them. The man who had served tea was called Jitesh, his friend Arjun.

Jitesh was keen to talk to me, which he did partly with Deepak translating, partly with his own limited English. He was about thirty years old; he didn't know exactly. He was a murderer, or to be more specific, a *thrice* murderer – he told me with pride in his voice – but he had only been convicted for one; they hadn't got him for the other two. These three had become his enemies, because of some family feud. They came after him once and attacked him, left him for dead. He rolled up his shirt to show me thick, jagged scars from knife wounds on his chest and stomach. He had let things pass for three months, working in a blacksmith's foundry. Then one night, he went to where the three lived, and killed all of them. 'Do you have any regrets?' I asked. 'None,' he said and Deepak translated: 'It was either them or me.'

Six months ago he was imprisoned for life, but he had been in prison for three years; it took two and a half years for his case to come to court. He was appealing to the High Court and hoped to be out in a couple of years. 'But you're guilty?' I ventured.

'Yes, he's guilty,' said Deepak, 'but there are ways. This is India.' Jitesh was very trusted by the prison authorities and they asked him to do many responsible tasks. 'He's really the one in charge here,' joked Deepak.

We turned to his companion. Arjun used to be a cycle rickshaw puller. Yes, I might have guessed that. On the backstreets of Hyderabad you see them, every sinew in their body straining, pulling at their ridiculously heavy loads, stoically manoeuvring across roads while every other motorist contrives to marginalise them. Beasts of burden, almost. He still looked lean and overburdened. Deepak told me that he'd struggled hard, saving all his earnings to purchase his own cycle rickshaw so that he could be independent of the big bosses who owned multiple rickshaws. Getting a licence for a cycle rickshaw is a huge scandal, Deepak said. Something had gone wrong for Arjun. Perhaps, mused Deepak, one of the big owners who had many cycle rickshaws felt snubbed by him, so had bribed the police to get him off the streets. These things happen, he said. Whatever the reason, the police had demanded ever-higher bribes for Arjun to renew his licence, which he'd not been able to afford. So his licence expired, he was arrested and his vehicle impounded. But because he'd put all of his spare cash into buying the rickshaw, even going into debt to do so, there was nothing left for him or his family to pay to get bail. Getting bail costs a lot of money; you need sureties, court fees and, of course, lawyers' fees. His only asset was his cycle rickshaw, which the police had seized. So there he was, stuck in prison.

'For how long?' I asked. Deepak asked the question to Arjun. 'Three years,' he said. Jitesh butted in, 'We came, same time.'

'He's stuck here *for three years*, awaiting trial?' I said, having difficulty processing this information.

'No, not waiting *trial*. Waiting to be charged,' Deepak said, shaking his head. 'None of us have been charged, have you?'

Until that moment I assumed I had been. It seemed incomprehensible to me that I could be in prison without being charged with anything. 'We're all under investigation. None of us have been charged. Arjun has been here for three years *without charge*. He's an undertrial, just like us.'

I'd not heard that word before, 'undertrial'. Now I guessed I was one myself. And his family? He hadn't heard from his family for two years. Without him as breadwinner they surely were destitute.

I quietly vowed to help Arjun as soon as I got out. His case – and his innocent toothy smile – sat on my heart and hurt me every time I thought about him.

Deepak steered me away, seeing my concern. He told me what would happen on Monday. A visit is called an 'interview'; we were allowed two per week. We were also allowed two phone calls per week, but only to local numbers, and we had to buy tokens first – that's why we needed to deposit money on our arrival. It took a couple of days to get tokens, and I had to wait until Monday to apply. I then had to register two numbers, the maximum allowed, and these were the only numbers I could ring. A similar system applied to the canteen, where tokens also took a few days to arrive and we could buy things like soap and biscuits.

Sunday progressed. Aditya had some chess pieces and we made a chess board out of a piece of old card, colouring the squares with my newly acquired pen. The day was then spent playing chess with various men; some played quite well, others didn't know the castling rule, or that when a pawn gets to the other side it can become whatever you want it to become, typically a Queen. I went along with their rules, and if I saw I was winning too easily, I made deliberate mistakes so that no one lost interest or face. Aditya's younger brother was especially enthusiastic, and we played a number of games. We sat in the shade of a jackfruit tree, on a sheet of dirty cardboard. Sitting with murderers and drug fiends, I felt no fear, only friendship.

Deepak brought a young man over to me, a Christian: 'He wants you to pray for him.' It is taken as given that a white man will be a Christian and able to double as prison chaplain. The man's bail petition was being heard the next day. He had done nothing wrong, he said; the police were corrupt and he needed me to pray that the judge would not be corrupt too.

As we finished praying, someone came past us and very quietly said that I had to go to the front entrance. I didn't know the status of this remark – only later did I realise that there was this grapevine that somehow got instructions around, done in exactly this low-key fashion. So I ignored him at first, until Jitesh, the thrice murderer, found me and said urgently, 'Go!'

Near the entrance to the admissions block, a senior official in immaculate prison khakis, whose rank I think was Assistant Superintendent, was waiting for me. There were several jailers nearby, standing with their lathis ready. The Assistant Superintendent was in his thirties and very tall. He stood erect, his face grim. He called me over to him. As he did this, one of Aditya's friends was walking by. The jailer made a jokey comment to him and the friend replied in kind. At this, the jailer suddenly swerved around, yelling at one of his juniors to get hold of the boy and beat him. The junior did so rather half-heartedly, beating him with his lathi on the backs of his legs, not really wanting to inflict too much pain. This angered the Assistant Superintendent, who marched across and snatched the lathi from his junior. He held the lathi high and with a wild sweep, he beat the boy hard on his legs, on his shoulders, and then up from the ground between his legs, causing the terrified boy to collapse onto the ground, groaning. His crime, I learnt, was chewing gum in front of the official.

The Assistant Superintendent then turned back to me. He told me to stand up straight and fold my arms, 'You're prisoner, not on holiday,' he barked. He asked me where I was from and my 'crime'. I told him England, and it was to do with foreign currency. 'You Britishers, all evil,' he shouted. 'You took all money from us. Now you are stealing from us again.' As he spoke to me, I could see Aditya's friend lying on the ground.

I protested that it was not like that, that I'd been funding schools for the poor. That was a mistake. 'You missionary, stealing our children,' he said, furiously. In the lead-up to the election, there was a lot of paranoia among Hindu nationalists about Christians coming in and funding schools to convert children. It was something he latched on to, and shouted some more vile insults at me. Suddenly he was distracted by another, convicted prisoner, a wizened old man sitting minding his own business on the low wall by the compound entrance.

The Assistant Superintendent strode over to him and shouted, gesticulating in a calculated manner, raising his arm as if to beat him, as the old man cowered in fear. He then grabbed him by the throat, shouting in his ear, and pushed him onto the ground. Turning to his jailers, he instructed them sharply in Telugu, and they went across and took it in turns to beat the old man with their lathis as he lay prostrate in the dirt.

I didn't know what to do. It was inconceivable that they would let me intervene, but I felt cowardly not doing so. This poor old man was writhing in pain as he was being brutally beaten by three jailers, coldly taking it in turns as they stood around him in a triangle. The Assistant Superintendent was yelling at me again to stand up straight and focus, focus on him. 'I'm talking to you,' he said, his voice raised. 'There's nothing going on to do with you, evil Britisher.' After a while, he dismissed me, 'Now go. We'll meet again tomorrow.'

I walked off, knowing the beating was still going on, unable to do anything except turn my back, crying inside for the poor old man and Aditya's friend, ashamed of my cowardliness, but also wary that my own manner of walking may be breaking unknown rules and the Assistant Superintendent could descend on me again at any moment.

I could not get the image of the beatings out of my mind for some time. They woke me every night, for months afterwards, my heart palpitating madly. I flinched every time I saw that sadistic jailer, who had delighted in emphasising his power and my powerlessness.

CHAPTER 3

THEY CAN'T TAKE THAT AWAY FROM YOU

ON MONDAY MORNING THERE was to be an inspection by the Prison Superintendent and everything had to be in order.

Perhaps this was because of what had happened in the night? In the early hours, alone in my cell, I'd heard a disturbance; lots of banging of plates against bars, and shouting. I'd gone to my cell door and others had appeared at the cells opposite. What was it? No one seemed to know. After some time, the noise calmed down. In the morning, over chai, Aditya told me that there was a son and father together, in room 1. The father had been ill and coughing badly. His fever had shot up during the night. The son and others in the cell had called for the jailers, but no one came; the prisoners were ignored. By 6 a.m., when the jailers came to unlock the cells, the father was in a coma, and was taken straight over to the prison hospital.

Was he OK? I asked. No one seemed particularly concerned. And how was the young man who had been beaten the day before? He was fine, Aditya said dismissively.

As I had my chai that morning, I was brought a bag that Sara had deposited for me on Sunday, the day before. Bless her, she came out all this way to the prison, even though she knew she wouldn't be allowed to see me. I was deeply touched. It was a shopping bag containing a spare pair of trousers, a shirt and some apples. That was it. She clearly believed that I had everything I needed inside, I thought (unfairly) at the time. (Later I found out she had brought many other things, including an Egg McMuffin sandwich, but that was all that got through to me.) So now I had two pairs of trousers, two shirts and some apples. I tried to share the apples with Aditya and friends, but Aditya told me to keep them for myself; my need was greater.

So I changed my shirt and trousers; it was the first time I had taken off my clothes (but not yet my underwear) since Thursday and my arrest. It felt wonderful to be out of those dirty black trousers in particular. However, soon the news was relayed to me (Deepak now seemed to have become the appointed channel for conveying instructions to me, perhaps because the system used before hadn't seemed fool-proof) that

I had to change my trousers, as they, being khaki, were too much like the prison jailers'. So I went to my room and changed back into my dirty black trousers.

There was to be an inspection of the whole compound, starting with the thirty of us new boys. After receiving my instructions, I went to join the group, but one of the convicts came with a bucket and disinfectant and sprayed water around, and so we were hustled away to another place to wait. Then came the instruction that I had to be shaved. One of the convicts was a barber. I hadn't shaved since Thursday, and indeed had thought I might start growing a beard. However, despite me motioning I was happy as I was, the jailer supervising indicated that it was not up to me, and one of the convicts took me over to join the queue.

Jitesh sidled up to me and mischievously told me that the barber was also a convicted murderer, on life imprisonment, though only for the murder of one person. When it was my turn, I was nervous. The barber used a full open razor. What had this life prisoner to lose by slitting my throat? Especially if the aggressive Assistant Superintendent had put him up to it with an offered reward? Thankfully, I was left beardless and unharmed.

We thirty new boys were made to line up. Fortunately it was cloudy, so no baking sun as there often was in March. We were handed out our admission cards – I saw with a sinking feeling that mine was green, not white. Green means up to thirty days; mine was not a straightforward case. I took a deep breath. For the first time, I realised that I might not get released that day.

You have to numb yourself. You have to endure this for as long as it takes. But I realised something standing in that queue. You cannot feel anything for yourself. If you felt your own pain, you'd end up wallowing in self-pity. So you numb yourself to your own pain. But your emotions don't simply disappear. You have to feel something, so you focus on others. Perhaps this is why everyone was so kind there. We couldn't be selfish, focused in on ourselves like people beyond the wall, because then we wouldn't survive. So instead, we felt empathy for others.

We were all made to stand in order of our prison identity numbers. One of the junior prison officials went down the line and barked the same questions at each of us. He did this in Telugu for most, but for me he reverted to English:

- Name?
- Father's name?
- Address?
- Crime?

Somewhere near the front of the queue, one of the new guys mumbled his answers a bit, nervously. The jailer thumped him several times in the chest, and slapped him around the face. The prisoner took it, swaying a bit, but made no other response. No one else moved, no one protested. We were all powerless. Now, when asked, people shouted more vigorously, not wanting to be caught out in the same way. But then someone was shouting too loudly, and the jailer thumped him too, and whacked him on the side of the head. Not too soft, not too loud; like children in a school we had to guess what was 'just right' for our teacher/jailer. But the goalposts kept moving: not too soft, not too loud, and not too detailed. The guy immediately before me was beaten for going into too much detail; they didn't want details of the wiring that he had thought he was selling, which turned out to be something else, or whatever it was, but simply that his crime was Section X of the Y Act.

We were all there only waiting bail; no one had even been charged with any crime, if what Deepak had told me was true – all supposedly innocent until proved guilty. But that didn't seem to carry any weight with the jailers, who treated us like scum to be handled in any way they wished.

I didn't get thumped or slapped; they barked the questions in English and I answered, not too loudly, not too softly, without too much detail:

- Name? T. James Nicholas.
  That's how I was referred to. It's an odd custom, found in South India only, to shorten your proper surname to an initial, and use your first names only. If anyone had tried to find me in prison by my surname, they wouldn't have succeeded.
- Father's name? T. Arthur Henry.
  I hated most of all having to mention his name in this vile place.
- Address? Daisy Cottage, Ewesley, Northumberland, England.
  I thought of the swallows about to arrive, and how they'd

soon be nesting under the eaves and twittering in the soft breeze of early summer.

• Crime? Section 35, FCRA.

But was that my crime? At most, there was a small sum of money that came in without prior permission, but that couldn't have led to me getting a green card, to stay in prison for thirty days. What was my real case? Why was I there?

We stood and waited – for how long? It was probably twenty minutes, but time had already ceased to be marked off accurately in my mind. Finally, the Prison Superintendent and his entourage arrived.

He was middle-aged and distinctly pear-shaped, his prison belt only just holding in his big belly; he had officious-looking spectacles and was wearing an imposing uniform, including a peaked cap and bulky military boots. He was surrounded by maybe ten other senior officials, not including Karan, the Deputy Superintendent, but including the tall jailer who had brutally beaten the young and the old man in front of me the day before.

The Superintendent was brought food to taste. A cook brought a varied selection of gourmet dishes in small, clean, stainless-steel bowls. The Superintendent sampled a little of each, using a clean stainless-steel spoon. I realised that a game was going on: he was pretending to be checking the prison food, to make sure it was up to scratch. But it was a complete farce; what he was tasting was nothing like the slop that we were given. He surely knew that, as did his whole entourage.

He and his entourage then approached us, but stopped some distance short, so that we all had to shuffle towards him to make up the distance. Each one of the new prisoners in turn stood before him, and one of the jailers barked at us the questions we had already rehearsed; in English for my turn. As we finished, we were pushed roughly by another jailer to go and sit on the ground on the other side of the entrance. They pushed me as roughly as they pushed anyone.

The Superintendent and his retinue then toured the prison compound; Jitesh, the convicted murderer, supervised us to keep order until the big boss was out of the door. We sat in the dirt, six rows of five, heads bowed in silence, like so many naughty schoolboys. After some time – how long? Perhaps half an hour; time had lost its precision – the Superintendent's retinue appeared from out of the block, and marched down the path to the entrance. Jitesh motioned his hand gracefully, as if he was a learned judge, for us to get up.

Deepak had told me that he could help me make a phone call that day, as Aditya had given me one of his spare tokens. ('Take it, you need it, we have others.') But then Deepak came back from the administration block to tell me the telephone was out of order. The realisation was that I could do absolutely nothing. I could not phone Sara; all I could do was wait. Would I get bail? How long would I have to stay there?

I stopped dwelling on these fearful questions; in prison, there could be no self-pity. At about 3 p.m., I decided it was time to wash. Deepak had told me that it was best to wait until mid-afternoon, because by that time the water in the pipes had heated up, so you could get warm or even hot water. It was true: the cold water pipe was now running very hot. I took off all my clothes for the first time since Thursday, stood naked in my narrow cell 'bathroom', filled up the small bucket and threw this over my head, scrubbed myself furiously with my hands. No soap, no towel, but bucket after bucket I threw over myself; a ritual cleansing. I dried myself with my T-shirt. It was warm outside, and I went into that warmth. This was a turning point; I recognised that I may be there for some time, and so needed to make it all as normal as possible. That meant getting cleaned up, as much as I could.

At 5 p.m., the evening 'lunch' arrived: rice and sloppy curry. I tried a bit of it, a taste. I had to do this; by now I was feeling incredibly hungry – my last meal had been Friday. I knew by then that I wouldn't be leaving before the end of the day. I had a few cautious nibbles, nothing much, but I broke my fast. The drugs crew had told me that they would be getting bail that day, Monday. Aditya, Harish and his team had been sitting on the steps by the entrance, waiting for that moment to arrive. They didn't look forlorn, though, now that they knew it wasn't going to happen; they took it all in their stride.

'I thought you were leaving today,' I said.

'Tomorrow,' Harish said firmly, as they walked back together to their cell.

At 5.30 p.m., one of the convicts came to me and said quietly, 'Interview', and walked away. What was I supposed to do?

I found Deepak and he told me I had to go to the administration block. I had given up hope, thinking that visits stopped at 5 p.m.

As the normal prison meeting hours were over, the interview hall was empty. The room was divided in half by two metal mesh screens, 2 feet apart, reaching from ceiling to floor. The door at the back of the room opened and Sara was admitted to the other side. Oddly, the prison jailer then locked the door behind her. We both rushed to the metal mesh, but could not touch each other across the divide.

Seeing her, all my strength vanished; all the routines that I'd been building up over the past days, all the friendships I'd made, all vanished into nothing. I choked back my tears, as she did hers. But we urgently needed to share our news. She told me that they had presented my side of the case in court; the judge had seemed sympathetic, but he'd asked to hear the CID's case the next day and then he would decide. She was convinced I would get bail then.

Suddenly I was not convinced any longer. I told her the things I needed her to bring; I had written a list in the front of my Gandhi book: biscuits, bread, fruit, mosquito repellent, books, writing paper, pen, soap, blanket. I told her the names of the people she must phone; she must cancel my talks in Delhi and Dubai. But she mustn't tell the university or my family, yet. And she would need to bring ₹50,000 next time she came. She guessed what it was for. All links to the outside world were embodied in this one person. I had been practising my speech to her all day, and now it rushed out mechanically.

Two of the long-term prisoners – one the political prisoner who read *The Hindu* – came and stood by me, gate-crashing our conversation. Sara was impatient with them, looking at them in such a way as to make them feel embarrassed and go away. That's what you do in the outside world, but to me they were like saints, who had looked after me and welcomed me, and I wanted to share them with Sara, and to share her with them. I could see they were diminished in their contact with the outside world.

A jailer came to separate us after ten minutes, unlocking the door and leading Sara out. Meanwhile, on my side, I was told that the Deputy Superintendent, Mr Karan, wanted to see me.

Earlier in the day, one of the political prisoners had told me that foreigners were kept in a different block, by law, and that he had heard I would be moved there urgently. Deepak had told me that the foreigners' block is full of Nigerians on drug offences and that they were very abusive to everyone, and would be doubly so to me if I was sent to be with them. He was very worried for me, and said I must arrange the bribe so that I could stay where I was, in safety. So I'd been waiting for Karan's call, to ask me for the ₹50,000 bribe so that I could stay in the admissions block. I was certainly going to arrange payment; I too was worried about what the foreigners' block might offer, so nasty was the picture of it that had been painted for me.

I was taken to Karan's office and allowed the great privilege of sitting on the chair in front of his desk. His task was indeed to tell me that I was to be moved to the foreigners' block.

'We have to treat foreigners differently, it's the law,' he said. 'So you will be moved to the foreigners' block.'

'I'd like to stay where I am,' I said. 'I've made friends.'

'I have to move you,' he said.

'Is there no way I can stay?'

'Well,' he said. 'There is a way. Sara can bring some small gift...'

I interrupted. 'How much?'

He waved his hand, murmured something about not wishing to push us in any direction really, but, well, ₹50,000 would do the trick. 'Then I can talk on your behalf to the Superintendent, to see if special concessions can be made.'

I readily agreed. 'So stay where you are tonight,' he concluded kindly, 'and I'll see what I can do tomorrow.'

Dismissing me, he asked, 'Is everything OK?'

'Everything is fine,' I said.

'That's good,' he replied. 'You cannot fight your destiny.'

I walked back to my block, to cell 13, just making the 6 p.m. deadline as the doors were being locked. The conversation seemed livelier that usual in some of the cells.

'The man, the father who was taken to the prison hospital: he died,' Aditya told me, talking across the corridor.

The sick father had died. He died because the jailers didn't respond to the alarm in the middle of the night. The cold loneliness of the night was creeping up on me. He was probably innocent, like me, certainly not charged with anything, if Deepak was right. Yet he'd died a miserable death in prison.

I sat on my blanket and did nothing. But too many thoughts come when you do nothing, so I opened my Gandhi biography and read.

Gandhi is still in South Africa. He is leading a march of 4,000 striking coal miners – all indentured Indian labourers – and their dependents, protesting against the £3 poll tax on Indians. Gandhi is arrested and imprisoned again. Meanwhile, the South African government declares the mines are now prisons, the European staff prison warders, and the labourers must work, not now as indentured labourers but in effect as slave labourers. From his own prison cell, Gandhi railed against the injustice of this – how the brutal South African government was offending the very rule of law that was the foundation of English justice.

Eventually, it all got too embarrassing for the British; Gandhi was released from prison and a commission of inquiry was set up that was to lead to the Indian Relief Bill and at least some measure of justice for the Indian population.

I stopped reading. It was enough for one night; I had to ration my one book. Then I was disturbed. The jailers had come for me, unlocking my door. I was to be moved to the foreigners' block. But Karan, the Deputy Superintendent, had said I didn't have to be shifted! I protested. They were not moved. I went obediently, with much trepidation.

The jailers handed me over to Jitesh, the thrice murderer, who would take me there. He was very worried for me. He said 'very black', referring to the Nigerians, turning his nose up and clicking his tongue against his teeth in disgust. 'Tell Karan, come back, quick.'

He took me along the road inside the prison perimeter, alongside the high double wall with look-out posts at intervals and guards with machine guns at their posts. The grounds were lovely, trees coming into flower; a beautiful day in nature coming to an end. We went through several checkpoints and gates, and then arrived at block C, the foreigners' block.

The jailers opened the block gates and I was pushed in, carrying my worldly belongings in a plastic bag. You had to be brave in circumstances like this. You had to make it feel mundane, as though you were going into a conference seminar room, nodding to the new people you've not met before. Or a coffee bar in a new town.

The block was one room with a veranda in the front, the room 25 by 15 feet. Along one wall, there were five Africans – Nigerians, I correctly assumed – boisterously playing a board game that involved much slapping down of pieces and shouting; along the other wall were two other Africans sitting quietly – they turned out to be from Ghana and South Africa – and then three Yemenis and a Sudanese. Everyone had got their blankets and some belongings on the floor, each with just about enough room to lie in plus about one foot either side. There were shelves at the far end of the room, where plates and cups and snacks were stored, and then an entrance to a partitioned back room, where there were two holes for toilets and two taps that leaked.

Perhaps I should have gone to the Nigerian side to even up the numbers, but they didn't offer to create a space; it was one of the Yemenis, the oldest of the three, who beckoned for me to make myself comfortable, creating a gap between himself and the South African, and making his fellow Yemenis move up a bit. Seeing my one blanket, he offered me an additional one; 'I have too many,' he said, when I protested. I was so happy to have an extra blanket. Tonight perhaps I would not be cold. The room was permeated in any case with the warmth of bodies. The Yemeni helped me lay my blanket on the floor and then offered me an orange.

The two younger Yemenis also warmly welcomed me. Yasser was in his late twenties, and Jamil had just turned twenty. They were arrested for bringing qat from their home country to India. In India, it was classed as a narcotic drug, but in Yemen, chewing qat was just a normal part of everyday life, like chewing pan here, Yasser said. I'd been to Somalia years ago, and I'd seen how qat was chewed there, so recognised what they were saying.

'We didn't know it was illegal,' Yasser said.

They had been in jail for 123 days so far, still awaiting bail – no charge yet. I now asked people this, realising the significance of what Deepak had told me earlier. They'd been in prison for 123 days without any charge, for a minor drugs infringement. Both were charming and friendly, and I enjoyed sitting and talking with them about Yemeni life.

The Sudanese's name was Al Sadaq. He had come to India

to get married. He said there were close links between Muslims in India and his country, and it wasn't that unusual. He had met his bride for the first time the day they were married. But then police came to arrest him; her family had reported that he had raped her, and denied that any marriage ceremony had ever taken place. 'But they were there at the ceremony!' He had no self-pity. He was a practising Imam and led the Muslim group – all the Yemenis and one Nigerian – in prayer each morning and night.

The third Yemeni, Ahmed, was in for murdering his wife. He was a major in the Yemeni army and would be fired soon, he feared. He said that his Indian wife committed suicide – hanged herself – and had even helpfully written a suicide note. Her family agreed with him, said she was crazy. But the police had arrested him anyway and thrown him in jail, where he was awaiting bail. Again, he had not been charged. He had been locked up since 12 February; he said the date, rather than the usual prisoner custom of saying the number of days imprisoned. He was the most depressed prisoner I'd met so far, but he had been the one who had made a space for me when I had arrived. Perhaps he was being extra kind to compensate for his extra pain.

I moved to talk to the other Africans. The Ghanaian, Valentine Joseph, had been caught in Banjara Hills with cocaine on him. It was a small enough quantity, so he believed he would get bail, but he'd already been there for 130 days. The South African, Johnson, was also there for drugs, although he said they had been planted on him. The Nigerians – their names were Michael, Peter, Godwin, Smart and Olaoye – were all arrested at the house of a fellow Nigerian they were visiting. They were brought to the prison together, but their fellow Nigerian had been taken to Kolkata for some reason, and he may or may not have been guilty of the cybercrimes they were all accused of. They didn't know him well, and had been visiting him as they had newly arrived in India.

'We were arrested because we are Africans,' said Olaoye; older than the others, he appeared to be their leader.

'This is India,' said Smart.

The room felt comfortable; cosy, even. The Ghanaian and South African quietly read their Bibles, the Nigerians were boisterous, one (Michael) giggling uncontrollably at any small joke. Then they stopped their games and banter, and all started doing gymnastic exercises on their blankets, competing with each other to show off the extent of their physical prowess.

Later in the evening, Olaoye yelled out, 'Cybercrimes!', and they fell about laughing at the absurdity of their alleged crime. 'This is India,' they cried. Then all the Muslims – the Sudanese, the Yemeni plus one Nigerian – got up to do their evening prayers at one end of the room. When they had finished, one of the Christian Nigerians went to the same place and conducted a long service all by himself, complete with hymns, (hectoring) sermon, Bible readings and prayers.

I was trying to sleep, but failing, the mosquitos attacking viciously. But eventually it all quietened down, and I drifted in and out of sleep until the Muslims woke up to do their morning prayers at 5.30 a.m., standing, kneeling, prostrating themselves before God, foreheads touching the concrete floor next to where I lay.

|||||||||||||||||||||

Quickly I learnt the routine in the foreigners' block. The prison day officially started with the jailers arriving at 6 a.m. Three came to check up on us, shouting at us if we were not already up for this roll call. The Nigerians would shout back, full of venom at being disturbed. 'Can't you count us as we sleep?' they would cry. 'How do we know it is you?' would come the response. There was none of the deference of the Indian block.

The doors were unlocked, and we were allowed outside.

Chai was served at the adjacent building, the VIP block, where someone said they even have beds. But no one was important enough to be there at this time. The urn of sweet, milky chai was brought over to the veranda each day by one of the convicted prisoners, who never stopped to talk. The Nigerians had a reputation for being a bolshie lot, and no one wanted to hang around.

We would drink our chai on our own veranda and sit outside to chat as the sun rose. The South African, Johnson, then went around with one of those Indian brooms made of sticks, sweeping and tidying. 'Is he on punishment?' I asked the first time I saw this. No, apparently he just liked to keep things tidy.

Michael, the youngest Nigerian, meanwhile, would go for a run around the compound. I joined him for a brisk thirty-minute walk. It was good to be getting exercise. At home, I was always just arriving back from some travels to exotic places, so never got into a proper routine. In prison, I had time for a routine.

After that, I would take my ablutions – throwing a bucket of cold water over me, using a slither of soap, which made me feel fresh. I would clean my teeth and shave. It was important to keep standards of cleanliness high, and one can demonstrate this above all by shaving and cleaning one's teeth.

At 8.30 a.m. or so, our English-language newspaper, the *Deccan Chronicle*, would arrive. By this time, we'd all be sitting under the trees. Olaoye would share the newspaper out, page by page. If I was lucky, I'd get the news pages first; if not, then the fashion or gossip pages were there to be digested – reading every word – until others had finished. We'd swap the pages around between us as we finished them.

Valentine Joseph, the Ghanaian, was very keen on discussing the news with me, being a fellow news addict. We were following two stories closely throughout our time together: the missing Malaysian Airlines Flight 370, and Russia's annexation of Crimea. One morning, we learnt that mobile phones on the flight appeared to be ringing, as reported by passengers' families; and that Crimea had voted in a referendum to join Russia. Valentine thought that this meant a Third World War. I cautioned that it might be more like the Korean War in the 1950s, where the Chinese and the Americans were fighting each other by proxy, through the North and South Koreans respectively. Perhaps this would be the Russians and Americans fighting by proxy through East and West Ukraine. Later, I heard him give a similar exposition to the Nigerians.

At 9 a.m., the first of the two daily meals would arrive, identical to the meals served in the admissions block; contrary to what I'd been led to believe, there was no favouritism about food, except, on occasion, there would be milk curd, only in the foreigners' block; it was the best thing I ate all the time I was there. A convicted prisoner would bring this, and we were strictly rationed to four spoonfuls each.

Days blurred into each other. Something struck me, though. All my life, I had always combined pleasures: a cup of tea *with* a biscuit *and* the newspaper, or a glass of wine *and* cheese *and* the new *Economist*. Now, I realised, when I was sipping my milk curd, I wanted to savour that for as long as I could, *before* I savoured the newspaper, and *then* a cigarette – I started smoking in prison, some extra pleasure to fill up time. Time was long, pleasures were few, and so they had to be rationed. It started making me more intensely observing of life's simple pleasures.

One of these simple pleasures was a proper chessboard, which we were fortunate enough to have at our disposal. Peter, one of the Nigerians, the proclaimed winner among them, suggested we play together first, to test my mettle. It was actually rather beautiful, sitting on the veranda, playing game after game in the mild morning sunlight. I didn't play aggressively, but as I'd won a few games with him a little too easily, I began discussing his moves – why did he do that, when two moves later I could take his Queen? After a dozen games like this, he legitimately beat me. That was very satisfying.

At 5 p.m. on my first evening in the foreigners' block, I was called back to see Karan. He said that he had consulted with the Superintendent, and was pleased to report I could stay in the admissions block, assuming Sara would come with the gift. I told him that I had already been shifted. He was surprised and clearly put out. Quickly, however, he regained his composure and took it all in his stride: 'Fine,' he said. 'Then bring the gift and you can be moved back to the admissions block.' He added, smiling, 'I know how comfortable you were there.'

'No, thank you,' I said. 'I will stay where I am. I accept my destiny.' I was not going to pay a bribe to him.

'We all have to accept our destinies,' he agreed, nodding.

On the second morning, different prison guards arrived to take away 'six Nigerians', but there were only five present, the sixth being the one transferred some time ago to Kolkata. The guards wouldn't believe the Nigerians, and went hunting for the missing man. This was the subject of great mirth for some time to come.

The second evening in the foreigners' block: I had been waiting the whole day, but expectancy peaks around 5 p.m., because after that you know there will be no visit, no news from outside, no bail. Those of us who were optimistic would sit on the stairs by the main entrance, waiting for a message of interview or bail to arrive, but nothing came. No one had come, there was to be no bail. No news from Sara. I assumed that the court had decided against me. Sara could only visit twice a week, so she was saving it for later in the week.

That night was a low period for me, my dark night of the soul. It was harder being in the foreigners' block than with the Indians, because we were alone in this country, it was all unfamiliar; most of all we knew that even when we got bail, we would still be trapped, because they had our passports. And if it went on for a long time, as we'd heard Indian justice did, then those of us with jobs could lose them. Major Ahmed, the Yemeni under investigation for murdering his wife, was the most depressed, perhaps because he had a lot to lose. I too had a lot to lose.

I lay on my blanket, surrounded by snoring men but alone, thinking how I could lose everything. I would be there for some time. The CID wanted me in prison for thirty days, that's what my green admission card meant. I'd miss five international lectures, dinners, fund-raising events. But worse, who could say there would be an end at all? I was in prison – they could throw something else at me. Deepak had affirmed that this happened; you're in for one case and they pile a few others on top for good measure. It could happen to me too.

There was a maximum five-year prison sentence for my alleged offence – abusing foreign currency received without permission. Perhaps this would be simply seamless – no bail, just staying on in prison, but then as a convicted prisoner.

I thought terrible thoughts: if I was there for five years, or even for five months, the university would have to fire me. They might be sympathetic initially, but they surely wouldn't be if it lasted too long. So I would lose my professorship. And because I had a mortgage, I would lose my home, Daisy Cottage – my source of sanity and peace. I'd lose my friends, too: I imagined telling them that I'd been in prison, and felt a shiver of shame shoot up my spine. They would surely think 'no smoke without fire', that some guilt must attach to me. And, I thought, I would lose Sara. She was there for me, valiantly fighting for my freedom in court, but even she wouldn't be able to tolerate it for long – not if I was there for months or years. She was not the kind of person who suffered fools gladly. I liked that about her. But it meant I would lose her.

I would lose everything: my job, my home, my friends and Sara.

I got up and walked to the side veranda, a small space away from the others. I was trying to be aggressive to myself, but this kind of self-hate didn't seem to work as well as it always used to. Instead, I started to feel a certain, odd calm.

Yes, you will lose everything, I thought, but there is something they can't take away from you. See how you love these people; see how you respond with love to everyone: the Indians in the admissions block, the Africans here. Feel your empathy for the suffering of people all around you, for the prisoners stuck in much worse situations than you. Think of poor Arjun, the innocent rickshaw puller, and those like him: innocent, but here for years because they're too poor to go to court. Think of those being beaten, of their powerlessness.

You feel empathy for them all. And they can't take that away from you. No one can take away your love of people, individual people. They can't take that away from you, your freedom to love.

And another realisation welled up inside me and made me calm, a huge wave of warmth filling my breast. One day, however far away that was in the future, one day I would regain my freedom. Even now, writing it makes me smile again, and chuckle and feel happy. For freedom very definitely is not just another name for nothing left to lose.

In the night, I slept deeply for the first time, and woke up feeling calm.

That evening I found a new place to sit, in the last hour before lock-up. Near the compound entrance was a pillar, close to where some prisoners and one of the friendly jailers were playing volleyball. A prisoner came to stand with me, interested in the book that I was writing in. He spoke no English, so I showed him the photos of Gandhi's life. Another convicted prisoner came to join us. His case was murder: 'Two persons. Illegal meetings.' I tried to understand what he meant.

'My wife. Other person,' he said.

'Oh, sex?' I asked.

He nodded. 'So I kill them. Both. I am honest, is that wrong?'

'No, it's not wrong at all,' I said, referring more to the honesty than the murder. Making what connections I could with him, I showed him the picture of Gandhi's murderer in my book, which he appreciated. We stood musing on his case by the garden gate, as if reflecting on the weather or cricket scores. Another man arrived, who spoke English even better. He told me that an Englishman used to sit exactly where I was sitting. It was a prime position, as close to the entrance as you could get, on a concrete block that was slightly more comfortable than the ground, and in a position where you could be on your own but still sharing in what others were doing. I told him my case was to do with foreign currency and a trust.

'Ah,' he said. 'The Englishman was in for exactly the same. He married an Indian woman, they lived in some village.' It was an idyllic life that I too would have loved. 'But he was arrested and brought here. He was a nice man, just like you.'

I had to ask the critical question: how long was the man in jail for, waiting for his bail? About three months, he answered. I was getting used to feeling a sharp pain in my stomach on hearing such things, and ignoring it. I turned to watch the volleyball game.

I was resigned to losing everything. My worst case scenario really could come true. Watching the ball jump forward and backwards was soothing, as were the smiles, especially on the face of the young jailer: an innocent smile, shiny white teeth. I'd noticed him a few times; he stood out by being consistently kind and understanding, even with the rowdy foreigners. People like him could help lead prison reform one day, I thought, if only he didn't lose his idealism, if it wasn't stamped out of him by people like Karan and the Assistant Superintendent. And for me, if I lost everything, I would still have the capacity to love others, and one day would have freedom again, to start over, to learn something else. Some freedoms could not be taken away.

At 6.35 p.m., after we'd been locked up, the Nigerians were brought back from court. All were subdued, but especially Michael, the youngest. At last they had been granted bail, apart from Michael. But they were not jubilant, because they had also been told the costs, and it was totally out of their reach. They needed ₹1 lakh (£1,000) each, to pay the lawyers, the sureties and the court fees – presumably bribes. Where were they going to get that sort of money from? Michael was in the worst position of all. He had no contacts here, and was just taken along for the ride; he had no lawyer to represent him in court. I could not stand his pain, so went and put my arm around his shoulder. I told him I would help him, if I got out before him. I would try to find a lawyer sympathetic to Nigerians. I would help him and I would help Arjun.

(The next morning, as we did our brisk walk around the running track, I discussed the Golden Rule with Michael – we always talk about some topic or other, and I'm forever the teacher. A teacher who wants to know that his pupil has understood, I asked him to relate back to me what the Golden Rule meant. He said, 'If *you* get bail, then when *you* are outside you will think of the one left behind and so help him as if you yourself were still left behind.' I inwardly chuckled at this somewhat selfish interpretation of the Golden Rule.)

I sat with Valentine Joseph, the Ghanaian, and asked if we could read the Bible together. 'The Psalms?' he asked. His Bible was the New International Version, but I soon realised that he was reciting from heart rather than reading, because he kept slipping back into the language of the King James Version. We read Psalm 31:

> O Lord, I have come to you for protection; don't let me be disgraced. Save me, for you do what is right. Turn your ear to listen to me; rescue me quickly. Be my rock of protection, a fortress where I will be safe. You are my rock and my fortress. For the honour of your name, lead me out of this danger. Pull me from the trap my enemies set for me, for I find protection in you alone. I entrust my spirit into your hand. Rescue me, Lord, for you are a faithful God.

Reading the Psalms in prison was unlike reading the Psalms anywhere else. The words hit me with a power I had never experienced before, or have since, and which I find hard to explain. Was it that, uttering those words, our voices were linked with those suffering down through the ages? We were pleading with God for help in overcoming our enemies using the same words as people suffering throughout history. We were praying to overcome those who had entrapped us using language that had been honed in times of desperation. Reciting the words, we were linked as one with the suffering of humanity across space and time.

My future is in your hands. Rescue me from those who
hunt me down relentlessly ... In panic I cried out, I am
cut off from the Lord! But you heard my cry for mercy
and answered my call for help.

We told God that we needed an answer to our cry for help.
We moved to Psalm 22:

My God, my God, why have you abandoned me? Why
are you so far away, when I groan for help? Every day
I call to you, my God, but you do not answer. Every
night, you hear my voice, but I find no relief.

And finally we came to Psalm 23, which even I knew by heart.
Tears streamed down my face as we recited together, sitting on
his blanket, powerless but pleading to a power that generation
upon generation had put their faith in:

The Lord's my shepherd, I'll not want. He makes me
down to lie. In pastures green, he leadeth me, the quiet
waters by.

Yea, though I walk in death's dark vale, yet will I fear
none ill; For Thou art with me; and Thy rod and staff
me comfort still.

Goodness and Mercy all my life, shall surely follow
me. And in God's house forevermore, my dwelling
place shall be.

I was taken back to my childhood, to nights at church camp, sitting around in a similar hut, all boys together, away from our homes, singing this Psalm to the accompaniment of a melancholy accordion, overcome by homesickness.

Later, on my own, I read Psalm 50. I could feel the soaring melodies of Allegri's *Miserere* as I read. Those high notes scaling the prison walls pointed to the freedoms we had lost but which we would one day regain.

They can't take that away from you, the freedom to love one another, or even to love oneself. I had found a place to lie down in the afternoon, to try to get some sleep to help me through the night of little rest. The others took naps inside the cell during the afternoon, but I couldn't bear to be there outside of lock-up. Under a tree, someone had laid two concrete slabs on stones, forming a makeshift bench. I lay there, my precious Gandhi book as my pillow, my hand over my eyes, and was surprised when I woke myself up gently with my snoring. It felt so much better that I had found a way of sleeping in the afternoon. I could add it to my repertoire of things to do. From that little place under the tree, I watched the birds – the babblers, the shrikes, the doves and some amazingly beautiful, colourful small birds that hovered by the bark of trees, descending, then flying off again to hover and repeat the manoeuvre. I would ask Sara to bring in our Indian bird book so I could identify them.

I was lying on the bench in the afternoon. My tokens had arrived earlier that day, so I'd been able to buy soap and a tiny portion of washing powder, and had hand-washed my clothes;

they were drying in the sun near to where I lay. I felt like I was really getting myself organised again, achieving some measure of control. The smell of the washing powder, its harshness on your hands as you scrubbed your clothes, the satisfaction of seeing clothes drying on a bush, all took me back to the time when I was a young man, in my late teens, travelling across Europe, and there was a similar savouring of simple things, like finally getting around to doing your washing and drying your clothes in the sun. Thinking these thoughts, something odd happened.

I'm an underachiever, that's how I always think of myself. I even sometimes recalculate my age, controlling for wasted years: I'm really several years younger than I am, achievement-wise, because I wasted so many years, including between eighteen and twenty-one.

In prison, as I lay there in the heat on that hard surface, waiting for sleep, listening to the birds and the flies and the distant chatter of people, enjoying the simple accomplishment of doing my laundry, I found myself drifting back to these years – but this is dangerous! I tried to stop the thoughts, because, before my time in prison, whenever I'd let myself think about the past, I'd get angry at myself for being so self-indulgent and time-wasting.

But I couldn't stop the thoughts, because I liked what I remembered. By a stream near a highway on entering Spain from France, in the high Pyrenees, my washing spread out to dry in the warm October sun. Marseille, Barcelona, Granada – those were the exotic places you could reach by hitch-hiking

in those days before budget airlines. I used to be totally uninterested in anything like architecture, museums or art galleries
– things you're supposed to absorb as a traveller. Instead, all
I wanted to do was to meet people, hear their stories, share
their joy and their pain. There was that old guy who ran the
Marseille youth hostel, who took me and two young women
out drinking. He tried first to seduce me, then when that didn't
work, each of the women in turn; after the others had gone to
bed, he sobbed on my shoulder about his failed life and dismal marriage. Then there was Klaus, the German I met by the
autoroute. We hitch-hiked together across the foot of France,
from Marseille to outside Barcelona, before parting because
he was in more of a hurry to cover distances than I was. And
Lili in Barcelona, who had come to the railway station that
evening, having drawn a picture on the wall of her bedroom
of me, she said. She knew she was going to meet me, and took
me home for a while, where I shared in her bringing up her
younger brother because her parents had died, and met with
her friends who were planning freedom for Catalonia.

In prison, I enjoyed the memories of those sounds and smells
and laughter and tears of the people I had met. And instead of
castigating myself for wasting that time, I felt kinder towards
myself; why not take delight in those small things? Why was
I always in such a mad rush? Had the world even noticed me
not being there?

In prison I learnt to like parts of myself that I'd despised
until then. In the peace of that afternoon garden, I was in touch

with my eighteen-year-old self, lying in the shade, listening to the birds, waiting for the rest of my life to begin. At eighteen, I had no idea how it would all turn out. Now in my early fifties, I was in much the same position. I immersed myself in that state of not knowing.

|||||||||||||||||||||||

Suddenly it was all over; the prison part, at least.

That afternoon, lunch arrived at 5 p.m.; lightly curried tomatoes with the rice. It tasted good and I devoured it eagerly, wiping my plate clean with my fingers. Then I went to watch the prisoners and friendly jailer play volleyball in the neighbouring compound. Someone was sitting on 'my' stone block, so I moved over to a tree, where the volleyball bounced and hit me in the face to great mirth from everyone. One of the convicted prisoners was expertly leading the game. Seeing me arrive, he stopped and came to sit with me, bringing a very smart chess set.

He was a good player; I'd met my match. I was enjoying the soft breeze, the fading heat, the laughter of the volleyball players, thinking that I could bear being there another day or two or three. It was just half an hour before the evening lock-up and the torture of the mosquitoes and failing to find a comfortable position for bones on stones, and the noise of the Africans and Arabs; I dreaded the night a bit, but the days were becoming bearable. One of the convicted prisoners sidled up to me and said, almost in passing, 'Bail'. I didn't hear him at first, absorbed as I was in my chess move. My bishop and rook were being threatened by my opponent's knight; how had I let myself into such an obvious trap? 'Bail,' the other man repeated, looking at a torn piece of paper with my name scrawled on it.

Suddenly, my emotions welled up. I didn't want to leave this security, this routine, for an uncertain future where I would have to face up to being trapped in India without my passport. And I didn't want to leave my friends behind in the foreigners' block and many, many more in the Indian cells. How unjust that they should remain in jail while I was freed. I'd tried several times to get the innocent rickshaw puller Arjun's full name and his prison number, but had not been allowed back into the Indian blocks after being relocated. How could I help him without those details if I left now? It was all too soon.

Seamlessly, someone else took over my chess game. My friends, who were happy about my news, accompanied me back to the cell. I divided up all my jail possessions and coupons, hugged each of them, and prayed for each that they too might find release soon. I was choking back tears for the beauty of these people and the unjust incarceration of the innocent.

My heart heavy, I walked down the lane by the high prison wall to the administration block, jailers in observation posts training their machines gun down on me, because it was getting late. One of Jitesh's older friends was expecting me, and took me through the procedures.

It was not straightforward. There were formalities that ended up taking two and a half hours – partly because the power kept going off and we couldn't do anything in the total darkness. I read the bail document; it said I had to report twice a month to Hyderabad CID Police. 'You'll have to do it for at least two years,' the jailer said, not to reassure me. 'You won't be allowed to leave the country during that time.' Hearing my sigh, he said, 'It's your destiny. You can't fight your destiny.' As I signed the document, the pen ran out of ink. 'Is this a good or bad omen?' asked the jailer. I could see my troubles beginning again. But at least I would be free to face them.

And perhaps, in a funny way, it would solve the problem of my long-distance relationship with Sara. It was hard sustaining a relationship while she lived in India and I was a professor in England. Our plan before I'd been arrested was that I would move to India in two to three years. After handing over my savings to her for her first new school, I'd been busy raising investment so that she could build a chain of low-cost private schools. When I felt confident enough that they were working well, I planned to give up my professorship and join her in the task. Perhaps I could start living with her now, if I had to be in India. Was that what our destiny was contriving? That could make me very happy indeed.

While I waited, I wrote notes in the margins of my Gandhi biography. I'd managed to keep my 'prison diary' secret from the jailers, hiding my pen in my book whenever one had come near. But I was bolder now that my release was pending. One jailer was intrigued about what I was writing, so I told him it was notes for a talk in America, the first thing that came to mind.

He nodded, but actually didn't understand what I'd said. When his superior asked him what I was writing, he told him something, and the superior came over to see me too: 'Writing prayers?' he said. 'That's good.'

All of us being released on bail had to go before many and various senior officers, including Karan the DSP, to identify ourselves. Each time we had to shout the answers to questions that had now become routine:

'T. James Nicholas

'T. Arthur Henry

'Daisy Cottage, Northumberland, England

'FCRA Section 35.'

In the accounts section, the convicted prisoner with the withered arm gave me back my remaining funds: ₹300 from the ₹1,300 deposited. As I walked back to join the prisoners about to be released, Jitesh's friend asked if he could have my money. I agreed, of course, but recalling that having money was one of the things you could be seriously punished for, I found a place to surreptitiously pass it over to him.

The twenty of us being released who had finished our formalities were made to sit down in the entrance hall, among the probing mosquitoes. We were lined up in one place, then made to sit down again, then lined up in another place – none of us knowing why or what for, but accepting it like children in school assembly.

One of the younger prison officers approached me and asked, 'How much money you have?'

'None,' I said.

He looked at my prison card, which said ₹1,300, the amount I had deposited, and repeated his question, to which I gave the same answer, my throat tightening.

Suspicious, he rushed over to the accounts office to check how much money I had been given. As he stood in front of the prisoner with the withered arm, we started to be led out of the opening prison door. I saw him gesticulating in frustration to find out exactly how much money I should have on me. I tried to move along as fast as I could, desperately willing the prisoners in front to move forward more quickly. I feared that I would be in big trouble if he found out, for if having money in prison was a punishable offence, presumably giving money to another prisoner would also be an offence.

I got out before he had found out if any money was missing. I walked away down the long drive as quickly as I could without running, but then heard my name called.

'T. James Nicholas!'

I was terrified, had to turn back, feared a bullet in my back from the armed guards if I didn't. But it was only a sympathetic jailer who assumed that the taxi waiting by the entrance was for me. It was for someone much grander than me. Almost crying with relief, I strode towards the gates, and met Sara coming in towards me, but I only hugged her briefly before saying, 'Let's go, let's go!', laughing, crying, sobbing, marching as quickly as possible down the road to freedom.

In her taxi, we drove back to the Taj Banjara, a nice business hotel a few kilometres from where we had stayed before. I knew a lot of people there; it used to be my regular when I stayed in India from 2007 to 2009. I was absolutely overwhelmed with the beauty of the hotel lobby – the cleanliness, the shininess, the prettiness. And it was so wonderful to be greeted by a junior manager, Khem, who I knew well.

'Good evening, Professor.'

Professor! Not prisoner – professor! Perhaps the outside world would be manageable after all.

MAGNA CARTA, 'UNDERTRIALS' AND THE RULE OF LAW

IN PRISON I READ how Mahatma Gandhi had successfully struggled for the rights of Indians in South Africa. Due to his efforts, in June 1914 the Indian Relief Bill was successfully passed through the Cape Town Parliament, abolishing a poll tax on Indians and establishing the sanctity of Hindu and Muslim marriages. Gandhi celebrated with an article in his weekly magazine, *Indian Opinion*. He described the Indian Relief Bill as 'the Magna Carta of our liberty in this land'. It 'confirms the theory of the British Constitution that there should be no legal racial inequality between different subjects of the Crown'.

Magna Carta. It's one of the most celebrated documents in global history. Exactly 800 years ago as I write now, in 1215 in Runnymede meadow, barons who had captured London forced their king, John, holding out at Windsor Castle, to set his royal seal on this document. Magna Carta established for the first time the principle of the rule of law. From then on, the nation would be governed by the law rather than the arbitrary decisions of the King and his officials. Even the King would be under the rule of law, just as his subjects were.

The principles of Magna Carta were directly invoked in July 1776 in the American Declaration of Independence. As Eleanor Roosevelt signed the Universal Declaration of Human Rights in December 1948, she said that it 'may well become the international Magna Carta of all men everywhere'.

Many see Magna Carta as iconic, totemic, symbolic, rather than as a living document. Introductory notes to a recent exhibition in the British Library in London describe it as 'a powerful *symbol* of the rule of law and individual liberties'. In a video at the same exhibition, President Clinton said its 'words and ideas have power to stir the mind and the heart and to keep the struggle for liberty enduring'. And the British Chief Justice Lord Bingham opined, 'The significance of Magna Carta lay not only in what it actually said, but in what later generations claimed and believed it had said.'

However, it's of more practical importance than that. Two of its most significant clauses, Chapters 39 and 40, are on the statute books in England today:

Chapter 39: 'No free man is to be arrested, or imprisoned ... save by the lawful judgement of his peers or by the law of the land.'

Chapter 40: 'To no one will we sell, to no one will we deny or delay, right or justice.'

Together they assert the rule of law, that there must be due process and no one can be held in prison without trial; justice delayed is justice denied. Demanding bribes for freedom or making people pay court fees ('To no one will we sell ... right or justice') is completely out of order.

These key principles were novel in England in 1215. What I began to realise, especially when I encountered the notion of 'undertrials' in prison, was that the principles appeared novel in 21st-century India too, 800 years after Magna Carta.

When I was sent to prison, I assumed that I'd be charged with something: perhaps that had happened as I was brought before the judge that fateful Saturday afternoon. It did not occur to me that I could be in prison without any charge being brought against me. In 2008, a celebrated British politician David Davis MP had resigned his seat in Parliament to demonstrate his contempt for government attempting to extend the number of days that terror suspects could be held without trial: the whole incident had brought to my awareness that, under normal circumstances in England, you could only be held for twenty-four hours without being charged. After that, you were free to go.

So when Deepak had told me about undertrials, those in prison waiting to be charged, and that I myself was one, it was a shock to me – and I didn't really believe him. It was not until I'd been out of prison two months that it was confirmed to me by my new lawyers that I hadn't, in fact, been charged with anything.

I'd been an undertrial for only a week or so, but most of those around me had been undertrials for many weeks or even years. It's a scandal.

The word 'undertrial' is actually potentially misleading, suggesting that the person is under*going* trial. In fact, it covers three groups:

First, there are those whose alleged offence is bailable but who have not been charged; they are under police investigation only. I was in this category, as were the majority of people I met in prison. Why, if their offences are bailable, had they not got bail? Some cases were like mine and Deepak's: we hadn't satisfied the informal 'minimum periods' that somehow were applied for bail applications. Others, like Arjun and Michael, most shockingly, were because they couldn't afford court fees, sureties, lawyers and other requirements to get bail. They were being denied justice, let us be very clear about that. Even in the days of Magna Carta it was realised that you should be assumed innocent until proven guilty. These people are being abused and beaten in prison. Their presence absolutely offends against any notion of the rule of law.

Second, there are those whose alleged offence is bailable and who have been charged, but who are awaiting trial. Again, the usual reason why they can't get bail is that they can't afford to do so. If they could afford it, they would be free until their trial. Again, their presence in prison is a scandal.

Finally, there are those whose alleged offence is non-bailable. They may or may not have been charged. Depending on the seriousness of the crime, for example, murder or attempted murder, such people would likely be kept in custody under any jurisdiction, so this category would not be unique to India. Jitesh, who had been waiting two years for trial, would likely have also been kept in prison elsewhere.

Around 38 per cent of undertrials are in custody charged with murder or attempted murder. In England and Wales, where pre-trial detention is used relatively sparingly, only half of such detainees are eventually imprisoned for the crime. In other words, even in a relatively benign prison regime, only half of these people are likely to be guilty. In India, given the level of corruption, there's likely to be a higher proportion of people unjustly accused, like Adit whom I'd met on the manhole cover and who had been accused of murdering his brother-in-law. In India too, the delays in bringing cases to court would also constitute a human rights scandal. In any case, even if all of these prisoners were removed from the equation, that still leaves the remaining 62 per cent of undertrial prisoners who shouldn't be there at all.

Most of the people I met in prison were undertrials. That's not surprising, given the astonishing official figures: in 2011, fully 65 per cent of all inmates of Indian prisons were undertrial prisoners (241,200 out of 369,792). Two out of every three people incarcerated in India have not been convicted of any crime; many will not even have been charged. They are imprisoned while they are under investigation, too poor to furnish bail. Most horribly, many of these people are there because of police corruption itself.

Even more appalling is that (again for 2011) 1,486 undertrial prisoners have been in prison *for more than five years*, while 7,615 have been there for three to five years. Arjun is certainly not alone; across India there are 13,592 undertrials who've been in prison for between two and three years, and 30,261 for between one and two years. There is the bizarre situation that some undertrials have been in prison for longer than the maximum stipulated sentence for the crimes for which they are under investigation.

The Supreme Court of India seems powerless to deal with it. Exceptionally, it did intervene in one extreme case of a young man in 2013 who had been in prison for more than twelve years awaiting trial for a drugs offence. The Supreme Court judgement read: 'The laxity with which we throw citizens into prison reflects our lack of appreciation for the tribulation of incarceration; the callousness with which we leave them there reflects our lack of deference for humanity.'

Think of all the misery this is causing. I met some of them – like Arjun – who had been in prison for years, not charged with anything. Like him, 40 per cent of all undertrials are illiterate. Their families are mostly destitute with the main breadwinner locked away. Their children – whom they haven't seen for so long – are now likely delinquents or being exploited by others.

The Supreme Court earlier noted the problem:

> It is a matter of common experience that in many cases where the persons are accused of minor offences punishable not more than three years – or even less – with or without fine, the proceedings are kept pending for years together. If they are poor and helpless, they languish in jails for long periods either because there is no one to bail them out or because there is no one to think of them.

It's a shocking scandal.

I'd been going to India for seventeen years. No one had ever mentioned this scandal to me. Even when I had visited the Hyderabad prison back in 2000 to help with literacy, no one had pointed out the awful reality. (It's not because it is a new phenomenon either, although it is increasing year on year – back in 1975, 58 per cent of all prisoners were undertrials. Many of the prisoners I had seen in locked cages like dogs back in 2000 were probably undertrials, supposedly innocent unless proved guilty.)

No one back in England has heard of it either. The British human rights organisation Liberty has commendably been campaigning against anti-terrorism laws that could have you in custody for *fourteen days* in England without trial: 'Fourteen days is still the longest period of pre-charge detention of any comparable democracy. In the USA the limit is two days, in Ireland it is seven, in Italy it is four and in Canada it is just one,' a recent pamphlet from the organisation says. 'Extended detention without charge flies in the face of our basic democratic principles of justice, fairness and liberty.' Indeed. In India, there appears to be no limit, however. You could be in prison for twelve years awaiting trial and hardly anyone seems to care.

Gandhi was excited to invoke Magna Carta as he fulfilled the dreams of freedom for Indians in South Africa. What would he make of this scandalous suspension of its principles in modern-day India?

A famous British comedian, Tony Hancock, lampooned the ignorance of youth about the rule of law in his 1957 comedy 'Twelve Angry Men': 'Does Magna Carta mean nothing to you?' he asked, 'Did she die in vain?' In present-day India it looks very much as if she did.

CHAPTER 4

THE DIFFICULTY OF DOING GOOD

SIX WEEKS AFTER I'd got out of prison I was to feel like I'd walked onto the set of a gangster movie and been mistaken for one of the cast. Leading up to that weekend, I became increasingly isolated. No more the love and empathy for prisoners to buttress me; no more inner strength from knowing I was surviving something difficult. Replacing it was the heavy, day-to-day realisation that someone high up in the police was after me, that I was powerless to do anything about it. Possessing my passport she also possessed my freedom.

After prison, once we'd realised it was not going to be a

simple task to get my passport back, Sara helped me set up in a rented room in a serviced apartment up a narrow lane, walking distance from the Taj Banjara hotel, where at least the staff knew my name and rank.

My bail conditions said that I had to go for interrogations at CID headquarters with Mrs Mantra 'between 9 a.m. and 5 p.m.' on the 'second and fourth Sundays', plus any other times at her pleasure. My first interrogation was set for Sunday 23 March.

Knowing India well enough, Sara and I figured that 9 a.m. was impossibly early for any government employee, especially on a Sunday, so we arrived at CID headquarters at 10 a.m. Up the sweeping staircase to the main entrance, we followed the same route I'd taken a few weeks earlier when I'd been brought there on my first night of custody. Even in the light of day, with Sara beside me, it felt deadening. The whole building was completely quiet.

No one at reception knew who I was, or what I was there for. Mrs Mantra was not around. A sickening realisation dawned on me: if there was no one to sign my notebook, brought on instructions from my lawyer, then there'd be no proof that I'd come in as required. Then she could claim I had broken my bail conditions and so send me back to prison. Surely it couldn't be that easy for her?

The security officers would not let us go into the building. Being less afraid of Indian authority than I was, Sara made us double back when out of their field of vision, and led me upstairs past the library where I'd spent my first night in

custody, to some offices where fortunately we found someone
in. It was Mr K. Ashok Chakravarthy, Inspector of Police, a
kindly, patrician fellow with white thinning hair and wearing
blue flip-flops.

He offered us chai and biscuits, found Mrs Mantra's number and put me on the line to her. Mrs Mantra was warm and
breezy: 'Tooley (she alone called me this), nice to hear you!
How *are* you?' It was a bit odd coming from someone who
had banged you up in prison. I felt my blood pressure rising,
but forced myself to be pleasant, although Sara glared at me
for being so: 'Mrs Mantra,' I began ('Why did you call her *Mrs*
Mantra? Don't flatter her,' Sara said later), 'How are you? I am
here for my interrogation.'

She seemed put out: 'You should have phoned me.'

'I don't have your number.'

'I gave it to you,' she said. In prison, perhaps? She said I
should wait for her; she'd be straight over.

We finished our chai with Inspector Chakravarthy.

'You had no business being sent to prison,' he said, shaking
his head. 'It's a straightforward case.'

Sara said that Mantra must have sent me to prison because
she wanted a big bribe from a naive foreigner. Inspector
Chakravarthy was noncommittal. But he kindly agreed to sign
my notebook, so I had proof that I had come in, should Mrs
Mantra not turn up. That was a great relief to me.

We sat outside and waited for Mrs Mantra. At 11 a.m. we
phoned her again; she was on her way. At 11.30 a.m., she didn't

pick up the call. At 12.30 p.m., she said, 'Go home and have your lunch. Come back and see me at 3 p.m.'

It was a refrain I was going to hear many times over the next few months: go home and have your lunch. As if (a) I have transport that will easily enable me to move around this heavily congested city, (b) I have a home to go to, where (c) a nice lunch is awaiting me. It also emphasised that (d) I am at this person's mercy and (e) my time is not my own.

We took an autorickshaw back to my rented room, sat miserably for a couple of hours, returning at 3 p.m. to wait downstairs in the security reception on broken chairs in the stifling heat. Mrs Mantra arrived at 3.45 p.m. with her son, the young man who needed a place at a good British university.

She took us up to the third floor. Here the space was divided into corridors by tall filing cabinets; leading off from these were staff cubicles. Piles of paper were stacked everywhere, most leaning heavily, some capsized altogether onto the dirty floor. It was gloomy, hot and stuffy, filthy and depressing. The electricity was off, so there were no fans to cool us.

We sat in her cramped cubicle, she at her desk, her son to one side; he said nothing the whole time, did not even catch my eye when I tried to be friendly. Sara sat by my side. Mrs Mantra started writing on her blank sheets of paper in her slow, laborious scrawl. It was as if someone had discovered writing for the first time, sitting there with her head bowed over the paper, concentrating intensely. Like a child at school, she started by writing the date of my visit at the top of the paper – but slowly, after consulting her wall calendar, forgetting what she'd read, going back and checking. And then she stopped and said, 'You are supposed to come on the second and fourth Sundays. So why didn't you come last week?'

'That was the third Sunday,' I said. She thought for a moment, then said, 'So why didn't you come on the 9th, the second Sunday. You've missed one interrogation.'

'I was in prison, ma'am,' I said.

For a moment it looked as though she was ruminating on whether she would allow this as a relevant excuse. I began to feel panic rising in me. Eventually, however, she let it pass after looking several times at the calendar on her wall. She began her interrogation proper.

Why Hyderabad? Why did I come here? In a cooperative mood, I told her the full details. It was in the slums of the Old City fourteen years ago that I'd first found low-cost private schools, showing how the poor were helping themselves improve educationally. I needed an organisation to conduct my research, so in 2002 I'd co-founded the Educare Trust. Our research found the majority of poor children in low-cost private schools outperforming government schools for a fraction of the cost. Following the research, we wanted to help the schools and their children, so we created a scholarship programme and a revolving loan fund.

'It's all there in my book, *The Beautiful Tree*,' I said, pointing to the copy I had just noticed sitting on her desk. 'Educare Trust is mentioned several times.'

When I had finished, she looked up from her page, said, 'Fourteen years ago?', and I realised she'd hardly taken anything down. I started again, painfully slowly, checking that she had written key points before moving on.

At the beginning I asked if I could sign to show I'd been there. 'It doesn't matter,' she had said, 'I know you've been here.' I had let it drop for a while, but later, I asked, 'I wonder if I could sign your register to show I've been here, and if you can sign mine,' producing my little notebook. She pushed it back to me.

'I am Deputy Superintendent CID. I don't sign prisoners' notebooks.'

'I'm not a prisoner,' I said.

She looked at me closely and her smile broadened, 'You are on *conditional* bail. At my say, you're back in prison.'

Mrs Mantra then fixed her stare on Sara. She asked how old she was. Where was she from? What was her relationship with me? What was she doing in Hyderabad? She seemed to know a lot about the trust. What was her involvement? What was her *real* involvement?

Sara had become the object of interrogation. In court she had said that she was an old friend of mine who happened to be in Hyderabad and so was helping me, and this was the line she stuck to now.

'I'm only allowing you to be here because I'm being kind,' Mrs Mantra had told Sara at the beginning, although Sara had proven useful in translating my English accent to her

– presumably the real reason she had allowed her to stay. Now Mrs Mantra said, 'I think you're more involved with the trust than you're telling us.' Looking at her calendar, she said to Sara, 'When can you come in and talk to me about your involvement?'

There's absolutely no way I could have *her* being arrested. Sara must not come back to Hyderabad. She was scheduled to leave the following day, but had intended to return a week later. I now realised this was impossible. Mrs Mantra wanted to send her down too; that was where all her questioning was leading. I couldn't take that risk, not with beautiful Sara.

I interjected, 'You're supposed to be interrogating me. I'm the one you put in prison.'

She turned and fixed her smile on me and said, 'You mustn't have ill-feeling towards me. I was only doing my duty. We must do our duty before God and accept our destiny.' As she said this, her hands came together in a respectful Namaste greeting, and she brought her thumbs to touch her heart, her forehead, before raising her hands towards the ceiling or, I suppose, the heavens.

I said, 'But I'm innocent.'

'*Achaa*,' she said. 'But if you're innocent, why were you in prison?'

'Because you sent me to prison,' I said.

Talking to her made me feel like I was running through quicksand. She shook her head, 'I have to follow my duty, before God.' She did the same elaborate hand movements again.

All the while, her son sat there quietly, giving nothing away.

Eventually, she did find a book for me to sign – a scruffy notebook used for many other purposes. But she adamantly refused to sign my book. With only her book signed, I was at her mercy; if she chose to say I hadn't come in, I could not prove that I had.

She let us leave at 5.30 p.m. We'd only been with her for two hours, but we were both exhausted. Trying to cheer ourselves up, we took an autorickshaw to the hotel where we'd been staying before, the Park Hyatt, because we had been so happy there with my niece and friends. But all I could see was Mrs Mantra in the lobby with her fixed smile, arresting me. At least I had the opportunity to thank the duty manager for being so kind on the night of the arrest in giving Sara the use of a hotel car without charge. His view on the whole incident was very straightforward. The whole thing was a set-up by the police for a large bribe, nothing more. 'It happens a lot,' he said, 'to us and our families.' It was a refrain I was to hear many times.

||||||||||||||||||

On Tuesday 25 March, two days after my first interrogation, I was in court. My lawyers had put in a petition to get my passport returned.

I arrived at the criminal court at 9.30 a.m. It's an old, colonial building, with stately palm trees spanning out from its grand column. Battered old prison buses arriving shattered the calmness of the scene. Prisoners were led up the grand stairs, two or three shackled together, chained at the wrists and the ankles, their chains dragging in the dust behind them. Their faces were not resigned, but defiant. But I knew how powerless they were. That sense of powerlessness overwhelmed me as I entered the court building. I followed the prisoners as they were led upstairs by the jailers in khaki uniforms with rifles and sub-machine guns at the ready. They were taken to the locked cells at the end of the corridor by the stinking toilets.

I waited on an old metal bench with no back support for Prandakur – Vashnu had assigned the case to his junior, and I never saw him in court. The corridor was dirty, the stairs leading up to them doubly so. The walls were covered in the dried red spit of men chewing pan. There was litter everywhere on the floor and scattered piles of pigeon droppings. No one else seemed to notice the pigeons nesting in the corridor on the metal pipe supports. There were no fans in the corridor, which made even the March heat hard to bear.

After a while I spotted Prandakur with a group of other lawyers, and stood with them as they talked in Telugu, in the forlorn hope that he might talk to me about my case. A beggar with crippled half-limbs came across to our group. He went straight to the lawyers and tugged at their arms, ignoring me. In the world I used to inhabit, beggars usually went straight to foreigners, to the white man, ignoring Indians, more certain of what they might gain. Here, he went for the people with power, ignoring the powerless.

Prandakur directed me to court 6, to let the judge know I

was there. Sara had been sitting every day in the courtroom while I had been in prison, to remind the judge that my case was waiting to be heard. So I sat and tried to catch the eye of the judge so that he knew I was waiting. In my suit and tie I hoped he could see I was respectable and deserving of attention. I didn't recognise him, but I'm hopeless at recognising faces.

At 1.30 p.m., the judge retired for lunch. We all stood up; as the court crier called 'Court stand!', everyone did the respectful Namaste greeting, placing both hands together and making a slight bow. I bowed only, worrying that putting my hands together might look a tad pretentious.

I didn't fancy staying in the court grounds for lunch, so I wandered along the road and found that one of the stores doing legal photocopying and the like also sold cold drinks. The kindly owner invited me to come inside and sit more comfortably under the fan on a plastic chair. I felt safe there.

I returned to court at 2 p.m., only to find I'd been making eyes at the wrong judge. Prandakur had sat me in the wrong courtroom. Now he directed me upstairs, to court 9, also on recess. The court clerk, a rather rotund man in his early thirties, was finishing his lunch. Every day I saw him bring out his tiffin of biryani with two halves of boiled egg on top and curry to the side, tucking in with relish, mashing it all together in his right hand.

I waited on one of the chairs along the wall, where the sign read 'Witnesses', but where Prandakur said I should sit. There were broken plastic and broken wooden chairs; I selected the hardest-looking wooden one. For some reason, which I wouldn't have been able to articulate at this point, I felt the need for penitence.

Waiting for the judge to return were exactly twelve lawyers, all dressed in white collars and distinctive white ties, white shirts, black jackets and black academic gowns. One dozed, some read case notes, but most just sat in the terrible heat, which the fans didn't do much to quell, waiting. Seeing them in their uniforms, I yearned for my life as a professor, resplendent in academic gown for graduation processions. I yearned for the comfort of knowing my status in a hierarchy, the comfort the lawyers were exhibiting in front of me.

The judge returned at 3.30 p.m. We all stood, they Namaste-ed, I bowed.

Now I remembered the judge clearly. He had a rather exuberant walrus moustache. He was certainly a handsome man, but he looked either totally disdainful or had severe indigestion after a heavy meal. He flicked away the numerous papers that were brought to him after signing each page with the maximum nonchalance, as if he really was above all this petty nonsense.

The court crier was friendly enough to me. He was wearing a white Gandhi cap, a *topi*, like that worn by a Mumbai tiffin wallah who delivers lunch to workers across the city. He was also wearing a red silk sash diagonally across his shoulder and a neat white shirt and trousers. Apparently, he was the one who had visited me in hospital; he asked after my health. He took turns with another in the same role, with the same uniform. His alternate, however, scolded me whenever he could, told me to sit up straight, not cross my legs, just like being back in prison, back in school.

The judge sat on a raised platform. Above him was a portrait of Gandhi, modestly attired with a shawl over his shoulders. Below the judge, on the mezzanine level, were a couple of old school desks groaning under the weight of piles of papers. At one, the court clerk sat; the other was set aside for witnesses. On the lower level there was the horseshoe table for lawyers, with the seats for witnesses on the side furthest from the door, by the windows. At the back of the hall, there was a wooden balustrade, behind which the defendants stood when called.

My case came up at 4.25 p.m. It lasted precisely two minutes. Prandakur, my junior lawyer, and the CID lawyer – the public prosecutor – stood together by the mezzanine level. The public prosecutor had jet black hair, like most Indian men, but it was a very glossy full head of hair that was brushed forward just over his ears, in an unusual fashion. Perhaps it was a wig, I thought; a wig not quite fitted properly? I also noticed that he appeared to have a mild hunchback, but it was probably because his black gown was too small, so it bunched up over his shoulders. He was a short, fairly squat man, with thick fish lips. Later, Sara told me that he was the spitting image of a comedian in a famous TV soap opera from her region.

The public prosecutor rested his arm on one of the mezzanine desks. He said that the CID needed more time for a counter argument to my petition. The judge wrote something on my papers, pushing them nonchalantly across to the court clerk; '28th March' was called out. Prandakur beckoned for me to leave.

The judge had given them until Friday to get their arguments ready.

It was only another three days – Wednesday, Thursday and Friday. But it felt like a huge blow. I had been away from my home and job for over a month. Each day was hard, each night harder still. The day in the stuffy heat of the courtroom was emotionally draining. At the end of it, all I felt like doing was getting rip-roaringly drunk.

On Friday I was back in court again. I got that same sinking feeling on arrival, seeing the prison buses being unloaded, the shackled prisoners taken upstairs, feeling everyone's pain as they sat in the dirty corridors or in the stuffy courtrooms.

As I sat and waited through the court all morning, I began to feel increasingly disturbed. If my case went to trial, then I would be tried through the 'part-hearings' I observed all morning. It was very hard to see how justice could be done. The part-hearing I was watching went as follows.

To begin, the court clerk at the mezzanine desk said *sotto voce* the name of the case, the court crier bellowed the same down the corridor.

The defendants stood behind the wooden balustrade. Meanwhile, witnesses were called to the mezzanine level, where they were quizzed by the public prosecutor or one of their own lawyers. I didn't see a single witness who seemed engaged with the process; they all seemed cowed, heads bowed, saying as little as possible, as if they knew they were at the mercy of the court to interpret their words in any way it wanted. Often, during the questioning of witnesses, the judge would intervene and wave the person away, exasperated.

One lawyer, quizzing a witness in a bright turquoise shirt, had amazing wispy hair growing straight out of his ears, sticking out about two inches on either side. His questioning was uncharacteristically clear compared to that of the other lawyers I heard. However, it was all to no avail: after a while he realised that the witness didn't speak any English. He rehashed the same questions again in Telugu, in a highly irritated manner.

Usually, however, the questioning was far from clear. I estimated that I was at an equivalent distance from the witnesses as was the judge. I could hardly hear anything. Not only the witnesses, but also most of the lawyers mumbled inaudibly. I leant in to try and catch what was being said, but only caught snippets. The judge also leant in trying to hear what was going on; at one point we caught each other's eyes as both of us were tilting forward, straining to hear.

As the questioning of witnesses continued, the judge relayed a précis of salient points to his court transcriber. (Once he had finished typing, the transcriber would print it out on the ancient dot matrix printer, zip, zip, zip, the noise screeching its way around the courtroom; the printed version would be torn off and handed to the judge to check.) But while the judge was relaying his points to the transcriber, the lawyers continued to question. Several times I saw apparently important points being made that the judge missed because he was still relaying earlier points to his transcriber. Other court clerks also presented papers for signing to the judge, which he flicked through in a perfunctory manner, paying little attention neither to what was in the papers nor to the interrogations going on beneath him.

Once, I saw one of the lawyers, proud at having secured significant concessions from his witness, looking up to see the judge otherwise engaged, so missing these important points. The lawyer back-tracked and asked the same questions again, hoping for the same reaction. The witness wouldn't play the game, though, and just shrugged that he'd already answered, so the lawyer's triumph was overturned.

It was all reminiscent of an Indian grocery store, where the shopkeeper, perhaps to be helpful, serves three or more people simultaneously. The outcome: no one gets served quickly and everyone feels deprived of proper service.

Part of the reason no one could hear was the noise of people mingling in the corridors outside. And between the defendants and the judge, the lawyers sat around their horseshoe desk and chatted to each other, often quite noisily, oblivious of the effect this had on people, especially defendants, who wanted to hear what was going on.

It all seemed so unfair on the defendants. What was happening at the far end of the room appeared to have very little to do with them. But it was their freedom that was being deliberated. It seemed so unfair especially to those who were poor, because they were paying for lawyers, who most of the time sat and did nothing. At any one time, you would see nine or more lawyers sitting around the horseshoe table, waiting for their cases to come up, greedily devouring the funds of the poor. The poor may have also had to take a day off work, because you wouldn't know when your case was coming up; you had to budget a whole day, arriving as I'd done in the morning, but perhaps not being seen until the afternoon.

At 2.30 p.m., Prandakur suddenly stood up in front of the judge, and I was ushered to stand nearby. I stood bolt upright in suit and tie, guessing that my case had been called. The judge relayed to Prandakur a message from the public prosecutor. He wanted more time.

Prandakur sat down at the horseshoe table, I sat down on the broken wooden chair, the court clerk said something to the court crier, who cried out a date and motioned for me to leave. And that was it. My hearing had been postponed for another week.

|||||||||||||||||||

Between court appearances and my interrogations, a typical day started at about 8 a.m. I would drag myself out of bed and go upstairs to the rooftop patio, where the serviced apartments' kitchen was based. I'd greet the Nepali kitchen supervisor and breakfast on greasy but filling south Indian food. After a shower, I'd try to do some work. I had my laptop computer set up on a tiny desk in a grubby cubbyhole in one corner of my room. It was by a small window with a filthy curtain and net curtain, looking out over wasteland and building sites where work had long been discontinued, sites overgrown with bushes and small trees. Alongside were other apartment blocks with washing hung out on balconies, and an oddly placed street lamp, where once there must have been a street before building work took over. If I looked to one side, I could see a tiny temple with an ornate golden lotus rooftop; to the other side there was a modern mosque.

Once I realised that my case was going into April, I finally plucked up the courage to tell the university. By email, my colleagues, dear friends Barrie Craven and David Longfield, helped me write a letter to the pro-vice chancellor, Charles Harvey, who immediately passed it on to John Hogan, the registrar. John helpfully organised a conference call to discuss the next steps. In those early days, it all seemed so hopeful; after our second call, I quipped to John that he must deal with cases of wrongful imprisonment every week, so confident was his approach as to what needed to be done. As time went by, however, both of us became increasingly out of our depth.

If possible, each day, I tried to do some university work – I had a couple of doctoral students getting ready to submit their theses, so going through these documents was something I could manage. Or I'd try to deal with a few of the 200 work-related emails that were arriving each day, to give the impression that I was on top of things.

More often than not, I had to spend time on legal matters, going through documents concerning the Educare Trust that I'd found in the schools, or that Barrie and David had found in my home, preparing summaries of these to demonstrate my innocence.

My capacity for doing this kind of work, however, rapidly decreased as the days and weeks passed and my isolation and growing despair made me increasingly depressed. By about the third or fourth week, after an hour or so of university or legal work, I'd collapse, exhausted. I'd make myself some eggs for lunch, sleep a bit, then at about 4 p.m. if I didn't have an appointment to see my lawyers, I'd walk down the narrow lane, Road No. 13, through the Taj Banjara back gates, along the stinking lake, on to Road No. 1, to the 'City Centre' shopping mall, where Crosswords bookshop was situated on the first floor. There I'd have a coffee and try to raise some enthusiasm to explore new books that had arrived. After a couple of hours of this, I'd retrace my steps back to the Taj Banjara for dinner and a drink, before walking back up the lane to my room, where I kept some gin for late nights, and then fitful sleep.

It sounds easy, walking down lanes and along main roads, but the reality is far from it. Pedestrians are the lowest form of human life in India. The back lane, Road No. 13, has no street lights, of course, so at night it's pitch dark. In England we'd think this narrow lane had room for only one car to pass at a time, but here two cars drive towards each other and somehow make it through. There are no pavements. Walking along on the lane, a car comes behind you, or towards you, at speed and beeps its horn. There's no chance it will slow down to take into account you being there. It beeps its horn and it's your responsibility to get out of the way. You have to step into the rough edges of the lane, where there are rocks, stones, boulders, gravel, mud, dirt, rubbish and shit.

That's Road No. 13. It feeds into Road No. 1, the main road, which is extraordinarily congested, polluted and noisy. It does have pavements at least some of the way, but these are used by local men as urinals, and they stink. So you have to walk in the road. Often traffic comes the opposite way from which it should, so you not only have to worry about the traffic behind you, but also random vehicles speeding at you in the wrong direction. Woe betide you if you want to cross Road No. 1 – which is one of the reasons I generally kept to the perambulation described. There are traffic lights, and even supposed crossings for pedestrians, but these are in name only. There are always thick lanes of traffic moving, and pedestrians have to dodge cars and two-wheelers, buses and trucks and the ubiquitous autorickshaws to get across. But even staying on the same side of the road, you have to cross junctions where lanes join, and here too you take your life in your hands as you struggle across while vehicles indifferent to the presence of humans come at you from all directions.

I had to do the legal preparation work for my case by myself. My lawyers, Vashnu and Prandakur, had delegated this to me, themselves having more important matters to attend to. Many afternoons I would arrange to see Vashnu to show him how I was making progress summarising the chronology of the Educare Trust. I would phone him in the morning, get told to phone again in the afternoon because he was at court, then make an appointment for the late afternoon or early evening, prepare a hired car only to be told just before leaving that I should come tomorrow instead. Most frustratingly for me, day after day I would ask to see the legal documents – the court petitions, the remand notes, anything that could help me understand the current case against me – and each time I would be told by Vashnu, 'Let's do one thing; Prandakur will bring these to you tomorrow.' But he never did. In the whole time I was using Vashnu and Prandakur as my lawyers, I did not get to see one single document from the court or prison or CID to help me understand anything about the case against me.

Occasionally, I would manage to see Vashnu in his office, in a residential apartment building an hour across town from where I was staying. He was frequently dismissive, doing the south Indian thing of shaking his head and sucking on his tongue, dismissively saying, 'Not like that' or 'That's not the thing, you see'. On the other hand, if you said something with which he agreed, he would say 'taken'; I didn't cotton on for some time that he meant 'point taken', and so would ask for clarification. But he wouldn't get my question and would assume I was challenging him on some of the finer points of the law, and so often we'd fall into hopeless misunderstanding of each other. He had terrible difficulty comprehending my accent, and me his.

He couldn't understand Sara well either, and both would usually resort to speaking in Hindi rather than English.

My friends back in England, Barrie and David, had found some Educare Trust documents at Daisy Cottage, and apparently spent several days with papers all over the floor of my university office scanning these and sending them across to me. One day I managed to find boxes of documents about the trust that had fortunately been stored in one of the schools in the Old City. Filthy, tatty boxes, full of rat droppings. So, slowly I was able to amass papers in my room – over 11,000 pages of trust documents, letters, receipts, invoices, cash books, etc. – which clearly showed, thankfully, there could be no case against me. At one of our meetings I told Vashnu that I had found all these documents.

'Let's do one thing,' he said. 'Let's not tell the lady about this.' He always called Mrs Mantra 'the lady'. Prandakur then told me that I must neither show any of these documents to the CID, nor even tell them I had found them. So in my interrogations, I had to keep saying I had no documents. I couldn't see the reason for this, and he would never say why, which was infuriating. This meant that, in my interrogations, I ended up looking furtive, guilty. In frustration once I did show a few documents to Mrs Mantra during an interrogation, the ones that showed I'd resigned from the trust in 2004, and so was not involved at all when foreign currency was received without permission. I was neither managing trustee, nor even a trustee. She completely ignored the evidence. Was this because she didn't understand what it was saying? Only later did I discover the cunning way that she and others in CID could simply dismiss it as irrelevant.

My lawyers' nervousness about my documents did, however, make me realise that I'd better get copies of them all, whatever the reason for their anxiety. In any case, that made good sense – supposing there was a fire or burglary in the room, and the documents were destroyed or stolen? Fortunately, one of my few remaining friends in Hyderabad – his name was Praveen – knew someone who ran a small photocopying business, who came around with four young colleagues with laptops and scanners and spent one day and night sitting there in my room, scanning, before realising this job would take longer and so removed them all to his office to continue the job, for another four days and nights.

So you want to do good in India, bring in funds to help the poor? Setting up a trust is a route fraught with dangers. Here's what I managed to piece together from the documents I found.

With a local Hyderabadi, I'd got the trust registered in January 2002. Because I was putting in the initial money, it was agreed that I'd be managing trustee; the Registrar in his office near, as it happened, to the criminal court agreed that this was fine. We made our first application to the Ministry of Home Affairs to receive foreign currency, using the correct application forms, at the end of 2002. A few months later, a letter came back saying the application 'was considered but the same was not agreed to'.

That was it, nothing more; no indication of what we could do. Time after time, we got a similar letter back, after many months of waiting, repeating the refrain that the application 'was considered but the same was not agreed to'.

Sometime during this period, we got wind that registration was not being granted under the Foreign Contribution (Regulation) Act because of me – a foreigner – being managing trustee. It was definitely not illegal; we checked again and again with lawyers and with the Registrar of Trusts. However, the Ministry of Home Affairs would not allow it, and apparently they had discretion over matters like this.

But this led to what I now saw as a very happy outcome. On 15 January 2004, I tendered my resignation, both as managing trustee and from the board of trustees itself! I found my letter to this effect, and the board minutes acknowledging my resignation and appointing a local woman, Gita, as managing trustee in my place. (These were documents I showed to Mrs Mantra, and which my lawyer later submitted to the court.) So surely this demonstrated my innocence, even if nothing else did.

It was Gita, not a foreigner, who made applications for permission to receive foreign currency. One application led to an inspection by a director from the Ministry of Home Affairs at the beginning of February 2005. Everything was found to be in proper order. The director wrote a very favourable report, which noted that the inspection had not revealed any 'mis-utilisation or misappropriation of foreign contribution by the trust', and hence that the central government had come to the conclusion that if there had been 'any contravention of the provisions of the Foreign Contribution (Regulation) Act', this 'was not a wilful act' on the trust's part, and therefore that 'a lenient view of the said contravention appears warranted'.

So far, so good. But then it started to unravel.

On his inspection visit, the director had been kind, had written a good report, but on departure had finally stressed to Gita that she needed to 'assist' him. Gita told me the story as I was trying to piece together exactly what had happened. By 'assisting' him, she had known exactly what he meant – he was after a bribe – but instead of 'doing the needful', as the Indians say, she gave him a Jolly Phonics kit – one of the literacy tools we were using in the schools – because, Gita had told me, he seemed really interested in this as a way of teaching his own child. He had politely accepted, but told Gita that she should come to his office in Delhi, and he would continue to do the right thing for her and the trust. She had gone in May 2004 – I had her entrance tickets to the Ministry of Home Affairs among my piles of documents – where officials from the Ministry of Home Affairs asked for bribes of ₹2 lakhs (£2,000) to get foreign currency approval. She didn't pay. Whenever I enquired about foreign currency, her response was always, 'Professor, don't worry, it's all fine.' I assumed that she had sorted it all out, somehow, perhaps in ways that she didn't want to tell me about.

But looking at the records, I could see it was not all fine. Two tranches of foreign currency, each of ₹17.5 lakhs (£17,500), had never been granted permission. Combined, these were the £35,000 that formed the basis of the CID's case against me. When I realised this, my heart sank a little. So there was a genuine case, at least against the trust (but surely not against me, because I was nothing to do with the trust during that period).

The letters around the application for permission were horrible to read. For the first tranche, Gita had applied for prior permission on 17 June 2005. A letter from the Ministry of Home Affairs was received in early October, which said: 'We expect to take a final view on your application within ninety days.' A further letter was received on 16 November 2005, which noted: 'Due to certain difficulties, it is not possible to dispose of your application within ninety days. Accordingly you are informed that it will take another thirty days from 29/11/2005 to dispose of your application.' In other words, three and a half months after receiving the application, Gita was told to wait another three months – that is, six and a half months after applying. Any cheque received would now have lapsed. Finally, a letter arrived dated 22 December 2005 from the Ministry of Home Affairs saying that 'the Central Government have decided *not* repeat *not* to accord permission under the said Act'. No reason was given; there was simply the one paragraph and nothing more. But the reason was clear now: the delays were given in the expectation of the officials receiving bribes. As bribes were not received in the allotted time, the request was thrown out. All very simple.

So the trust had indeed received foreign contribution amounting to about ₹35 lakhs (£35,000) during the financial years 2005–2006 and 2006–2007. This is indeed an offence under the FCRA. But it was 2014 – so why had it taken nine years to bring this to court? That's a puzzle that I didn't manage to understand.

There was good news and two pieces of bad news here. First, the good news. Given the complexity of the regulations, the discretion the Ministry of Home Affairs has in their interpretation, plus the tardy way with which the Ministry deals with cases, offences by trusts are commonplace. So common, indeed, that the Ministry publishes a list of penalties that can be paid for such violations, without the need even to go to court, certainly not to prison. Think of these being like speeding tickets. For the violations of the Educare Trust, the penalty would be £1,750.

The first piece of bad news was that my lawyers had no idea about this, nor did the public prosecutor, nor the judge, nor anyone else involved. It was only by chance that I uncovered these penalties later.

The second piece of bad news was more severe. What Mantra had accused me of went beyond this – the only legal document I'd seen against me was the arrest warrant she had laboriously written on my first day of custody in the library. This had spelled out, yes, the offence of receiving foreign currency without prior permission. But she had not stopped there. She had gone on to say that I had used the funds not for their 'specified purposes', but for my own 'aristocratic, lavish' life-style. This was a big problem. If this was the case, the law did not allow you to pay a penalty. Instead, the courts could impose five years in prison for this offence.

A chilling thought. That's why all the rest of the documents were of such importance – and I was so thankful that somehow they'd been kept in one of the schools. The invoices, receipts, letters from schools and children, they were the key documents showing that Mrs Mantra's serious allegations were not true; they showed that we had been using funds for the 'specified purposes', providing scholarships for the poor and loans to help schools improve, providing teacher training and building schools, not for any other purpose at all.

It was rather like I'd been stopped for a minor speeding offence, but then the policewoman had added on extra things she'd made up, like I stole the car and, oh yes, as I was speeding, I had knocked people over and killed them.

That, I realised, was the situation I was up against.

||||||||||||||||||

On my second interrogation, Mantra reminded me again that I was on conditional bail and she could have me back in prison at any time. To demonstrate her power and my powerlessness, she called a junior officer in to her airless cubicle. He asked me what I was doing at the main bus station at 10 p.m. last night and who was the African I was with? It was Michael, the young

Nigerian I had promised to help in prison, keeping my side of the Golden Rule bargain. I had managed to pay for bail for him and gone back to prison to pick him up as he was released. I had put him on the bus to Mumbai, where he had been told other Nigerians might be able to help him. But how did they know? Clearly they had been following me. I felt increasingly vulnerable.

She asked about people I'd seen all week and where I'd been each day. She asked me further details about Sara. 'Where does she live? When is she coming back to Hyderabad? What is her father's name?' I was cagey about answering any of these questions. 'Don't worry,' she said in response to my silence. 'We can find all these things out. We are the CID. Don't think we can't find out everything.'

But then in the middle of her questioning, her eyes closed and she fell into a deep sleep. I didn't try to wake her; it was a tremendous relief. Then her head jerked down and she woke herself up. I knew she was always eager for distraction, so took her nap as my cue. 'It's Telugu New Year tomorrow?' I asked. Immediately she and her son – who was, of course, present at this and most interrogations – perked up.

'Ugadi,' she said. 'That's what we call it. We celebrate the day our senior god Lord Brahma created the universe.' In detail, she told me how they will prepare special food called Pachadi, with six tastes representing all our emotions: jaggery (sweetness), bitter neem (sadness), hot chilli (anger), salt (sourness), lemon (bitterness), and the taste that comes from really young tender mangoes, not sweet but not bitter. She told me how Pachadi brings together all the nutrients that are needed in this hot time, but which you wouldn't want to eat normally. 'Who would eat bitter lemons?' she asked. 'But if they've already been offered as Prasad,' that is, gifts to the gods in the Temple, 'then you eat. It's clever, can you see?'

They would go to the Temple for puja early the next morning, when the priests would unveil the Panchangam, the 'book of the year', cataloguing on a day-by-day basis all that was going to happen. 'The big thing now is who will win the election, both state and national,' she said, 'which we'll find out tomorrow.' I thought one didn't need high priests to tell you that; everyone knew Modi was going to win, but I said nothing that might dampen her enthusiasm for talking.

'And then we worship our gods,' she continued. 'Did you know we Hindus have *three crore* gods?' she asked. (Three crore is the Indian way of representing 30 million.) I didn't know that, I told her. 'And you know where they all live?' she asked. She told me that she and her son had watched something on the Discovery Channel about it, something about 'physics' missing dimensions', all to do with string theory. I knew something about that. The two major scientific theories, quantum mechanics and relativity theory, contradict each other. The first works for the very small and the second for the very big, but they are not compatible when trying to explain the same thing. To solve this problem, scientists have created string theory. But, the scientists say, it cannot solve the problem in three-dimensional space, only in eleven dimensions. In these missing eleven dimensions, I inferred from what Mrs Mantra was saying, the gods lurked.

This all fortunately took a fair chunk of our interrogation time. At 5 p.m., she went to find the book that I had signed in last week. She couldn't find it anywhere. She enlisted her son to look in her cupboard and various other filing cabinets, but the book could not be found. I asked her to sign in my book; again she refused. It was still her word against mine about whether I'd satisfied my interrogation bail conditions.

Two days later, against my wishes, Sara came to Hyderabad. It was a national holiday. Terrified of her being arrested by Mantra, I insisted that we couldn't stay in my rented room; we were far too easily located there. We took off to a distant part of town to stay in a relatively inexpensive hotel that Sara had found, surrounded by beautiful tropical gardens where she felt I could relax. Unfortunately, I had to go through the whole rigmarole of explaining to the receptionists why I didn't have my passport, as it's a legal requirement to hand these over in any hotel; eventually, because Sara was persuasive on this as on many things, they agreed to me sending a scanned copy by email. But then they explained that they had to submit passport numbers to the police every evening. My heart sank as I realised that running halfway across town had not hidden us from my persecutors at all.

So I was not at all relaxed. The humiliation, the loss of control over my life seemed to have left me without any libido. My testosterone levels had diminished, beyond repair it felt. Instead of an intimate time together, which would have helped so much, I couldn't even raise a smile. But she was loving and forgiving.

I kept saying to Sara that we had to be as inconspicuous as possible. In the evening, however, there was an old man playing the piano and I'm a sucker for a sing-along. We were both in need of a lychee and vodka, and after a few drinks we were leading the singing of songs from the 1940s as well as Beatles' songs, into the small hours. I loved Sara as she sang, hopelessly out of tune, with gusto. We did talk seriously for a bit – Sara said that her father and mother were probing why was she going to Hyderabad all the time, asking what was going on.

'They need to be told; we need to deal with this,' she said.

'Yes, yes,' I said, my whole being recoiling from having to deal with anything else at the present time.

In the morning, I woke with the anxiety of a hangover.

'We didn't make too much of a scene last night?' I asked. Sara did her usual calming thing, saying, 'Of course, no one would have noticed, you're fretting unnecessarily as usual.' We went down to breakfast and the restaurant hostess called out in recognition, 'The singer! Mr James!', a refrain repeated by the food waiter, the drinks waiter and the chef who made eggs to your specification.

That morning, I was due in court. We ordered a taxi and Sara insisted she would come. I was nervous, but she said she didn't want to leave me on my own. Fortunately, we bumped into Prandakur as we climbed the stairs to the courtroom, and he said it wasn't wise that she was there. I insisted she go back to the hotel and pack up, and book a flight for that evening. She saw how concerned Prandakur was and took her cue from him. That was to be the last time she was with me in Hyderabad.

It was my third court appearance. I sat there on a hard broken wooden chair on the side, and for the first time I thought it might be all right after all. Perhaps I'd been too overwhelmed on my first couple of visits to court, and could not make head nor tail of what was going on. Now, I watched my judge and began to admire the way he dealt with cases, his sensitivity. He held my future in his hands, yes, but I could be safe with him, I thought.

Awaking me from these reveries, a familiar but dreaded figure walked into the court room – like a small songbird responding to the shape of a raptor, my stomach lurched even before I could recognise who it was. It was Mrs Mantra. Her shape, her form, her demeanour, they all filled me with dread; she was the embodiment of all that was keeping me there against my will. I was so relieved that Sara was not there. Mantra had come to the courtroom to show the judge that she was taking my case very seriously, and that she didn't want me to be able to leave the country. My heart sank. The kindly court crier came over and said, 'You'd better find your advocate', for the case wasn't supposed to be heard until afternoon; Mantra's arrival as the CID Deputy Superintendent meant that it would be heard forthwith.

Prandakur arrived just as the public prosecutor stood up. He seemed to mumble, so that I had to lean in to understand what he was saying. The case against me was simple, he said: if they granted me my passport, I would simply 'abscond', never to return.

My lawyer stood tall, talking loudly and clearly. As he spoke, the courtroom seemed to come to a standstill as people looked up to watch his performance. He demolished their case, said that of course I would come back, that I came to India knowing there was a case against me (not quite true, I thought), so why wouldn't I do so again? He talked long and passionately; the judge listened, but made no move to show more interest in one side or the other, as a judge should. Prandakur took him through the documents that showed I had resigned from the trust when the foreign currency offence was supposed to have taken place – the one set of documents that he'd agreed I could submit to the court, as copies, not originals – so any case against me was unfounded.

Mrs Mantra then made the public prosecutor stand up again, like a wife pushing forward her reluctant husband. He said, 'If he resigned, why did he keep coming back to India?', as if he had uncovered something rather important. The judge nodded his head in apparent agreement at its importance. Then it was over. There were hushed comments and the court crier called out, '4th April'. The judge had postponed his decision until Friday.

As we left, I bowed to the judge, holding back any emotions. But I felt so drained, because it was clear that Mantra was fighting tooth and nail to keep me in India, and I was aware that the obvious and easiest thing for the judge to do would be to side with her.

Friday 4 April arrived. It was exceedingly hot and stuffy in court. I sat in my suit and tie from 11 a.m. until 1 p.m., when suddenly the judge, through intermediaries, asked me to get my lawyer – the court attendants told me, very specifically, that this was for 'counselling'. Later, Prandakur said that there had been a misunderstanding and that I'd been told to get my 'counsel'. I really don't know what the truth was. Unfortunately, Prandakur wasn't in the building. Here was the judge, apparently being sympathetic to me, inviting my lawyer for private discussion while the public prosecutor was not present, and Prandakur wasn't anywhere to be seen.

Prandakur told me later that this was the way the system worked, that he was pursuing 'seven to ten cases' that very day, and so he couldn't be expected to be in the building for me. Nevertheless, I did note that, at one time, there was a record of twenty-two lawyers sitting in the courtroom, awaiting their cases. I felt very let down that mine wasn't among them. Prandakur said he would be there 'in five minutes'; he had not appeared by the time the judge went for lunch at 1.30.

This started the process of me losing it. On the phone, I shouted and swore at Sara, who took the brunt of it. By the time Prandakur came to court at 2.30 p.m., I had calmed down. We sat together in the courtroom.

At 3 p.m., the judge reappeared and immediately called our case. Again, this seemed very significant, as the public prosecutor had not yet arrived. Instead of calmly going through the documents we were presenting to the court as we'd planned, Prandakur went straight into ranting mode, covering all the same ground as before, about what a good man I was, how I'd served the poor. Then – where did this come from? – he said that I earn ₹70 lakhs (£70,000) a month! That's twelve times more than I earn! As I earn lakhs of money and stay in expensive hotels, why would I need to steal money from a trust? The judge meanwhile seemed impatient, but still Prandakur ranted, not picking up any of the signals. And then, after ten minutes or so of his ranting, the public prosecutor arrived, accompanied by Mrs Mantra, and he stopped.

It was almost as if he was deliberately ranting until they had arrived. Why would he do that?

The public prosecutor took over and very calmly and clearly did everything that I thought Prandakur was going to do, except in his case he explained the irrelevance of the documents we had put before the court. He then said, so unfairly given the time I had spent in interrogation, that I had made myself unavailable to the CID and was refusing to cooperate with their investigations. The judge seemed to be very clear that this was the kind of discussion he was interested in, not my lawyer's histrionics.

Prandakur came back and, to my horror, simply continued his outburst, shouting at the public prosecutor even when the judge had silenced him and was writing his verdict, and the other lawyers were laughing at what was going on.

I followed Prandakur out and yelled at him when I heard the news that the judge had postponed his decision for another full week, until the next Friday. How was I going to cope with another week of this?

Then I remembered miserably what Sara had told me about the day I got bail. The CID's lawyer – a junior public prosecutor – had also gone over the top in court, at my lawyer Prandakur's request, to put the judge on *my* side rather than *theirs*. Sara had had to supply ₹20,000 (£200) for these efforts. This couldn't be what was happening in front of me now, could it? – except the other way around – them paying my lawyer to alienate the judge against me?

The following Friday, 11 April, I was back in court again. In the corridor, I had met the public prosecutor on his way to another courtroom. I had smiled at him, albeit weakly. There was no point in having enemies, I had thought. Whereas others might have hinted at some element of empathy in catching my eye, he had none; his eyes cruelly refused to give me any ounce of recognition. He coldly and brutally ignored me as he walked past me.

The judge summarised the case for and against me getting my passport back. The key thing, he opined, was that it looked 'suspicious' that I was trying to leave so quickly, given the early stage of the investigation. If he allowed me to leave India, he risked me never returning. So the petition for the return of my passport was rejected. On the plus side, he did alter the conditions of my bail so that I could go for interrogation on the second Saturday and second Sunday rather than second and fourth Sundays. It was no consolation at all. I was faced with being stuck in India for some time – how long? I had no idea.

I shouted at my lawyer, swore at my auto driver and cried myself to sleep when I got back to my room, with the help of quite a bit of local gin.

CHAPTER 5

OUT OF HYDERABAD

SOMETHING VERY DIFFERENT HAPPENED at my next interrogation, which seemed to presage the beginning of something rather hopeful.

After I had flipped out when the judge ruled my passport should not be returned, my lawyers got a little worried. They said it was highly unusual for a senior CID officer like Mrs Mantra to come to court. It was clear she was trying to put undue pressure on me and the judge. They seemed to understand my pain, so for my next interrogation, Vashnu first of all promised he would accompany me, but then (inevitably) dropped out. He did send a younger colleague, however, Nelson Matthew, a Christian from Kerala. It was a relief to find at last some legal person who understood my English and me his.

Mantra arrived at around 2 p.m. (We had been waiting since 10 a.m.) She was in a very breezy mood. As she took us upstairs to the third floor, she talked happily with Nelson. I refused to engage with her. I'd been helpful in the past, but I could not be helpful to her now that she had denied me my passport and forced me to stay in India with an uncertain future.

The electricity was off, as per usual, and the office was overbearingly hot and stuffy. She searched through the pile of folders she had brought with her to the desk. As she could not multitask, she stopped shuffling her papers and told me that she had been in Mumbai for the past two weeks seeking out Gita (the woman who had taken over as managing trustee from me). She had heard that Gita was Tamil. 'All Tamilians are Christians, either Protestants or Catholics, do you know that?' she asked. I grunted in reply, not caring whether I was agreeing to the first part (false) or the second part (true, if you exclude Orthodox and Coptic Christians). She had decided that Gita must be Catholic (as it happens, not true) and Catholics go to church regularly, did I know that? I mumbled noncommittally. So detective Mantra had been to every Catholic church in Mumbai for fifteen days, searching for Gita at morning, midday and evening mass.

All this clever detective work had been in vain; she hadn't found her. But the fifteen days away had been valuable, she told me, and so we moved to the real point of her story: her time away had given her empathy for what I must be feeling. It is hard, she could now see, being away from home, having to stay in hotels (or serviced apartments, she added), spending money you can't afford, having no home cooking, and so on. 'Now I understand what you are going through,' she said. 'I am a lady with a heart, *as you know*. I want to help you.'

She got up to leave the cubicle, taking with her the big file of folders, leaving behind only a copy of my book *The Beautiful Tree* on her desk. Perhaps she had brought the wrong folders? After she had gone, Nelson said, 'I know what she wants.' He said he would tell me later. As we waited, he pointed to my smartphone and told me I must not bring that to CID or anywhere near the police – they could seize it at any time. Did I have a laptop? Then they could seize that too; I mustn't let them know I had one. I had to be very careful. Every time I heard things like this repeated, I got more frightened, felt more insecure. Everything felt increasingly shaky and nebulous, even my possessions vulnerable.

The big pile of folders had demonstrated that we were in for the normal gruelling questioning. But then Mrs Mantra returned without folders, instead with just the signing-in book. It had only just gone 3 p.m.; she usually only brought that out at well after 5 p.m. She took a phone call, and gave directions to her office. As we waited, she and Nelson spoke in Telugu. I sat there trying to escape in my head, thinking of Daisy Cottage in the soft summer sun to calm myself. The phone went again and she went downstairs, I assumed to meet someone.

While she was absent a man wandered in. He was quite chubby, cuddly almost, with thick glasses, jet black unruly hair, a cherubic face and a smile that seemed nervous, innocent. I introduced myself; he said his name was Jivan. I asked him what he did and he must have said 'ma'am will tell you', but I heard 'Mum will tell you', and so I assumed this was Mantra's eldest son. I knew the older son was studying at an Indian business school, so I began asking him about this; he looked embarrassed, tried to shake me off this line of questioning. Then ma'am arrived and I said it was nice to meet her eldest son, and she was very put out. 'Do you really think I'm that old?' she chided and then huffed, 'I'm not ancient you know.'

Jivan turned out to be thirty-six, she less than ten years older. I apologised – the usual sort of stuff one has to say when one offends ladies about their age, even ones who have imprisoned you and taken away your liberty.

Regaining her composure, she refocused on the matter at hand, reminded me again of her big heart and newly acquired empathy, and introduced Jivan. Jivan said simply, 'We'll talk for ten minutes and I'll let you know how she can help you.' He then picked up the copy of my book from her desk and it opened at Chapter 8, 'An Inspector Calls'. I'd forgotten how explicit that chapter was about official corruption in Hyderabad (among other places), how school entrepreneurs have to pay bribes to officials and the police in order not be closed down or harassed. He read aloud the chapter title to Mrs Mantra, who scolded him, 'I'm not Inspector, I'm Deputy

Superintendent.' It happened very quickly, and I didn't know whether he had opened to that chapter by chance, or if he knew about it already, so turned to it deliberately.

She smiled sweetly, endorsing Jivan's remark that he was going to tell me how she could help me, and then got me to sign the book – it was only 3.30 p.m.; was she really going to let me go so early?

She was. But not before she said, 'This week we must visit schools together.' My heart sank. We'd finished early that day, only so that she could torture me during the week. 'On Tuesday, we will visit schools and continue our investigations.' I really couldn't bear the thought of spending any more time with her than I had to, sitting in a car with her, getting out of the car with her, walking up stairs with her, all the things we would have to do together if we visited schools, time moving so very slowly, having to be nice to her because she held my freedom in her hands. Anyway, I could not take her to the schools and incriminate others with my presence; I knew how afraid school entrepreneurs were of the police.

'I will talk to my lawyer,' I said.

'We will go. You don't need to keep talking to any lawyers,' she replied.

Jivan and I left. Nelson said this was 'just for the two of you', so departed on his two-wheeler. However, he phoned me a few minutes later (perhaps he'd spoken to Vashnu, my senior lawyer) and said, 'Don't you say anything, just listen to what Jivan has to say.'

In his car, Jivan was not modest about his achievements. He was a very successful businessman, he told me, who had founded an elite group of companies that included schools, colleges, hospitals, film studios, a fashion department, super-markets – indeed, most businesses you could imagine. He was especially proud of his company's leading international schools, which had a great reputation in the city and beyond. 'I'd love to visit them one day,' I said. 'It's my interest, schools.'

'Yes, I remember now, Mrs Mantra told me,' he said. 'Let's see, maybe I can take you now?' But of course, he then real-ised, it was Sunday, and schools were closed on Sundays. 'Well let's go in the week, perhaps after you've gone to your schools with Mantra?'

This elite group of companies, he told me, made ₹600 crore (₹6 billion) profit a year; that's about £60 million. Ask anyone, he said, if they know of Jivan, and everyone will know him and his elite group of companies.

'We can ask these people here,' he motioned to a group as we stopped at traffic lights. 'Ask them, do they know of Jivan.'

'No, no, we don't need to do that,' I said. 'I believe you.'

And I did believe him. Why shouldn't one believe this nice man, with the innocent smile and boyish charm, who said he was going to help you, when you're a broken man yourself? He suggested we go and have a soft drink at the Park Hyatt, the hotel where Mantra had arrested me. I asked, 'Is that on your way home?' As always, I didn't want to put anyone out, so only if it was on his way home should we go there. Conveniently, it was.

As we drove, he said that he was only trying to help me, and I mustn't tell anyone what he was about to tell me. So he began his story. He had also once been arrested by Mrs Mantra. She had thrown him in prison, just like me. Yes, he'd got out after a week or two, just like me, and gone straight back to business. Later, he became very successful, and now he needed her, because the police were like the mafia; you couldn't do anything without their permission, and so he did her favours like this. 'I'm a very busy man,' he said. 'I could only come between 2 p.m. and 4 p.m. today, I told her.' He did things like this for her, and in return she helped him with his businesses by making sure he didn't get arrested again.

'She's helped me too,' he said, 'by getting me this position.' He got out his wallet and showed me his identity card, which read 'Vice President, Anti-Corruption Bureau, State of Andhra Pradesh'. I looked at him incredulously. 'This is India,' he said. 'You must know everyone is involved with corruption, even in the anti-corruption bureau.'

We were not yet at the hotel, but having finished telling me about his businesses and his relationship with Mantra, he decided he might as well tell me how he could help me.

'She has completely made up the case against you,' he said.

'What?' I asked. 'She's told you?'

'Of course,' he said. 'She told me she made up any lies she could think of about you.' Seeing how perplexed I was, he added, 'It's normal; don't look surprised. But she also told me she deeply respects you – all the great work you've been doing around the world for the downtrodden.' I had difficulty taking this in. 'But now,' he continued, 'you are the downtrodden, because she has downtrodden you.' He enjoyed his own little play on words.

'What Mantra wants is very simple,' he said. 'She has a debt of 12 lakhs (£12,000), and she wants you to pay it off. But a bit more too, because she knows you earn a huge amount, so 15 lakhs is what she wants. She knows you earn 70 lakhs a month.'

Oh God, not that figure again, which Prandakur had bandied about in court. So she thinks I'm very rich, I realised, and has her expectations set high because of that.

Forgetting completely that Nelson, my junior lawyer, had told me not to say anything, I told him I couldn't afford more than ₹3 lakhs (£3,000).

'No, that won't be enough,' he said. 'That won't be nearly enough. It's 15 lakhs she is after.'

We had come quickly to the point, so we didn't really need to go to the Park Hyatt after all. But we had arrived, and so walked into the lobby area anyway, where my heart sank with the memories of my first meeting with Mantra, and getting arrested at one o'clock in the morning.

But couldn't I be a bit relieved now? Wasn't Jivan showing me the way out of all this? That I could just pay a bribe, albeit a hefty bribe, and then I'd be free and home?

We sat down. Jivan said, 'Let me see your phone. Put it on the table; I need to make sure it's not recording.' Of course

I complied immediately. We ordered juices from the waiter, whom Jivan gave the impression of knowing well.

'How does it all work?' I asked.

He said, 'We phone her now, and tell her you'll pay. Then you get the money to me – I know it will take a day or two – then she'll tell the court that the case is closed, the defendant – that's you – has been found to be innocent, and you'll have your passport back in two days. It's easy. We can phone her now, are you ready?'

Our soft drinks arrived. I hesitated.

'If you don't pay she will have you re-arrested. She knows you've done nothing wrong, we all know that. It makes no difference. She can make something else up. She's like a teacher in a school. You're the pupil, stuck in her classroom. She is marking your exercises. Whatever mark she gives you, that's the mark that stays. She can decide to give you a tick. Or she can decide to give you a cross.

'Do you want her to give you a cross? Her deadline is Tuesday to submit your papers. You've got to decide today. Tomorrow's a holiday. Whatever she writes on Tuesday, tick or cross, innocent or guilty, that's what you'll carry with you. Shall we phone her?'

I had some notion that I had to negotiate.

'I can't afford 15 lakhs. I'm not a rich man, I'm a poor academic.' He didn't look convinced. 'Look, I can give her 5 lakhs. That's all I can afford.'

He sipped on his juice and waved to the waiter to come by again, and ordered a coffee. Would I like a coffee too? No, I was fine with just juice. The hotel lobby was quiet on a Sunday afternoon; we sat in silence in that cool, cavernous space.

He changed the subject. 'I'll show you my elite group of companies' website – let's look on your phone. I'll show you my schools.' Unfortunately, though I had a BlackBerry smartphone, I was not on a data-roaming tariff, so I couldn't access the internet. His smartphone also did not have roaming. 'That's a shame,' I said. 'I was looking forward to seeing your schools.' I added, 'Can you give me the website address?' He was about to write it in my notebook, but then hesitated. Seeing that I had a couple of business cards tucked away, he picked one up and wrote the address on the back. The web address was www.dnbgroup.info.

'Look later,' he said. 'I want you to see our schools and colleges.'

He sipped his coffee. 'You know,' he said, 'that night you were arrested, I was here, in the Park Hyatt.'

'Really,' I said.

'Yes, I had a big party here to celebrate my sister's wedding anniversary.'

My mind drifted back to that evening; yes, there was a really big party going on – no, it was a fashion show, taking up all the function rooms downstairs, I recalled. Odd. But I wanted to believe him, wanted to believe *in* him. Instead of asking where his party was, I did my own mental apology for him, and thought that it must have been in a smaller function room upstairs, perhaps not quite as grand as he was saying; sometimes Indians do exaggerate.

'And you know what else,' he said. 'It was Mantra's birthday that same day!'

'Really?'

'Yes, it was her birthday, and I met her as I was arriving and wished her.'

'So.' Seamlessly he moved back to where we were. 'Are we going to phone her then?'

'Five lakhs?' (£5,000) I said.

'Offer her that. She won't accept less. But I can't guarantee she'll accept.' He picked up his phone, and pressed her number.

'Wait,' I said.

'It's ringing,' he said.

'Let me think...' I said.

I recalled Nelson's words. Don't say anything. But why not? What could the problem be?

'Let me find what I can afford, and phone her later,' I said.

I asked him if he would talk to Sara – by talking to him she could work out what to do, I was sure.

'OK,' he said. 'But on my phone.' I dialled the number, and handed the phone over to him. They talked for a while in a mixture of Hindi and English. When I took the phone back, Sara told me, 'he seems OK, but you might as well talk to Vashnu before you do anything.'

Jivan sensed it was all over for the time being, now that I'd spoken to Sara. He said, 'Don't mess with Mantra.' I told him I'd phone him the next day. 'You have to, before Tuesday,' he said, and gave me his number.

I took an autorickshaw. Although I had been hesitant at the end, I was feeling happier. Suddenly it seemed as though it could all be over soon. What had he said? Mantra would tell the court and I'd have my passport back in a couple of days. The young lawyer Nelson Matthew phoned me, and after I'd told him the news, he said that the case seemed simple, but I had to talk to Vashnu before doing anything. As I went back towards my neighbourhood, my happiness grew. The waiting was over, I thought; Mantra had shown her true colours. In fact, it all seemed quite clear what had been going on: she'd been grinding me down – first with prison, then with the interrogations – getting me on my own away from Sara and any other friends so that I was vulnerable, going to court saying terrible things about me, to make sure my passport was not returned. Then when I was a broken man, she turned all sweet, offering me this olive branch, to maximise her earnings. I knew that I was probably going to have to pay £15,000. I would have to borrow it. I went through a list of people in my mind, family and friends. But I would approach them the next day, not that night – I wanted to enjoy the feeling of relief for a while. I could be home in a few days, Jivan had said; a few days – perhaps by the weekend? If so, then I could still make the gig in New York the week after! And I could get back into the swing of my work and my life, and this hell could fade to a distant memory.

I decided not to go straight to my room, but to have a drink at the Taj Banjara. This added to my bonhomie. The waiter brought me the drink I liked even before I had a chance to sit down and order. The Indian Premier League T20 cricket competition was on the lounge television. I mused how five out of eight teams had names connected with royalty: the Royal Challengers Bangalore, the Kings XI Punjab, the Chennai Super Kings, the Kolkata Knight Riders and the Rajasthan Royals. It was funny, the way people living in republics around the world love royalty, I thought. Think of how the Americans dote on our British royal family.

Feeling lighter than I had done since my arrest, I walked back up Road No. 13 to my apartment block, and even the traffic didn't bother me so much.

It was about 9 p.m. by the time I got into my room. I put my notebook on my desk and the business cards dropped out, including the one that Jivan had written on. I should look at his website, I thought. Perhaps I could go and visit his schools this week, while I was waiting to get my passport back. You never know – he could even be a good contact to have in Hyderabad when I recommenced my work. I was certainly not averse to keeping close to rich, powerful businesspeople who could help with my work for the poor. (I have a bit of a Robin Hood complex.)

I poured myself a gin and water and booted up my computer, feeling as always the little electric shocks when my hands touch any exposed metal – the room was not properly earthed. I typed in the web address. It was a reasonably attractive website: 'Welcome to DNB Group, Elite Group of Companies.'

There was a moving bar in the middle showing pictures of the various companies in the group. Yes, they were exactly as he had said:

- Dr Jivan Pathlabs Pvt Ltd
- DevaFilm Distribution Pvt Ltd
- Jivan Fashion Brands
- Bada Paa Supermarkets
- DNB International Schools
- DAF DNB Fertilizer
- Jivan Television Network Pvt Ltd
- DNB Deva Hospital Pvt Ltd

I turned on my television and watched the cricket some more.

But I was restless, feeling a bit hopeful for the future. I was interested to see what Jivan was involved with. So I clicked on the web pages for the schools and colleges, and read through the details about them. It all looked interesting. Back to the cricket.

Still restless, I went back to the website again. I might as well see what else his group of companies was doing. I clicked on to the other web pages.

Every single one of them was 'under construction'. Every single one. There were no web pages on fashion or films or supermarkets or television. The only page with any links was the education one. This, of course, was the only page he had gambled I would look at.

I went back to the schools and colleges page. And then it

dawned on me. I realised that the web page was simply linked to pages of *other* schools and colleges. But these had absolutely nothing to do with his 'elite group of companies'. I scoured their pages, trying to find any mention of DNB Group, or Jivan, or anything. No, they were just other pages of schools and colleges that his website had fallaciously linked to in order to create the impression that something was going on.

It was a complete sham. The website was a scam.

Suddenly, I panicked. I'd fallen for it completely. I was sitting there with him, discussing bribing the Deputy Superintendent of Police. In a panic, I phoned my lawyer, Vashnu, and uncharacteristically he picked up straight away. I told him what had happened.

'Not like that, it's a trap!' he said, exasperated. 'She's known for it. Tell me one thing: did you offer her any money? Did she record you offering her money?'

I told him I didn't.

'We'll do one thing,' he said. 'Come and see me on Wednesday, when I'm back from Delhi.'

A trap? He told me they didn't want a bribe at all at this stage. What they wanted was for me to phone her, and record my conversation. And then I'd be back in court again, this time for offering the DSP of CID a substantial bribe to quash my case. I'd certainly be back in prison for that. And then they'd have me for a real, rather than a made-up offence. And this time, because I really would be guilty as charged, they could collect an enormous bribe from me.

I hadn't offered money on the phone to her, thank God; I'd had the presence of mind not to. But did it make any difference? For I'd been speaking with Jivan all the time about bribing a police officer. He asked me to put my phone on the table so that I couldn't record him – but why didn't I think to ask him to do the same with his phone so that he couldn't record me?

I went back over my words: did I say anything that could have incriminated me? Of course, almost every other word! I was not careful at all. I'd trusted him totally – I was back in the place where I'd been arrested, and was feeling vulnerable. That was why he took me there, I suddenly realised – in order to make me needful of him, to remind me of Mantra's power.

So now they had their tape of me talking about bribing a police officer. An inspector would surely call again soon.

The doorbell to the apartment rang. I hid away my laptop, hid it in one place, then a second, then a third, eventually leaving it in the shower cubicle, where it couldn't be seen from the door. The doorbell rang again. There was nothing I could do. They would know I was there; the guy at reception would have told them. I had no alternative. I had to answer.

I opened the door on the third ring. It was Praveen, the one friend who had remained faithful to me in Hyderabad, and who had helped me find someone to copy all my documents.

'Just checking all the scanning was done OK?' he said.

Seeing how anxious I was, he reminded me, 'You told me not to phone, that's why I came round.'

Yes, I'd told him not to phone, because someone else had intimated that my phone was probably being tapped. 'Don't stay here,' I told Praveen. 'I'll meet you in the Taj Banjara lounge. I'll be there in five minutes.'

In the Taj, we put on a jolly show of meeting each other as if by chance after some time, to avoid implicating him. I told him about Jivan. He took it all in, asking pertinent questions. 'Did he record you?' I didn't know. 'Did he have a smart-phone?' Yes. 'Did you check it was not recording?' No. 'Did you say anything about paying a bribe to a police officer?' Yes.

'I'm sorry,' he said. 'I can't be seen with you again. I have my own problems.'

It was to do with his wife; she was a foreigner, and he mumbled something about the police demanding bribes to process her immigration paperwork.

'I can't have any more run-ins with the police at the moment. Sorry.'

I agreed with him. He couldn't be seen with me. I was going to say the same thing in any case. I wished that I'd been able to say it first, though; it would have hurt less. I told him to go. He walked out of the Taj Banjara, waving hesitantly, and it was the last time I saw him. He was the last friend I'd had there. Now I was completely alone.

When he had gone, I sat and had a drink of water – I had to get sober. The cricket was coming to its climax and, as often with these T20 matches, it went to the wire, decided on the last ball. The waiters stopped and watched the ending while

I sat and reflected on what had happened. Mantra knew I was a broken man, so she'd brought in her con artist, Jivan (whatever his name was); they'd created a website *especially for me* – could that be true? They'd been planning this for a while – playing a long, calculated game. And now they knew I was willing to pay ₹5 lakhs; that's what I'd told Jivan. But it was nowhere near enough. Better to get me back in prison again – this time for attempting to bribe a police officer, a very serious offence – and then I'd be willing to pay the required ₹15 lakhs or more, whatever the amount they were after.

What to do? In England, of course, I'd go to the police. In England, I would know there was a protective edifice around me, the rule of law, a comfort and backdrop to all our lives all the time; we never even have to think about it. But in India, the police have hijacked the rule of law and without it, everything becomes terrifying.

I walked home carefully, aware that an accident could very easily be arranged in this little back lane and no one could prove it was anything other than an accident.

I locked my room door, bolted it. I did not fall asleep until my tiredness overwhelmed me as the first cockerel awoke and the night hounds stopped howling. Somehow, I slept through the call to prayer and only woke up when the kitchen supervisor called me at 9 a.m., saying that the kitchen was about to close, worried that I would miss my breakfast.

Nothing happened for a couple of days. Each night I'd lock myself in my room, not sleeping until the early hours, then crashing into a deep sleep before, inevitably, the kitchen folk – being concerned – phoned me at 9 a.m. I had unplugged the phone at first, so they couldn't do that, but then I realised the receptionist couldn't warn me if I got any visitors, so I left it plugged in.

Each night I had awaited the CID's arrival. On Monday night I was especially fearful; I got myself prepared, mentally and physically, as best I could, to be taken into custody again. Tuesday the same. By Wednesday, I was still there, and feeling slightly less nervous.

I went through different options: suppose Mantra and her conman Jivan realised, now that the Tuesday deadline had passed, that I was not going to give them any bribe. They knew I was a writer, that I even wrote about corruption. Jivan had gone straight to Chapter 8 of *The Beautiful Tree*, 'An Inspector Calls'. It can't possibly have been a coincidence. So they knew I wrote about this stuff. And if I was not going to give them any money, then I'd lost any usefulness. It would be better to bump me off, so at least I couldn't write about them – I could see that. But they'd not be likely to do anything in my room, surely. It would be so much easier to 'get rid of me' outside; a road accident would be easy to organise, especially in the narrow lane leading to the Taj Banjara. I mustn't go out at night at all, I realised.

By Wednesday, I was thinking perhaps their little sting operation on Sunday had failed. Perhaps they hadn't recorded my conversation with Jivan after all. So would they try something else?

And then it dawned on me exactly what they would try next. What's it called, a candy trap? No, a *honey* trap. Mantra knows I am on my own, can surely guess that I am a red-blooded male, feeling lonely. However much I love Sara, this terrible loneliness is hard to bear. So she could get me to meet a pretty young woman somewhere, not make it too obvious, even make me chase her a bit. And then have her accuse me of stalking or harassment or even rape; and I'd be back in prison again, for another offence.

Then I realised, oh God, it was happening already. In the bookshop, Crosswords, at the coffee bar, there was one young woman in particular working there, whom I chatted to when I was there most afternoons. Yes, she was pretty but shy, and I had been much too friendly with her. It was now clear to me that she was about to report me, have me arrested for 'eve-teasing' as they call it. Once, I even left with her as she finished her shift, and we walked down the stairs together before going our separate ways. I'd been taking too much of a risk. I'd have to avoid the bookshop at all costs. But it might've been too late.

Slowly I closed down all my options for human contact. I reflected on things that had been happening over the past few days and came to believe that the police were closing in all around me. The guy who had been in charge of scanning all my documents came back on Monday, bringing the three suitcases of documents to discuss payment. Meanwhile, he asked to top up his BlackBerry, so I lent him my charger. When I was going to bed on Monday night, I couldn't find it – I always charged my phone as I went to bed, in case I was arrested during the night again. I looked high and low, scolded myself for my forgetfulness. Then I remembered that the scanning guy hadn't returned it. Had he taken it deliberately, under instruction from on high, to make me especially vulnerable when they arrested me?

And then, John, an Anglo-Indian duty manager at the Taj Banjara, a propos of nothing, asked me, 'Where are you living these days?' I told him, but then when I was sitting down with my black tea and chocolate-covered doughnut, I thought: why is he asking? Had they been looking there for me? And I knew I must never come to the Taj Banjara again, because it was too risky; they all knew about my case and where I lived and my regular habits. I had to keep away, try to stay in the apartment, not go to any of these places where people knew me.

At one point, the lowest point in the middle of one night, I had perhaps the most terrifying thought of all. That I was like John Nash, as played by Russell Crowe in *A Beautiful Mind*, and I was *imagining* it all, that none of this was actually happening, that I'd flipped completely. How would I know?

I stayed in my room to avoid any of these risks.

On Wednesday night, the doorbell rang. I jumped, as I'd done several times in the past couple of days. I had a drill: I hid my laptop away in the shower, piled clothes on top of my precious suitcases that had been returned to my room, with documents inside that proved my innocence. The doorbell ringing was usually the kitchen staff bringing food for someone in one of the other rooms. There was no real need to panic; I had a drill that's all – it was good to follow. The doorbell rang again. I wished they would bloody well answer the front door if they were expecting food. On the third ring, I had to go and answer.

It was Jivan. He was smiling, and behind him were two unsmiling characters. Jivan was a small guy, about my height. The other two were both taller, gangly; even though it was very hot, one was wearing a leather bomber jacket over his black T-shirt.

'Nice place,' said Jivan, looking around the large living room.

'It's not mine,' I pleaded, aware that it was not in my interest to look too wealthy. 'I have just one room.'

'Which room?'

I pointed it out to him.

'Let's go,' he said.

I led them in. I was highly conscious of the three suitcases sitting there in the alcove. They mustn't seize them. I sat in the chair by the desk. Jivan sat on the bed; his two friends remained standing.

'Can I get you some water?' I asked. It was the normal way of making someone feel comfortable in India. Jivan didn't want any water.

'I told you Mantra needed to know by Tuesday; that was yesterday. You didn't phone. Did you not understand? Didn't I tell you she could do what the hell she liked with you? I'm trying to help you. You're not helping me.'

'I don't have any money,' I said. I realised at that moment that I had already decided I would not pay any bribe to her. I don't know when I decided it, but from that moment on it was very clear in my mind.

'You have no fucking choice,' said Jivan, his face angry for the first time. He quickly switched his boyish grin back on, but not until he had motioned to one of his thugs, who opened his jacket to reveal his handgun tucked in his belt. He took it out. I didn't have a clue what to do. I sat in my chair while the two guys stood there, one holding a gun.

I knew some did carry guns around there, although as an Englishman I was not at all used to such weapons. One wealthy businessman-cum-philanthropist I had got to know well through my work in schools in the Old City had a Smith & Wesson .22, which he carried in his belt sometimes – perhaps all the time. The first time I'd seen it, we were at his college for a graduation day, at the speaking podium, and it had dropped from his belt onto the floor. His assistant had picked it up and put it on the table next to us, the barrel pointing at me. He had chuckled as he saw my surprised reaction, and later told me what type of gun it was, and showed me his Winchester rifle, kept on a ledge in the back of his car, just in case his vehicle was attacked. It was nothing to worry about, he had reassured me. Jivan's thug had a gun like the Smith & Wesson. Was this also nothing to worry about?

Jivan waited a bit, waited for it all to sink in, then said, 'Get us the money, *theek hai*? It will be fine, as long as you pay. But if you don't, you know what will happen now,' and he motioned to the guy with the gun.

I thought that, in this nice quiet room, far away in the back of the building, he could shoot me and no one would know. Sara hadn't liked the room; she had wanted me to be in one of the apartments at the front of the building. A difference between the sexes, I had thought then; I wanted to be away from it all, she wanted the security of people around her. Now I yearned for people to be around me.

He got up, and so did I. The guy with the gun stood where he was, but the other guy pushed me, pushed me hard, back into the chair. 'We will show ourselves out,' Jivan said. 'Tomorrow night. The Park Hyatt. Come with money. OK?'

'*Theek hai*,' I said.

I sat in the chair for a long time after they'd gone. I could not move. Eventually, I got up slowly, every movement difficult. I retrieved my laptop from the shower and locked and bolted the doors.

I had to get out of there. I could go to a hotel, but hotels require passports, and although I had a scanned copy of my passport, which some would accept, in any case they would inform the authorities. So wherever I stayed, they would find me. But, I realised, only in Hyderabad: the Indian legal system is decentralised to state level. Yes, the police can go across state borders, but it requires special permissions, takes time. So if I could get out of Hyderabad, then I could be safe, at least for a while.

I schemed and planned all night – I didn't sleep at all.

In the morning, I started making my moves. I'd seen enough gangster movies to know the type of thing to do. I had to make it seem as though everything was completely normal. I would not use my phone to relay any details. Fortunately, the internet was working, and I managed to Skype Sara briefly to ask her to help me. If it all worked out, I had a code phrase to tell her on the phone: 'Swallows are back at Daisy Cottage.'

I had to make everything look as normal as possible. No one should be remotely suspicious of what I was about to do. Over breakfast every day, I read the newspaper, so that day I read it just as carefully. As I finished, I made sure the Nepali supervisor saw me leave at my normal time. 'See you tomorrow,' I called out in a sort-of-normal fashion.

There had been a lot of toing and froing with cases and bags this last week, because of getting the three cases of documents scanned. No one would be suspicious of me leaving with another bag, providing that my personal bag was left in my room. I went and purchased a travel bag similar to mine from the small suitcase shop on Road No. 1. I put a few clothes in it, but left the room as untidy as usual. I took only one book, Ramachandra Guha's brilliant *Gandhi Before India*; the rest I left on my table, with notebooks and paper to make it look as normal as possible. All my toiletries I left; I could buy these where I was going. My bed had already been made while I'd been out, so I messed this up a bit to make it look as though it had been slept in.

I went downstairs to the reception and paid for ten days in advance – it was something I did periodically, nothing odd about it. I'd ordered a car from one of the taxi companies that I used regularly, for a 'two-hour package', exactly what I'd been using to take my documents to the lawyers. Taxi drivers could never find the way there, and rarely understood my directions. This was good. I went to find the kitchen supervisor as normal and asked him to explain the address and where I was going. 'Tell him I'm going to my lawyers,' I said. This was good, all very normal.

Before the car arrived, I went down to the Taj Banjara for my morning chai – I'd not been for a few days, and I wanted everything to look especially normal that day. One of the junior managers I knew well, Khem, came to meet me, and told me he'd thought of someone who might be able to help me. Someone called Haridevan was staying at a nearby sister hotel, the Taj Krishna, in room 656.

'He's good friends with the Chief of the CID. He will help you,' Khem said, handing me a scrap of paper with these details on it. Was this another trap? I needed to get away. I left the hotel lobby before my tea arrived.

In the taxi, I ostentatiously gave the address of my lawyers, and we drove off down Road No. 13. I then pretended to get a phone call, and told the driver, 'Change of plan, need to go to the airport.' Fine – he changed direction.

Were we being followed? I believed Jivan had been keeping an eye on me – that's why John had asked for my address;

I thought they must have been looking for me already that day – that was why Khem was giving me these strange bits of paper. But I was making my escape. When we were halfway to the airport, I phoned Sara and chatted about the swallows arriving at Daisy Cottage. This was her signal to book me a flight from Hyderabad to Delhi. I wanted it to be booked as late as possible. Tonight, I would be expected with the money, 'or else'. They would surely be on the lookout for me. They might think I would try to leave town – although they would know that, as they had my passport, this would be impossible for me, as foreigners need passports for all domestic travel.

This is where I may have had a trump card. I had a second passport. The British authorities grant this to bona fide people whose work requires them to travel frequently. It's a little-known fact, but something that I've benefited from over the years – you can apply for a visa for one country while travelling in a second country, for instance. When I came to India, somewhat unusually, I travelled with both passports, as I was going to travel on to Dubai and then west Africa, and my west African visas were in a different passport from the Indian visa. But Mantra only seized one passport, the one with my Indian visa in it – of course, she wouldn't have guessed I had a second.

It was a trump card, but not quite as valuable as it sounds.

To get out of India, of course, you need to show your passport *and* your Indian visa *and* your arrival stamp. That was all in the passport they had seized, so my second passport was useless for that purpose. I'd gone through this many times, trying to think of any possible way of using it, but there was no way it could help me get out of the country.

But it had occurred to me that I might be able to fly domestically. To get into any airport in India, you have to show your photo identification and travel itinerary to the waiting armed soldiers at the entrance. Indians are allowed to show any photo ID, but for foreigners it has to be their passport. As with leaving the country, the soldiers are supposed to check your identity *and* your visa *and* your entry stamp, to make sure you are in India legitimately. But most times I'd noticed soldiers just look at the photograph and check the name in the passport against the name on the ticket. So with my second passport, I might be able to get past the soldiers and on to a flight.

It was worth the risk. I had to get out of Hyderabad. And if I could get to Delhi, I could go to the British High Commission and tell them that I was not safe anymore. My country would protect me. Having a second passport did make me feel I had the upper hand over Mantra in that one respect, because she would have gone through a similar thought process and decided that I was stuck in Hyderabad (or at least Andhra Pradesh), so totally vulnerable to her.

I went to the Air India ticket window to get the printout of my itinerary for Sara's online booking, showing my passport. With some trepidation, no doubt looking guilty as I moved down the queue, I handed across my passport and printed itinerary to the soldier whose queue I'd chosen – the older, more genial fellow, who was likely to be less conscientious than the younger recruit to his side. There was a moment of fear as he flicked through my passport. But he was only trying to find the photograph: British passports went through a phase of having the pictures at the back rather than the front, and so he was momentarily confused. He found it, looked at the photo, then at me, then at the travel itinerary, compared names and then waved me through.

It worked. At check-in, they also looked at my identification, but only the name and photo.

I phoned Sara, relief flooding over me. 'I am sitting in the lounge,' I said, ambiguously. 'I'll probably be here a few hours.' She knew I had got on the flight to Delhi.

Sara had booked me a hotel in Delhi too. I went there, bluffed about bringing the wrong passport – because in hotels they are conscientious about finding your visa and entry stamp – but said that I could get someone to scan the proper one and send it through.

'Yes, OK,' the receptionist said reluctantly.

The Delhi police would know that a James Tooley had arrived in Delhi, but there would surely be no connection with the Hyderabad police, especially since they thought I was stuck in Hyderabad.

In my room, I had a bath. It was baking hot outside, but somehow I felt like a very hot, deep, relaxing bath.

I had had one dealing with the British High Commission already, and it wasn't particularly positive. A good friend of mine in England, Sir Michael Barber, heard of my plight after

I'd got out of prison and immediately emailed the British Ambassador in New Delhi, someone he'd met on a few occasions. He told him about my arrest and being harassed for bribes. The stark response came back: 'It happens all the time, I can do nothing about it.' The British could not interfere in the legal system in any country provided that they were following due process. Had they taken me before a judge before throwing me in prison? Yes. Was an investigation proceeding into my alleged crimes according to the law of the country? Yes. No matter that the system was corrupt, that the due process in India would not remotely pass muster in England. It was a farce in which everyone had to appear to accept that what was taking place was somehow above board, because they must not be seen to be interfering in legal matters of sovereign nations.

The only exception was if the police were *physically* harming me. Quite why bodies are so much more sacrosanct than minds was no longer clear to me. The ambassador emailed Michael a private number that he could pass on to me if ever I was in *physical* danger.

This was the number I rang. It didn't matter that I'd been in psychological danger for months; now that I was in physical danger, they could come to my rescue. At least, I had assumed it was a private number, but it turned out to be the embassy's general line, and I had to go through various pressing of 2s and 1s and 5s before I was eventually through to someone who could help with 'passport-related enquiries'. I told the lady who answered the whole story, dwelling especially on what had happened in the past week – my passport petition being rejected in court, Mantra introducing me to Jivan at interrogation, him asking for £15,000. She listened politely, but then interrupted me:

'It happens all the time. We are always hearing from foreigners like yourself having bribes demanded of them. Your situation is not unusual,' she said.

'I was in prison, is that not unusual?' I said.

She demurred: 'Possibly. But you're not being physically harmed?' she asked. I was about to tell her about the visit from Jivan and his thugs, and the gun. But her tone was making me feel belittled. She clearly thought I was overreacting to something commonplace. No shots were fired, after all, I thought. It was only a gun. In India, like America, guns are not uncommon. Only an Englishman would be so afraid of a thug carrying a gun. So I said nothing.

'They're just trying to frighten you,' she said.

'I am frightened,' I said.

'We're concerned about your welfare,' she said.

We spoke for about thirty minutes. A few moments after we'd finished, an email arrived from her. It accurately summarised our conversation, including the possible 'serious repercussions' that could follow if I complained to the Indian authorities, even if I complained through the British High Commission. She had said that Mrs Mantra could think I was more trouble than I was worth and so move to have me silenced if I complained at this stage to her superiors. But then, to finish it all off, there was this chilling sentence:

'I'd also like to keep you informed that as this involves a possible bribery, we are required to notify the Serious Fraud Office/Crown Prosecution Service as you might already be aware that if you pay the bribe, under UK law you may be prosecuted in the UK.'

She'd reported me to the police in England. I had phoned her to tell her I was being harassed for a bribe and felt threatened because I wouldn't pay up; in any case, my freedom had been taken away from me. No matter – she had reported me anyway to the British authorities, just in case I eventually broke down and paid the bribe.

No one could help me, certainly no one from my own country. England had given birth to Magna Carta but now couldn't care less whether its fundamental principles were being followed in the countries it cosied up to. I was completely alone.

THE UBIQUITY OF POLICE CORRUPTION

THE BRITISH AUTHORITIES REFUSED to help me. Their reasoning in cases like mine is that what is going on in India must be respected, because the Indian authorities are following 'due process'. They are living in cloud cuckoo land.

They are turning a blind eye to what everyone knows is taking place, the very existence of which means that 'due process' can patently *not* be followed. It is time we admitted that something pretty awful is going on in India.

An excellent book – though a chilling read – is Debroy and Bhandari's *Corruption in India*. Corruption, the abuse of 'a public office for private benefits', they write, 'has become endemic ... hardly any interaction with agents of the state is devoid of, at the very least, an underlying thought of a bribe'.

They call corruption India's 'parasite'. Those in junior roles in the bureaucracy and police 'thrive on bribes and *baksheesh*', and those at higher levels 'on grease money and scams'. Meanwhile, the junior levels share some of what they have taken with their superiors; their superiors 'share with the politicians'.

The type of corruption I was caught up in they call 'small-ticket' or 'petty' corruption, labels that sound innocuous enough. But even this kind of corruption causes huge human misery. It's a terrible affront to human dignity; small-ticket corruption can put people behind bars for weeks, months or years in India, without any recourse to justice.

Small-ticket corruption is everywhere in India. I was very open with people I met about why I was stuck in India. Almost without exception, everyone I spoke to had a story about police corruption. John, the junior manager at the Taj Banjara who became a good friend of mine during my enforced stay, told me how corruption had worked in his interest (although very much against the interests of the poor woman involved): in the traffic chaos that I dread, he'd knocked over a woman who was trying to cross the treacherous Road No. 1. The case had gone to criminal court, where he'd managed to bribe the police and public prosecutor to change the evidence so that it was not his fault; he got away scot-free, while the woman had to pay her own costs and received no compensation for her hospitalisation. Perhaps the worst thing was that John saw nothing wrong with his story; he thought it on a par with my tale of wrongful imprisonment.

Abdullah, a friend from the Old City, told me the story of how his brother had been knifed when there was some 'communal' violence in his neighbourhood. (In India, 'communal' violence refers to clashes between different religious groups, often Hindu and Muslim – in this case, Muslim and Sikh.) Early one morning, outside the *Gurdwara* (Sikh temple), Sikhs found their saffron, triangular flag had been burnt. Duly offended, they went on the rampage. Sikhs are permitted by law to carry large knives, their *kirpan*, a tradition going back centuries. They used these knives to great effect, including on Abdullah's brother. I'd heard of the incident from several sources, and it appeared that the local police simply stood back and let mayhem unfold. (Things calmed down when the army arrived – the army is trusted not to be partisan, unlike the police.) The police arrested Abdullah's brother and took him into custody. The local officer called Abdullah in. He said, 'We've quietened the whole situation down, now we need something from your side.' Abdullah protested: his brother was knifed! The officer simply repeated, 'We've quietened it down, what are you going to do to assist us?' However much Abdullah protested, in the end he had to pay the bribe; if he didn't, they made it clear they would have kept his brother under arrest and eventually sent him to jail under investigation.

His friend, Alif, told me how a neighbour was murdered by

someone they knew. Ten days later, the murderer walked free, having paid a substantial bribe to the police to drop the case against him.

And so on, and so on. Almost everyone I met volunteered a story of police corruption affecting their families.

Overall, India is corrupt by international standards; its police corruption stands out as being particularly pernicious. Transparency International's 'Corruption Perceptions Index' ranked India eighty-fifth out of 178 countries (2014); only Argentina (105th) and Russia (154th) ranked lower among major economies. As Debroy and Bhandari put it, while India may lay claim to being an emerging economic superpower, its corruption levels keep it in the 'company' of mostly ... poor countries.

However India is perceived by outsiders, Indians themselves know well what corruption is doing for them and their country. An excellent series of studies conducted since 2005 by the Centre for Media Services and Transparency International highlights the problem. The latest study (2012) reports on corruption impacting the poor living in urban slums – Hyderabad is one of the nine cities studied. The report says that the 'daunting nature' of the problem of 'pervasive' corruption has 'generated a feeling of helplessness and apathy in the public mind, resulting in cynicism, fatalism or in arguments that rationalise corruption'.

Overall, more than 56 per cent of slum households paid bribes demanded of them simply to access public services. But over a third of slum dwellers were denied access to public services to which they were legitimately entitled, simply because they could not afford to pay the bribes.

In terms of perception, the police are perceived as the most corrupt of the public services, with 88 per cent of respondents indicating the police were corrupt. These perceptions were firmly based in reality. The highest level of corruption experienced by slum dwellers was indeed in their interaction with the police: 75 per cent of respondents had experienced police corruption.

Over a third of respondents reported that they had to pay a bribe simply to get a case registered, as in India you can't phone a number like 999 – you have to go to the police station yourself. The police seem to have utter discretion about whether or not they register a case, hence the extortion they can inflict. The Indian Corruption Study (2008) found that people had to go many times to the police station to register a complaint, as often their requests were 'dismissed or ignored' by those on duty. When people went to the police to learn the status of their case, they were often given a vague response such as '*inquiry chal raha hai*' ('inquiry is going on'), with no specific information forthcoming. This would be an overture to pay a bribe to get more specific details.

The study also notes that it was usual to pay the bribe directly to the police themselves rather than through a middleman, which would be quite common for other public services: this shows the complete 'lack of fear' among the police. Nearly 90 per cent paid bribes directly to police officers, while only

8 per cent paid a middleman and around 3 per cent a local political representative.

Transparency International (2012) pointed out that a significant proportion (26 per cent) of those giving bribes paid to get their name removed as an accused person. This sounds as though it is using corruption to do corruption, but their earlier study (2008) suggests that many such cases feature people 'falsely implicated in a crime as an alleged accused', often by the police themselves – exactly as I was. 'Finding no way out, these poor households end up paying a bribe to get out of the situation.' A further 13 per cent paid to have their name removed as a witness.

The India Corruption Study gives two reasons why there might be such an 'alarming level' of corruption in interactions with the police. First, because the police service is 'monopolistic in nature', households have no option but to use them and there is no private alternative to access. Secondly, poor households 'hesitate to complain for fear of further harassment and in that process end up being victims of corrupt practices'. The India Corruption Study (2005) spells this second reason out even more chillingly: the police 'are vested with substantial powers' so not paying the bribe could have serious repercussions.

These statistics convey the extent of the problem across India. Adding colour from a police perspective, I found an extraordinary account from an Indian Police Service (IPS) officer. IPS officers are on a par with the Indian Administrative Service (IAS) officers, the elite of the Indian civil service. They are trained at the National Police Academy in Hyderabad. One of their number, Superintendent Arvind Verma, had served twelve years as police superintendent in Bihar. He wrote a compelling and extraordinarily candid admission in an article, 'Cultural Roots of Police Corruption in India': The Indian police, he writes, 'have an unsavory reputation for extortion'. 'Every rank' from 'village watchman' to the 'Director General of Police is known to have tainted hands'. Police officers and inspectors 'prey upon the common people by misusing their powers to extort money from the complainants, witnesses and naturally the accused'. Money is extorted from 'hawkers, footpath dwellers, truck and bus drivers'.

This corruption extends to the top, to IPS officers like himself; one way they have of making money is by getting bribes from subordinate officers for transfers and postings. But then those who have paid bribes to get a position have to recover that amount; the obvious method is through extortion of the general public.

Overall, Superintendent Verma concludes, 'Corrupt practices are ... found in every department, in every rank and in every police institution including training colleges. The malaise has spread all over the country.'

Corruption can even help explain the atrocious driving I was experiencing every day as I tried to negotiate Road No. 13 and Road No. 1 on my way to the Taj Banjara and Crosswords book store: in *Corruption in India*, Debroy and Bhandari show how there is 'rampant corruption' around the getting of drivers' licences. In Delhi, people arriving to pick up their new drivers' licences were given a surprise driving test: fully two-thirds failed the test. The authors noted that 'many unsafe drivers were able to get the license'; indeed, of those who used an agent to acquire their licence, only 12 per cent had to take a driving test at all! Corruption, they say, 'has therefore overwhelmed the ability of the driving test to only put the better drivers on the road'.

As I was stuck in India reflecting on the extent of police corruption I had a small epiphany. In my simple-minded way, I suppose I had always assumed that peace and order required the presence of police and legal authority. But the peace and order (in general) that one sees all around, all the time in Hyderabad and in India, appear to have little to do with the police or any legal authority. In fact, the police are the anti-agents of law and order – they are 'anti-due process', as Abdullah put it to me, describing the situation with his brother. The peace we take for granted, the law and order, actually seems to be a *spontaneous* order, a self-organising system that arises through the everyday interactions of ordinary people. Sometimes it does go wrong, of course, although often when it went wrong in Hyderabad it was because some politicians were agitating and inciting communal mistrust and getting the police to intervene on one side or the other, as was the case with Abdullah's brother. Sometimes there will be a genuine thief or even a murderer. But then it's important to remember that the police neither stop that from happening nor even follow due process with these genuine cases; witness Alif's neighbour's murderer, who is even now walking free. The police in India seem to be on the side of disorder, not order – they foment trouble, then they capitalise on it. Ordinary people getting on with their lives, on the other hand, in general seem able to create a spontaneous order of relative peaceful-ness. That was a startling and unexpected realisation.

But the question kept on nagging me: *why* is there such corruption in India, and why in particular are the police so cor-rupt? I'd heard many people talk about their theories for this, from the malign influence of Indian religion, to the enduring but also malign influence of the British. None of them seemed particularly satisfactory. Weren't there any better explanations?

CHAPTER 6

MONEY OR POWER

DOWNSTAIRS IN THE TAJ Krishna hotel, Peter played the piano early evenings. One day, as he packed up his music, I told him my story.

'As a citizen of this country,' he said, 'I'm so ashamed. You've done such good work here for our children – how could it treat you so badly?'

And then, typically, he told me his own recent story. He's Anglo-Indian, his wife a foreigner, Malaysian. She had lived in India for thirty-seven years and their children now lived in Australia, so she wanted to go and join them. She needed a PCC – a police clearance certificate – in order to leave the country. Getting this should take just a couple of days. It took them three months.

'Did you pay a bribe?' I asked.

He hadn't. 'But only because I happened to have some friends who knew someone high up in the police force; he put pressure on the officials to relent. That's the only way you get things done in India,' he said. 'Money or power. Those are your only choices.' In the end, I too had to go the power route.

||||||||||||||||||

The two weeks in Delhi did me a great deal of good. I had to return to Hyderabad in order to meet with new lawyers; after my previous lawyers had failed to effect the return of my passport, the university insurers had decided I needed new support, so found me lawyers with international credibility (and prices to match). I had to meet them and plan the next stage of my case.

In Delhi, I'd been able to spend some time with Sara and with other friends. There was a conference of the National Independent Schools Alliance, the umbrella body for low-cost private schools across India. They made me chief mentor, which helped restore some of my lost identity, at least for a while. Sara and I met with my friend Gurcharan Das – the best-selling author of masterpieces such as *India Unbound* and *The Difficulty of Being Good*. He was shocked by my story and said it was absolutely disgraceful that this could happen in 21st-century India. 'Corruption is our scourge,' he said. He promised that he would think of ways to help me.

Also, the consensus among Sara's friends in Delhi seemed to

be that Mantra had sent Jivan to frighten me into paying a bribe, but it was all a bluff; he was never threatening any more than that. Yes, there was a gun, but only the English are so horrified by guns – in India, they're not so unusual, more like America. Now that I had refused to pay up, Mantra would simply lose her interest in me, they thought. 'It happens all the time. You're not the biggest fish they have to fry,' one friend told me. 'You've refused to pay the bribe. Mantra will now move on and find someone else to exploit.' In other words, calm down, dear!

I returned to Hyderabad on 28 April feeling much better. Until my aircraft landed in the brand new International Airport, that is, and I feared that there would be police waiting for me. I braced myself. But there was no one, and no one had called at my apartment (the receptionist confirmed) and I began to feel rather foolish – perhaps I had overblown things a bit.

So I was feeling calmer, but also becalmed, because I was stuck in India for the foreseeable future.

I had an introductory meeting with my new lawyers; it was a tremendous relief to sit with people who could communicate with me in English, and who were willing even to share my court documents with me! They solved the mystery of why my earlier lawyers didn't want me to show any original documents to the police. The police, I was told, would deliberately lose any documents given to them, knowing full well that only originals are acceptable in court, thus destroying any case I had instantly. That was really worrying, especially as I could easily have handed over document after document to Mantra, without realising this. Why on earth didn't my earlier lawyers tell me this?

My new lawyers affirmed that I couldn't go to court to get my passport back for a while yet – it was too early after the last rejection. In any case, the court closed for the whole month of May, the long summer holidays in Hyderabad. So Mantra was still in control of my freedom for at least a month more.

A day after I returned, I did a little bit of work in my room, feeling quite virtuous for getting through some emails, making at least an impression on some of the university work piling up. And then I walked up to Crosswords, the bookshop in the City Centre mall, and even the woman at the counter didn't seem frightening any more. I'd really been paranoid, I thought to myself. I had really overdone it!

I felt restless, however, so I walked across to the Taj Krishna, the slightly more upmarket hotel, part of the same chain as the Taj Banjara, opposite the City Centre mall. Unfortunately, the bar was closed – of course it was a 'dry' day in Hyderabad because of the election the next day, as prescribed by the Prohibition and Excise Department of the Commissionerate of Prohibition and Excise. In fact, it would be three dry days: election day and the days before and after. I braced myself for the emptiness of a drinkless night alone in my room.

Suddenly, I recalled what Khem, the junior manager at the Taj Banjara, had told me the day I had fled Hyderabad. There was a person I should meet at the Taj Krishna, he had said, who was friends with the Chief of Police. I surprised myself by remembering his name, 'Mr Haridevan', and even the room number, '656'. When I'd been given his name, I'd thought it was all a set-up, too paranoid to think anyone could be on my side. But feeling that I had nothing to lose, I asked for him at the reception, and to my surprise, was asked if it was Mr Haridevan *Jivan* I was looking for? Yes, of course, I replied, not knowing if it was him at all. I was told I should go up to the seventh floor and ask the 'butler' for him.

The receptionist came across to the lift to insert his card, as the seventh floor was the restricted-access club floor. In the lounge, the butler greeted me warmly as if I was a regular, and phoned Mr Haridevan's personal assistant, who shortly came along the corridor to meet me. He gave me a number, which I phoned, and Mr Haridevan, without any question as to who I was or what I wanted, agreed to see me in one hour. Was that fishy? Or normal? I really didn't know.

After an hour and a half, Mr Haridevan still hadn't arrived, so I asked the butler again, and this time was led down to the sixth floor, to the luxury suite at the far end of the corridor. I was admitted into a large sitting room, with a corridor leading away on one side and a large patio window with a balcony on the other side.

Years ago, I had arranged to meet with Rahul Gandhi, leader of the Congress Party and son of the assassinated Rajiv Gandhi. I hadn't thought the unassuming young man sitting to one side was the person I had come to see, so aimed my smile at the person who seemed to have more gravitas, but who turned out to be his personal assistant; the unassuming young man was Gandhi. I made the same category mistake in Haridevan's room. This time, I made no effort to smile at the man in untucked shirt and slacks and no footwear, mistaking him for the personal assistant who had come upstairs earlier. However, as the man started to assert himself, ordering food and directing me to sit down, and then the personal assistant returned, I realised my mistake. I was already with Mr Haridevan.

He volunteered some information about himself. He was a businessman with a strong involvement in national and regional politics. He lived in the Taj Krishna when in Hyderabad; his other home was a hotel in Bombay (like most Indians I know, he didn't call the city Mumbai).

'So what do you want?' he asked.

I jumped in without any preliminaries, surprising myself at the velocity of my launch. 'I'm in big trouble,' I said, quickly listing that I'd been arrested, imprisoned, passport confiscated and was being pursued by Mrs T. Mantra, CID DSP – at which point he interrupted me. The butler had returned with snacks, and Mr Haridevan said, affecting an appropriate gesture, 'It's very hot in here; the air conditioning is not working,' and so we went outside. On the balcony it was of course much hotter than inside, but out of earshot. He swept his hand across the landscape, telling me he could see three-quarters of Hyderabad from there, and three of India's great religions: there, the city's great lake, the Hussain Sagar, with the ancient statute of Buddha on its island; above that, the magnificent Hindu

Birla Temple; and then across to the Muslim Old City with its sixteenth-century triumphal arch, the Charminar, and the adjacent grand mosque, the Mecca Masjid.

'Tell me,' he said, indicating for me to continue.

'Mrs Mantra is sending people around for a bribe,' I said.

He shook his head. 'Don't use words like that. You foreigners always make that mistake.'

How could I describe his tone? He was dismissive of me, but in a sophisticated, pleasant way. It was a tone I hadn't heard before – not like Jivan's, for instance, which now seemed pathetically self-serving. This was more like an ornithologist describing a bird that was commonplace to him in his country, but which he recognised must seem exotic to outsiders. 'Don't call it a "bribe",' he said. 'Just think of it as about satisfying ego, that's all.'

He asked why I was in trouble. I told him the rough outlines of the case, to do with foreign currency and a trust, of which I wasn't even a trustee, and that all the money was used to serve the poor in the Old City.

'OK,' he said, satisfied with what I'd told him. 'I'll speak to the chief of CID tomorrow. He's my friend. And then you can have your passport back within hours.'

Within hours! I stood there, feeling immensely grateful. But then cautious – this was all too quick.

'Why would you help me?' I asked.

'You're innocent, aren't you?' he said.

'Yes,' I said.

'Good. Then I will help you.'

'But why would the chief of CID listen to you?'

'He listens,' he said, lightly, shrugging off my probing.

Then he asked me if I had lawyers. Proudly, I started to tell him about my new lawyers, from the firm that we shall call 'Shuramarthy Law'. He stopped me straight away, sucking his tongue in disapproval in the south Indian way.

'*They* are the bad guys – they'll bleed you dry, take all the time in the world and extort maximum money from you,' he said.

I thought then of 'Old India' versus 'New India'. My new lawyers were most definitely New India; they did everything the correct, modern way, all due process, in swish and expensive offices in the poshest part of town, Jubilee Hills. But Mr Haridevan was clear: it was much quicker and less expensive to use the old route of influence and bribes – sorry, ego payments. On the heat of the balcony, Mr Haridevan even made it feel like an exotic natural history, rather than anything undesirable.

In my gratitude, I could have sat with him all night. But he said he had other visitors and I should come back at 10.30 a.m. the next morning, with all my documents, arrest warrant, remand reports, legal petitions and police and CID responses.

As I walked back, I knew that this had brought difficulties already. For I didn't have any of my legal documents; my old lawyers, Prandakur and Vashnu, had these. Firmly Old India, they'd never shown me any legal documents pertaining to my case, however much I'd asked for them. And now that I'd got new lawyers, the old lawyers were holding on to them, perhaps to extract some ransom payments for their exchange.

Anyway, it felt like a strong lead; perhaps we could move forward even without the documents?

Back in my room, I found that Gurcharan Das had emailed saying he had arranged a meeting with a director in the Ministry of Home Affairs the next day in Delhi. I reckoned that the meeting with the head of CID was more likely to come to fruition, not the official one, so I declined, although I felt bad about abusing Gurcharan's kindness.

The next day, Wednesday 30 April, was election day in Andhra Pradesh. The papers were full of it. 'Vote Modi,' said the cover of the *Times of India* in an advertising feature. I woke up uncharacteristically early, around 6 a.m., feeling invigorated. I checked my emails and found that Gurcharan was fine about rescheduling the Delhi meeting.

A few minutes later, however, I got an urgent phone call from a friend of Gurcharan's, a retired general, who told me that I mustn't spend any more time with the CID in Hyderabad. 'You must avoid them; come straight to Delhi, where we can sort matters out easily for you with the Ministry of Home Affairs. You must come quickly. We've uncovered a police scam, you are in danger.'

I felt out of my depth. Old versus New India again, but which path should I take? Which would give me my passport back most quickly? I felt an atavistic connection with Mr Haridevan and all he had discussed the night before – behind the scenes we could sort things out; why mess with transparency? But I also had this modern connection with Gurcharan, that we should do things properly, above board, in an open and progressive manner.

Then I realised it was more complicated than that. The reason why I was in trouble at all was because the Educare Trust had refused to pay bribes to the Ministry of Home Affairs; that's what Gita had informed me. The Ministry of Home Affairs in Delhi, then, seemed not to be part of Gurcharan's 'New India' at all. Not knowing what to do, I phoned Gurcharan and told him that I'd met with a businessman who had arranged a meeting with the head of CID. He agreed it made sense to keep this meeting. The general, Gurcharan's friend, phoned again and asked me to email him full details of who I was seeing, for my protection.

'Mr Haridevan Jivan,' I wrote, 'has arranged for me to meet Mr P. S. Subramanyam, Additional Director General of Police (the head of CID).'

'OK,' he replied, I sensed reluctantly. I'd got the green light to go ahead from Delhi.

(Later I told Haridevan about the general from Delhi being so concerned, and he chuckled: the Ministry of Home Affairs wants the case back, he said, because they're jealous of the police in Hyderabad getting all my bribe money. 'That's why they're saying these things. You can take your choice,' he said, shrugging. 'Go up to Delhi to pay more bribes and get the case stopped that way, or stay with me and we'll sort it out with the "boss".')

On election day, the roads were wonderfully empty, the

shops all closed. I could cross Road No. 1 easily without feeling I was taking my life in my hands. The roads were wonderfully *quiet*, too – no constant blare of innumerable traffic horns.

I walked down the corridor and waited outside Mr Haridevan's room. I could hear someone inside on the phone, but no one heard me knocking. Eventually, a cleaner arrived and let me in. Mr Haridevan's personal assistant greeted me, but suspiciously – throughout our meetings, he didn't lose his suspicion of me. Against his better judgement, he was instructed to invite me through to the bedroom, where Mr Haridevan was sitting next to the window. He motioned for me to sit. The unmade bed was between us, with four pillows that had been propping him up and the *Times of India* spread out on the bed. A portrait of Gandhi was hung to one side of his bed. The television was on with live election coverage; he turned down the volume when I arrived.

The other night it had all been such a rush – now I observed him more closely. He was wearing blue shorts and an open-necked shirt revealing a delicate gold chain. He had a boyish face, which made him seem younger than he was. Later, I found out he was my age, though he looked ten or fifteen years younger. He wore glasses, which he peered over at times, had buck teeth and a charming almost naughty smile that he flashed when he was pleased about something, as happened frequently when he was on the phone – or rather, on one of his phones. He had two gold-plated iPhones and one other smartphone, plus various tablets and an iPad.

He asked me, 'What is your view?' pointing to the election coverage on the television. I said it seemed likely that Modi would win, and that even people like my friend Gurcharan Das (name dropping for a reason, of course) thought that was a good thing.

He said, 'Yes, of course Modi will win, and he will be in for ten years, and will be a good Prime Minister. He is not interested in money, only in power. He is not corrupt, so will be good. What is the view from outside?'

'From England?' I asked. How would I know? Surely he realised I was stuck in India? I said nothing.

He continued, 'Modi will be like Margaret Thatcher was to England, for India. A power for good.'

I showed him the documents I'd brought about the trust, but not the court documents required. I did know my case number, however, and he asked his PA to find my bail conditions on the internet. He was unable to find them; the PA appeared disgusted with me for not even knowing my old lawyer's full name, let alone not having any of my papers with me. But Mr Haridevan seemed relaxed about it all – perhaps it added to my unworldly innocence.

He told me that everyone in the CID knew about my case. Mantra had phoned the public prosecutor at midnight before my arrest to get his consent, painting a vile picture of me. He also told me that Mantra's boss, Mr P. S. Subramanyam, the Additional Director General of Police (ADGP), had actually been there with him the night before, when we had met.

This meant of course he would have been in the bedroom, as I had been in the living room and then the balcony. There's nothing odd in India about meetings like this being held in the bedroom, although to Western sensibilities it seems strange. But there's no implication of sexual matters. At least, I think there's no implication. We were in the bedroom – was something else expected? I realised I didn't really have a clue.

Mr Haridevan made arrangements for me to go to CID headquarters the next day at 11 a.m. to meet with the ADGP. And within a day or two, I would have my passport back.

The butler arrived with coffee for us both; he was treated to a dismissive snarl from Haridevan as he tried to fit the coffee onto the table next to the iPhones. The butler found my face friendly, however, and told me that it was south Indian filter coffee, the best coffee you could get, and that the biscuits were locally made.

As we drank, Haridevan told me that when I went to meet the ADGP the next day I should take a letter with me, requesting the return of my passport, outlining the situation and inserting the crucial line: 'Whenever CID requires me for investigation, I will without fail return.' I nodded in agreement.

'So will you return?' he asked.

'Of course,' I said.

He smiled wearily, as if I was a pitifully slow learner.

I asked him about his gold-plated iPhones. It was an innocent question, just to keep conversation moving. 'They're from London. Gold & Co. The latest one might cost – what is the exchange rate? – about £1,000.' And then, 'You can bring me one as a gift.'

And perhaps that was it. Khem had warned me that Haridevan would be expecting something. But what could I give a man who had everything? What difference would a bribe make to him – perhaps pay for his suite for a couple of nights? Yes, he'd help me, and I could bring him a gift that was a bother to get, and would in any case be nice to receive *as a gift*. At least I understood the situation; it didn't seem too bad.

In the evening, I sat and wrote to the ADGP, something positive to be doing at last, adding to my growing sense that it may really be all over and soon I would be free.

IIIIIIIIIIIIIIIIIII

The day after the election in Andhra Pradesh (although it continued in India for a few weeks more), the newspapers were full of the low voter turnout in Hyderabad: only 53 per cent. The *Times of India* condemned the masses for not bothering about India's precious democracy.

I know many Indians are very proud of their democracy, and I hesitate to write what I'm about to, because I really don't wish to offend any of them. But the more I saw of what was going on, the more I tended to side with the man from a slum reported in the *Times of India*, who asked what the point of voting was when there was so much political corruption. The *Times of India* severely castigated his approach. 'It's only through voting that we can rid ourselves of corruption,' it railed. But how true was that? I wondered. Did an individual voter really have any power through his one vote to change the entrenched corruption, including that around elections?

Every day over breakfast, I'd been reading the newspaper. Every day, incredible India had stories of politicians bribing voters. In the *Times of India*, for instance, I'd read how politicians were going to ATMs, drawing out cash and handing it straight to voters, who formed an orderly line outside the cash machine. Handouts of liquor were especially popular among rural farmers. One enterprising politician had been caught by a journalist bribing voters, this time not with cash but with gifts of 'cell phones, pressure cookers, mixer grinders, DVD players, microwave ovens and gas stoves'. I read how some politicians had enlisted the ambulance service to ferry cash around to hand out to voters. In one district, the police station had received a complaint that some other policemen were assisting politicians by transporting cash for bribing voters in their own police vehicles.

I'd also read an article which explained something that had puzzled me – why on earth did the elections in India take so long? They were spread over a period of a month. That's very odd. Again, it is all to do with police corruption. No one, not even the central government, trusts the police. The rule of law has completely gone out of the window, and central government knows it. So the army is required to keep order during elections, because local police would be in the pay of some local politician or other. Because there are only a limited number of soldiers to go around, the polling has to be stretched over a long period, to keep the police away from the polling stations.

Mark Twain once observed, 'It could probably be shown by facts and figures that there is no distinctly native American criminal class except Congress.' He would have to add the Indian Lok Sabha (the lower house of Parliament) to his list. The *Times of India* suggested about 30 per cent of members of Parliament and state assemblies had criminal cases pending against them.

The day after election day, I couldn't muster much enthusiasm for Indian democracy, where politicians used police to bribe voters and the police had to be kept away from polling stations to avoid them skewing the result.

I went for my meeting with the 'boss', as Haridevan called him, the Additional Director General of Police (ADGP), Mr P. S. Subramanyam. Instead of an autorickshaw, I ordered a taxi, feeling that I wanted to be presentable but also feeling like spoiling myself. As I travelled, I saw billboard hoardings everywhere of poor peasants with their forefingers raised in what, at first glance, looked like a rather rude gesture – but they were showing their *inked* forefingers to prove they'd voted, that they at least could be counted among the *Times of India*'s worthy citizens.

When I arrived at CID HQ, the two men at reception greeted me knowingly, as if they were aware of why I was there. They took me to wait for the 'boss' in a narrow waiting room with two black faux-leather sofas and a fan pointing oddly towards the wall. It was very hot in there, and I wondered if I could move the fan so that it blew into the room, but decided the better of it. I was treated well, served a glass of ice-cold water, followed by black tea (not milky chai, as if they'd been informed of my preferences – Khem at the Taj Banjara would certainly know this about me).

I was taken into the boss's office. Mr P. S. Subramanyam was a big man with broad shoulders, a wide face, a plump double-chin and a thick moustache. But the effect was somewhat ruined because he was dwarfed by his huge desk spanning ten feet or more, and the huge library of books behind him, and the huge room.

He motioned for me to sit in one of the seven seats in front of his desk. One man – a very little man by comparison, doubly dwarfed by the room – was sitting directly opposite the boss in the middle seat. His bag was on the seat next to him, which meant I had to sit on the very end seat, making me feel already at a disadvantage.

'Tell me,' began Mr P. S. Subramanyam. By way of introduction, I presented him with a copy of *The Beautiful Tree*, but immediately he got a phone call and spoke election politics (or was it cricket?) in Telugu for ten minutes or so, while I sat waiting. Putting down the phone he said he knew all about me, that I'd done great things for the poor in Hyderabad and, he said proudly, really put the city on the map. He turned to the man in front of him and said I was an eminent professor. Finally, he said, 'We've got to review the case as Mantra' (he seemed to

mumble her name as if with embarrassment) 'has been looking at it.' Then my heart sank as he said, 'It's a very busy time
for me, so I want you to meet with Mr...' (he gave a Telugu
name that I couldn't pick up – there's something about south
Indian names and accents that makes them very hard to deci-
pher to an Englishman on first or even subsequent hearings)
'...and he will review the case and see what is going on.'

But then Mr (whatever his name was) butted in, and rattled off in the most horrible, officious voice, 'See, he has not
been cooperating with CID, he has not been coming when
he should, he has been trying to come on Saturday instead of
Sunday,' jumbling up things that had been happening, giving
Mantra's version, then saying that there was foreign currency
wrongly used amounting to crores of rupees – hundreds of
thousands of pounds!

I listened, horrified. Mr P. S. Subramanyam looked per-
turbed, but said, 'Let's see whether he is guilty or not,' and
then dismissed me. He told me to go upstairs and wait for Mr
(whatever his name was), while he talked further with him.

My heart sank. I'd been full of hope, but now my hope was
dashed. I shook his hand and that of Mr (...), trying to get his
name; after the second attempt, thinking I had some sense at
least of the sound and if I went quickly upstairs I would be able
to recognise it on one of the signboards. I climbed the stairs to
the third floor, saw signs for various names, but none resem-
bled the vague sound I had in my head, which anyway was
quickly disappearing in the heat and anxiety. The only other

thing I recalled was that the man was 'deputy' something or other. There were eight deputies on the third floor, including of course Deputy Superintendent Mantra, whom I was desperate to avoid.

I felt helpless, stupid to add to the burden of my lost hopes not even knowing who I should be meeting. And if I failed to meet him, then the lifeline offered by Mr Haridevan from the Taj Krishna would disappear. He wouldn't be happy if I failed to meet someone just because I didn't get his name; that would be stretching my naive innocence a bit too far.

I stood helplessly by the lift well, thinking I should just wait there until the required man came up. But people seemed uncomfortable with me being there, wanting me to move on, and in any case it was terribly hot, with no fans, and I was afraid Mantra would come by, and seeing her would be too terrible to contemplate. I allowed myself to be led into a waiting room attached to the offices of the three *deputy* general inspectors, who seemed to have names closer to the one I recalled from downstairs.

I sat there miserably. I'd forgotten how emotionally draining it was being in the CID headquarters. Away in Delhi, I couldn't recall this feeling. But it came back the instant I was there again. My stomach twisted and dragged down; I felt as though I was sinking into quicksand, my freedom, my life at the mercy of people who didn't understand me and who were trying to trap me.

Hearing this new guy, Mr (...), saying that I was not cooperating with the police, implying that I was an evil criminal

... all my carefully built-up calm disappeared in a moment of being upstairs in this building; this dirty, crowded, ugly, monotone building full of mediocrity and mendacity. There was a feeling of your own worthlessness, that your time didn't matter anymore – you could be at the beck and call of others who had more important things to do, you could sit and wait for as long as they wanted, and then respond to what they wanted you to do, irrespective of what you may have had to do. Mutually consulting diaries was out of the window, for ever. You were insulted, disbelieved, had stories constructed about you, but your time mattered no longer. It was a discombobulating set of feelings.

Thankfully – so thankfully! – one of the secretaries (male of course; in government offices all assistants are male) spoke good English, seemed very bright and was uncharacteristically helpful. He even seemed to empathise with how difficult it was to recognise names as a foreigner. Cleverly, he hit on the idea of showing me the police yearbook to see if I could pick out someone from their photograph. Of course, people all have photographs of themselves from a few years back, so I didn't even recognise P. S. Subramanyam, the boss, and in any case I'm notoriously bad at this – is there an equivalent of colour-blindness for not being able to identify faces from photographs? Perhaps it's called stupidity. But then the helpful assistant turned a page and I did immediately recognise the man from downstairs, or at least I said I did, even though a moment later I wondered how I could possibly have known it was him.

Anyway, the man in question was a superintendent, not deputy, adding to the confusion. But in the absence of anything better to go on, they took me along to his office, where the secretary was cold and unhelpful – as people usually were in that place. Wonderfully, I bumped into the kindly CID man who had sat with me on my first night in custody, and had rubbed my back as I cried when they took me into jail. I had wanted to see him to pay him back the money I found he had lent to Sara. I gestured to him (because he didn't speak any English, and me no Telugu) that I wanted to do this; he refused. I felt in the presence of a good man and wanted to hold on to his proffered hand for as long as I could.

Mr (...) arrived, and it was him – I had recognised the picture correctly. In his office, he immediately started where he had left off downstairs, saying that I was not cooperating with the police and that I was further refusing to cooperate by not bringing in all documents pertaining to the trust. I asked how could I be expected to have all my documents from ten years ago; was I supposed to carry them around with me as I travelled around the world all the time? 'Yes,' he said. 'Exactly. You should have everything with you, in case there is an inquiry.'

I sat, feeling hopeless. I started talking about Mantra, that it was her who was not cooperating, that she was not interested in the case, only interested in *other things*. I was about to say interested in bribes, but the terrified look in his eye, like a Victorian aunt afraid you might mention sex, made me stop.

Anyway, he said, I had to bring in all my documents; there

was no alternative. He would quickly review them. And I mustn't be afraid, he added, smiling ruefully, that they would find something else wrong and prosecute me, nothing like that would happen with him. This new possibility I hadn't even thought of, but now realised that it may have been an additional reason why my lawyers hadn't wanted me to give documents to the police. The police can always find *something* you've done wrong; regulations are so extensive that it wouldn't be too hard. Then they can prosecute you on that instead. (This was confirmed when I spoke to two of the people who ran schools in the Old City, Alif and Abdullah. Don't cooperate with the police, they had said. 'They will go through your papers with a fine-tooth comb, and find out which paperwork is missing, or which minor law you've offended. Then they'll descend on you for that,' said Alif. 'Cooperation is the *worst* thing to do with the police,' Abdullah stressed, reflecting on his life's experiences. 'They'll catch you out,' said Alif. 'The only option for you is pay the bribe.')

I took down his name and phone number in my notebook. Even in front of him, I couldn't get his Telugu pronunciation, and as he spelled it out I had difficulty with his pronunciation of the letters; it was most embarrassing. Anyway, he was Mr S. Rajan Gopala Reddy, but I could call him Gopala. He was Mantra's immediate boss, he told me. 'So bring in all your documents,' he said, 'and you will get your passport back.'

After the meeting, I phoned my new lawyers and they agreed that we should go through all the 11,000 pages of documents

I'd located, identify the most important and make a summary of these, to show my innocence. They would help me with this – and they would keep the three suitcases of originals in their office, so that I would feel less vulnerable in my room. So there was something positive to do. Mr S. Rajan Gopala Reddy, they said, seemed at least more professional than Mrs Mantra.

From feeling upbeat, however, I collapsed again on the weekend. It was May; I'd been stuck in India over two months. Time was ticking by – I was stuck and couldn't get moving. On Saturday, I couldn't get out of bed until 3 p.m.; I burst into tears when talking to my eldest brother Mark on Skype, just couldn't control myself. I hated being there, feeling trapped.

But I tried to pull myself together. I went to Crosswords bookshop. It had a whole jumble of books in a section called 'Philosophy and Religion', and it was this section that I was drawn to all the time now. I bought a book called *The Promise of Death*, which somehow seemed comforting. And then there was *Flatland: A Romance of Many Dimensions*, by Edwin Abbott Abbott, about humanoid creatures who lived only in two dimensions, but who realised that some of the two-dimensional objects they encountered were actually manifestations of objects in three dimensions. I read it sitting there with my coffee, and recalled what Mantra had implied about the millions of gods living in nature's extra eleven dimensions, and wondered what it all meant.

||||||||||||||||||

Submitting my documents to the CID was not as easy as it sounded. On our first attempt, I went with my new lawyer, who we shall call 'Kavitha'. She was a tall, big-boned young woman, I guess about thirty years old. She was highly Westernised, educated and sophisticated. She was very efficient, very quick to grasp points, very knowledgeable about legal matters pertaining to my case, and her English was excellent. She was New India to the core, as different from the Old India lawyers as you could imagine. She talked to me, she let me know what was going on, she understood my need to know! She was kind and accessible.

And she had all my arrest, prison remand and court documents, duplicates obtained from court (as my old lawyers had refused to hand the originals over). And, miracle of miracles, she shared these with me, so that I could read all that Mrs Mantra had written against me and what the judge had written in response. For the first time, I realised that I'd not been charged with anything – confirming what Deepak had told me in prison, but which I'd simply refused to believe. There were only Mantra's allegations against me. I was still under investigation – there were no criminal charges at all. That was the good news. The bad news was that an investigation can last for ninety days, longer if the judge agrees.

Our first attempt to get documents to the CID failed dismally.

The plan was to take the small subset we'd selected of the most important documents to Mr. S. Rajan Gopala Reddy.

In total these amounted to some 200 sheets. Kavitha had carefully colour-coded these, pasting coloured stickers neatly onto
different pages to indicate their link with our carefully prepared summary document.

At the appointed hour, we went to the CID HQ office in
my hired car to meet Mr S. Rajan Gopala Reddy on the third
floor. He began aggressively. I was guilty and the only way I
could prove my innocence was to hand over all the Educare
Trust documents going back to 2002. 'That's twelve years ago,'
I protested. 'The trust has been closed for two years, defunct for
five years, and I don't live here.' Again I asked, 'Am I supposed
to carry with me all the documents from all the organisations
I work in all around the world wherever I go?'

The answer again appeared to be 'yes'. He didn't even bother
to go through the documents we'd brought in. He said, 'You
have to bring *all* your documents; on their own these are worth
nothing.' He scoffed when Kavitha showed him the documents
proving I'd resigned from the Educare Trust, and that this fact
was intimated to the Ministry of Home Affairs. None of this
mattered one bit, he said, 'because where did the Ministry of
Home Affairs acknowledge my resignation?'

I was stumped. 'Resignation is a two-way thing,' he continued. 'If they haven't acknowledged that you've resigned, then
there has been no resignation. You can try to get out of any
problems by resigning!' he said dismissively.

Kavitha tried again. She stressed that I resigned before any
alleged wrongdoings took place. 'That's what you're saying,'

he said, 'but you've made it all up. Because they haven't ack-nowledged your resignation, therefore you didn't resign.'

That feeling of wading through treacle – no, that's too pleasant – of being stuck in a peat bog, sinking into the mire, suffocating as the black mud closed over my face, came back with a vengeance.

There was some positive discussion – at least, Kavitha told me later that I should feel positive about it – about whether we could bring *copies* of documents or whether only origi-nals would do. He had wanted originals, of course – Kavitha had said photocopies. She made up some story that I'd found scanned copies of the documents on a computer in Newcastle; we couldn't find the original copies anywhere in Hyderabad. He seemed to find this persuasive, and finally agreed that we could bring copies.

We should then take these to Mantra, he said. Emboldened by Kavitha's presence, I said I didn't trust her, so he agreed to receive them himself. He told us that his boss, the ADGP, wanted this case dealt with as soon as possible – it was a pri-ority. Mr S. Rajan Gopala Reddy was flying to Delhi the next day, but when he came back two days later, it would be his major focus.

Our second attempt was a few days later, Thursday 8 May, as we'd needed two days to get all the documents carefully printed out from the scanned copies I had made, and then there had been a holiday. We arrived at CID HQ at 3 p.m., Kavitha hav-ing come independently from the office, with three cardboard boxes of copies looking disappointingly less impressive than the three suitcases of original documents. Mr Reddy seemed chirpy, from which I took a crumb of comfort. He was keen to share with us that which explained his gaiety: the CID had just arrested someone of significance to the US, and the American Ambassador was coming in to thank them. Because he had to rush off to this celebratory party, he couldn't stay with us to receive the documents, so we should take them over to Mantra – 'Don't worry,' he said, seeing my face fall. 'I will come as soon as I'm finished.'

We went to meet with Mantra. She was not in her office and was not picking up her phone. It was 3.30 p.m. After a few minutes, however, she phoned me, and said that she was just coming back from her lunch and would be there in ten minutes. We waited in her cubicle with our three boxes. It was mighty hot, the muggiest day I'd known there. Rain was threatening. We sat and waited.

A woman in her late thirties with terrible burns on the side of her neck and hands arrived. She was Mantra's new sidekick. Eventually, Mantra returned from lunch at 4 p.m. She stormed into her room, not looking at me, steaming with anger and hurt. She rudely asked Kavitha what she was doing there (this was the first time she had met my new lawyer). She looked at the boxes, picked up one or two of the papers, and then proceeded to talk about me in the third person.

She was martyr and angel: 'I have only ever been kind to Tooley,' she told Kavitha, 'doing my job, my duty, but beyond my job and my duty. I have always looked after him, tried to help him, make sure he was comfortable. I didn't want him to go to jail and even gave him money so that he could have toilet paper in prison.' It was all lies, of course. But her tone made me start to feel her pain too now.

She turned to include me, bringing up that she has been waiting the whole day for me, since 9.30 a.m. 'You didn't phone,' she said. 'I was waiting by the phone all day.' She glared at me, and at Kavitha. 'So now,' she continued, 'you are going to the bigger people, the governor, the judges, is that right? Am I not good enough for you anymore?'

Kavitha tried to calm her down. She explained that Mr S. Rajan Gopala Reddy had asked us to see him first, then come over to meet with Inspector Mantra. At this, Mantra cut her dead.

'I don't know who this "Inspector" person is.'

Realising the error, I butted in, '*Deputy Superintendent, DSP* Mantra.'

Kavitha continued, 'Yes, we should come over to see *DSP* Mantra and now we are here.'

'Well,' said Mantra, sighing deeply, 'I think I will give up this case and hand it over to someone else.' She was the hurt girlfriend or wife, about to pack her bags and leave. It tore at my heart; I cannot bear to hear a woman talk so pitifully. She said to Kavitha, 'I am going to be transferred, all because of this case. Nothing like this has ever happened to me in my life; I am a poor widow with two sons to support.' She continued,

'I have only ever admired Tooley, and now he is treating me so badly. I even brought my son to pay respect to this great man while he was in hospital. And my sons have read his book, and they're accusing their poor mother of being the evil one, saying that they won't wear khaki [i.e. join the police force], because of what Tooley is accusing me of doing, my sons hear the rumours just as I do!'

She sat sobbing. I have never been good at handling crying women. I felt guilty, only wanted her to stop crying. The side-kick glared across at me, telling Kavitha what a bad man I was, how ma'am had only every tried to help me, and this is how I reward her.

The three women then settled down into a female-exclusive conversation, and Mantra's manner changed completely. Gently, she asked Kavitha where she was from and then, 'Spinster?' Indian women are keen on these sorts of details. Kavitha nodded and Mantra added, 'It's better. Managing a career and a husband – men will always let you down,' motioning towards me. Then there was more intimate discussion among the women, in Telugu, then more ranting in Telugu, which Mantra repeated in English, I supposed for my benefit:

'It's all because of my caste that I am going to be moved from this case; I feel as though 150 years of my history is coming back to haunt me.'

It was 5 p.m. I'd warned Kavitha how normal it was for Mantra to get distracted, so Kavitha gently tried to push her back on to task, handing over our documents. Mantra picked up some from the nearest box, and she said, 'These are photo-copies, I can't take them.'

Kavitha said calmly, 'Mr S. Rajan Gopala Reddy agreed we could bring photocopies.' Mantra said, 'Mr S. Rajan Gopala Reddy is not in charge of this case. While I am still in charge, I will not receive photocopies.'

Kavitha asked, ever so gently, if they could go and ask the public prosecutor, who sits in the same building a floor below, if he would accept photocopied documents. Much to my surprise, Mantra agreed. They were all away for about an hour. While they were gone I wondered whether I should fear Mantra more now; would she put her henchmen on me again for ruining her life? Or should I fear her less, because now her superiors would make sure I was out of India as soon as possible?

Eventually the women returned; the decision was that we could submit these documents but the CID would only acknowledge receipt of photocopies, not originals; this may cause problems later, but was fine for us for now.

It was gone 6 p.m., time for Mantra to finish her day. I thought we might have been able to simply hand over the documents then, but apparently she needed to check them. 'Can't we do that now?' I quietly asked Kavitha. But Kavitha knew not to push her; it was late in the day for her (even though she'd only come back from lunch at 4 p.m.), and we agreed that we'd come back the next day. Mantra wanted us to leave the boxes with her.

'There's a very secure cupboard here,' said her sidekick with the burns. 'You don't need to bother yourselves.'

Kavitha wasn't persuaded. 'We'll take them, and bring them back tomorrow.' (As an aside to me she said quietly, 'Of course they would lose even these, just to inconvenience us.')

Back in the car, Kavitha told me about the conversation with the public prosecutor. At first, he had been adamant that he would not accept copies. 'Even in the investigation, we need originals, and of course in court, originals only can be accepted,' he had said. This was of course why we were not going to give them the originals, said Kavitha; they would most definitely deliberately lose them, thus making it impossible to defend me in court.

After some time, however, Kavitha had managed to persuade him: Tooley was trying to cooperate, she had told the public prosecutor. It was totally unreasonable to expect him to have all the documents with him now; he wasn't managing trustee during the period in question– not even a trustee. What he had done was find some documents that were scanned as they went along; some of his colleagues had found them on a computer in Newcastle, and he was trying to cooperate, so please let him.

Eventually the public prosecutor acquiesced. He said that my case was a 'paradox' to him. 'So confusing. On the one hand,' he said, 'it's just a simple foreign currency case, and a very small amount at that.' He understood now – because Kavitha had explained to him carefully; there seemed to have been no knowledge of this law before she did – that this should have a simple outcome of a penalty being paid, nothing serious at all. It was all a bit like a speeding fine, he agreed, a simple penalty to the correct authorities and the case should be closed. 'But on the other hand,' he said, 'it all seems like a – a scandal. There's something much bigger going on with Tooley behind the scenes that you don't even know about.'

Where did he get this from? Kavitha had asked him. 'It's all that Mantra has uncovered,' he said. Mantra chipped in, 'Yes, he's not married you know; what's he doing here, gallivanting about the world, hanging out in posh hotels? Is he a philanderer?' she asked. 'Or gay?' added the public prosecutor.

Kavitha tried to explain to him that none of this was relevant to the case, which was simply about foreign currency. Mantra would have none of it. 'He was drinking alcohol when I first met him at the Park Hyatt,' she said. 'He is a deeply immoral man.'

The third attempt at handing over my documents was on Friday 9 May. We were supposed to meet Mantra at 10.30 a.m. It was raining heavily, a pre-monsoon shower, so when I had phoned her as she always wanted me to do at 10 a.m., she said, 'It's raining.' Emboldened I asked, 'So?' Because of the rain, she put back our meeting to 11.30 a.m. Eventually, at 12.30 p.m., Mantra arrived (for the morning shift). We sat in her little stuffy cubicle office with the documents between us on the desk. Mantra talked to Kavitha and peered over the boxes to see how I was responding at times. I tried to disappear behind the boxes, closing my eyes to think of Daisy Cottage.

The swallows and house martins would be building their nests, twittering in the weak spring sunshine.

She talked to Kavitha for thirty minutes or so, mostly in Telugu; we were waiting for Mantra's sidekick to arrive, the woman with the burns. When she arrived, Kavitha patiently began going through some of the documents, but then Mantra interrupted her.

'The pages are not numbered,' she said.

'Yes, they are,' said Kavitha politely, pointing to the documents we'd printed out, all paginated. 'No,' said Mantra. 'The documents are not numbered *consecutively*.'

What? There were 11,000 pages. 'They have to be numbered consecutively.'

I started to do it then and there, in front of her, just to make a point, huffing and sighing, feeling my blood pressure rising. I started to lose my cool. Mantra said, 'Why are you blaming me? I am only doing my duty before God.' And she put her hands together in the Namaste form, and touched her heart, forehead and pointed to the heavens. She would not be budged. The pages had to be paginated consecutively, and she would not accept them until that was done.

In the Taj Banjara, on my way home from the CID, I spoke to Khem, the junior manager who had put me in touch with Mr Haridevan. He was sympathetic. 'It's a shame the case is not moving forward. Can't your firm pay the bribe for you?' he asked. To him, the problem must have been that I could not afford the bribe, not that I was refusing to pay the bribe.

I spent the whole weekend numbering these papers consecutively, 10,532 altogether, once I'd discarded some that were duplicates. Like a school pupil, I kept wondering whether I was doing it right for her, aware that the goalposts could move again, and that however hard I tried I would fail, because that was the purpose of this exercise.

She'd given me a totally futile job – what on earth was this numbering for? – so that I would be shown not to comply and so that she could catch me out again, or at least keep delaying me. I knew that was what it was all about. When I had been in her office, she had told me to circle the numbers; as I laboured all weekend I felt sure I was not circling them properly, and for sure she'd pick me up on that, and make me do them all over again. Or she'd pick me up on my untidy numbers, or I'd make some small mistakes, any of which would enable her to tell me to do it over. All weekend I felt like some small schoolboy totally at the mercy of his fastidious but arbitrary teacher.

Our fourth attempt to submit the documents was on 12 May. At my interrogation on the Sunday, she had told me to arrive Monday morning at 11 a.m., and without fail she would be there – we could submit the documents and I could be gone in thirty minutes.

I arrived shortly after 11 a.m. She arrived at 12.25 p.m. There was the usual small talk as we waited for her assistant to arrive. And then, as we went through the documents, Mantra sat, totally bored. She was utterly uninterested, trusting her sidekick to check the page numbers. Indeed, she looked increasingly crestfallen as we went through them. For a while I thought that must be because she was thinking what a strong case I have, with this full range of documents in meticulous order. At one point she fell asleep, just as she did during interrogations. But when she perked up, she was all sunshine and light, wanting to engage me in banter. 'What is the weather like in England; do you have seasons like we do here?' she asked, lightly. It reminded me of the fable about the sun and the wind and the man in the overcoat. She had tried using the wind and failed to get me to remove my overcoat. Now the sun was coming out.

Because that was still the purpose of it all: to get me to do the needful. When we'd finished at 2.20 p.m. and signed and stamped the receipt, and the documents had been put in their boxes by the cupboard where I guessed they would remain untouched for some time, she had laughed with us that she would have a terrible job getting these accepted in court, because it was a difficult enough job getting five pages, let alone 10,532 accepted as evidence; and she had thanked and praised me for cooperating, and praised my organisational talent, saying, 'We need more people like you in India; no Indian could have done it like this'; when all this was done and I got up to leave, she motioned for me and Kavitha to stay.

She looked at me fondly and began to talk, 'I have always worried about you. I know that you are suffering,' she said, 'but I am suffering too, because I have this case, and you foreigners don't know how to behave. Your country is *pucca*, but here, everything is wrong. You Britishers created the laws, back in 1861, Macaulay and the Indian Penal Code. In those days it worked well. We need to put the clock back. We still live in the police houses you Britishers built 250 years ago. They've lasted, but the system you brought has not. We need you to come back again, because without you we are corrupt. We cannot trust anyone, not even our husbands or our children.'

Kavitha tried to get us to leave again, saying we had a meeting to go to, but Mantra told her to sit.

'He has to know this, he has the right to know everything,' she said. She continued, 'Everyone in any senior position in the police got there through bribes. In my case, I was denied promotion for ten years, because of my caste. Ten years ago I should have been promoted to DSP. I was top ranking in my year at police college. But then some of my fellow students bribed the authorities to promote them instead of me. I saw I was not on the list of promotions. Why not?, I asked. They told me there must have been a typing error. And sorry, by the time the typing error was found, it was too late. Try next time, they said. It took me ten years, and only now I have got this promotion. But everyone has to pay bribes. I paid 12 lakhs [£12,000] to get this position, and you have to understand, I have to get that back from my clients. That's why Tooley needs to give me that money. Even the senior-most policemen, my boss, his boss, the ADGP, they've all paid bribes to politicians, or to businessmen connected with politicians, to get where they are. Everyone is corrupt.'

She paused for a moment to answer some query from her assistant. Then she continued, 'The Ministry of Home Affairs raised this problem with us, but we know exactly what had happened.'

'What?' I asked.

She gave me the heart-to-forehead-to-ceiling Namaste hand gesture:

'God be my witness, because you didn't pay a bribe to them! We've read their letters to you and know what they were asking for. But you were innocent, and so got yourself into all this trouble. You *insulted* them for ten years, by not paying any bribes. Now they have their revenge.

'Everything you do in India requires a bribe – that's just the way it is. You can't register a birth or a death or build a house or buy a plot of land without bribing. It is simply not possible.

'We all know you are innocent, we know you are a great man who helps the poor. We must get you home soon. I know you are suffering. But we can't let you go. Not until you have assisted me.'

Then she sighed and turned to Kavitha. 'This whole case could have been resolved so quickly,' she said, 'if he had just responded at the beginning and made me happy.'

Brazen is the wrong word. It was natural and unembarrassed. She turned again to Kavitha, 'Try to impress upon him', she said, 'that that is his only way out.'

We got up to go.

'By the way,' Mantra said sweetly, as we were leaving, 'have you heard from Mr Jivan lately?'

I shook my head. 'Will he be contacting me?' I asked with a sinking feeling, remembering my last encounter with him in my room.

'If he wants to contact you, he'll contact you I'm sure,' she said.

Smiling, she waved us on our way.

CHAPTER 7

A MODEST PROPOSAL

A DECADE AGO, WHEN I was doing research in Hyderabad using the Educare Trust as my office, the Secretary of Education was Dr I. V. Subba Rao. We'd become good friends then – he'd been very impressed by what we had found in the Old City. He'd visited some of the low-cost private schools, amazed that they had existed without his knowledge. He had also been the main speaker at the Indian book launch of *The Beautiful Tree*, at Crosswords. He'd been promoted within government and then, five or so years ago, he'd moved to Paris, taking on a position high up within UNESCO.

I hadn't wanted to bother him with my problems; I thought, in any case, he would be far removed from it all, based as he was in Europe. But then I heard that he was mooted to come back to India as the chief secretary for one of the two new states that was being carved out of Andhra Pradesh, which suggested he might still be connected to things Hyderabadi. By this stage I was completely desperate, and my shame at being in this position had to take second sitting. I'd been told that all the delay was because the police were waiting for my documents. I'd been told that Mrs Mantra was going to be removed from my case. Once both were done, I'd be free in a matter of days. But getting the documents handed over was clearly irrelevant, and Mrs Mantra was still very much in control of the case – and so my life.

In desperation, I emailed Pauline Dixon at the university for Dr Subba Rao's email address; she got back quickly, and so I emailed him, briefly outlining that I was in trouble. Within minutes he'd responded, saying he would do what he could.

At 7 p.m., I got a call from Mr Haridevan telling me to meet him at the Taj Krishna straight away. I went, walking uncomfortably in the languid heat of the evening, not sure what was going to happen, nervous about bribes, nervous about what I may have done wrong. I went up to his room and was shown immediately through to the bedroom.

Haridevan said quickly, 'How do you know Dr I. V. Subba Rao?' I began to explain nervously, but it was soon clear that it was good that I knew him. 'He phoned Sir...' (he referred to the Chief of Police as 'Sir' sometimes, as well as 'Boss') '... while I was with him an hour ago. He spoke very highly of you. Sir was already minded to help you, but now he will very quickly. Don't worry. It will all be over soon.'

I felt so pleased that Dr Subba Rao had helped in this way. Why hadn't I asked him before? I kicked myself for this. But it was partly because I felt he was so removed from it all in Paris, and partly shame on my part for getting caught up in this. Now, with both Haridevan and Subba Rao on my side, it seemed as though I could see the light at the end of the tunnel. I felt exhausted, but positive.

And then Haridevan warned me: it was absolutely essential that my case got resolved before state bifurcation, because after that, inevitably, everything would slow down. State bifurcation – this political issue was a problem for me. Hyderabad was in the state of Andhra Pradesh, but some politicians had been agitating for many years to split the state in two, even going on Gandhi-esque hunger strikes, peaceful protests that had, inevitably, provoked considerable violence, and hence had made the politicians sit up and notice. A couple of years earlier, the Congress government had caved in and agreed to carve two new states out of Andhra Pradesh. One would be called Telangana and the other would eventually settle on the original name, Andhra Pradesh. Hyderabad was going to remain the temporary capital of both states for now.

Why was it a problem for me? Well, my case, like all cases, would fall under one of these states, but it was perfectly possible that Mr P. S. Subramanyam, the ADGP, or my judge would be removed to the other state. And in any case, state bifurcation would create huge delays in all government processes, including the courts. So I had to get it all done before that happened; it was only a matter of weeks away.

'It's good to stick to your principles,' Haridevan said, admiringly. Before, he had said, 'you foreigners – you don't know anything'; now he said it was good what I had done. He told me that people like Mantra frequently victimised foreigners. They knew we were easy game, because we had the constraint of needing to get home. They delayed everything in our cases, and everyone connived in this, because there was money in it for everyone, especially the lawyers.

'If you appear in court ten times, then clearly there is more for the hungry lawyers than if you appear only once,' he said. So foreigners normally paid up, because they had to. He laughed gently. 'You have to pick your targets carefully. Most foreigners are easy targets. You were not. Someone like Mantra is normally good at who she picks. This time she was not.'

Another man from CID Police arrived in the bedroom. This new guy asked me if I spelled my name TULLY, and said he read the BBC's Sir Mark Tully a lot. I would have liked to spend time with him, but Haridevan indicated, kindly, that it was time for me to go.

The next day, I went in for my meeting with Mr P. S. Subramanyam at CID HQ at the appointed hour of 11.30 a.m. He was not there. His PA was friendly, and asked me to wait for him. At 12 noon precisely, I was called into his office. There were two other people already there in front of his big desk.

He said to me, 'Who arranged this meeting? It certainly was not me.' He seemed to be saying it for effect, for the others present, to put me in my place.

Thinking quickly, I said, 'I've come in after your call last night with Dr I. V. Subba Rao, to say thank you for giving me hope.' At this, Mr P. S. Subramanyam was friendly enough. Friendly enough indeed to hand me a copy of his book, *Trafficking in Persons*, which I got him to sign. Inside there was a description of his career, along with a photograph of him looking resplendent in full uniform. A foreword was written by a Supreme Court judge, who noted, 'I congratulate Sri P. S. Subramanyam, for *very tactfully handling a sensitive subject*, like trafficking in humans, *given the fact that he is an officer of the Indian Police Service*' (p. iii, emphases added). With my new understanding of the police force, I took this to mean that the police could also be implicated in trafficking.

Mr Sudhir Kumar, the bookish CID officer I'd met at Haridevan's the night before, came into the office and Mr P. S. Subramanyam introduced me, in glowing colours, as a very famous man who had contributed well to education here. He would like, he said, 'to give me the benefit of the doubt, provided that my papers are in order'.

Mr P. S. Subramanyam asked me to wait in the waiting room. I went back into the room with the three black faux-leather sofas, and was shortly joined by many others.

It seemed as though I was just one of many using the 'power/who you know' route. Indeed, there were soon nine people waiting, three to a sofa. I talked to the guy next to me. He was dressed smart-casual, but his friend sitting next to him was in jeans and a T-shirt. (I was in my suit and tie, which I considered the appropriate sartorial choice for such an occasion.) He told me that Mr P. S. Subramanyam was his uncle, and he was there to get help for his friend, the guy in jeans and a T-shirt, about some land issue. I wanted to know how close he was to Mr Subramanyam.

'So he's your mother or father's brother?' I asked.

'Not like that.' He was only some distant relative, but this didn't stop him being asked to help.

This made me feel in much less exalted company. Especially when I waited for nearly two hours in the increasingly hot and stuffy room as everyone else got seen before me. Eventually Mr Kumar called me in – not to the office with the huge desk, but into a side, semi-open-plan office, where there was much noise all around, and many interruptions. Mr Kumar had some of my files on his desk. I sat in front of him as he opened one and proceeded to read through it one page at a time, all handwritten notes from one investigator to another. He finished reading this folder, and started on another. One of the CID officers whom I remembered from my custody in the library and hospital came to join us, greeting me like an old friend. Sudhir Kumar told him that Mantra was asking for ₹15 lakhs bribe from me. They both shook their heads. What enraged them all was her greed in asking for so much, not the fact that she had asked for something. The pair of them spoke in Telugu, and I could not see how anything could move forward in that noisy room, and started to feel despairing again. But at 4.30 p.m., Sudhir Kumar got a call from Mr S. Rajan Gopala Reddy, who conveyed the news that Mrs Mantra had finally been removed from the case. It seemed this was the news that he was waiting for, and why he had asked me to wait there with him. My case was being handed over to a Mr Rajshekhar, also DSP, who would take over all the documents the following morning and familiarise himself with the case. I should then meet with him at 3 p.m. on Friday.

'Is this good for me?' I asked Mr Kumar. 'Yes of course. Mr Rajshekhar is a very good, fair man.'

'Will he not just ask for the same bribe?'

'No, there will be no bribes. But you must prepare your best defence for Friday. But don't worry,' he said. 'Finally, you can be calm now, the case will be fine.'

He put the files away, job done, and we talked about books again. He recommended reading Jawaharlal Nehru's *The Discovery of India*, and also *The Autobiography of an Unknown Indian*. As I was leaving, he said, 'Don't bring your lawyers on Friday. We don't like lawyers here. Come alone, all will be fine.'

I left at 4.45 p.m. and took my taxi across to the government Secretariat offices. Dr Subba Rao had arranged for me to meet with the chief secretary, the most important civil servant in Andhra Pradesh. At the main gates I explained who I was going to see, and suddenly I was an important man again. It was a very strange feeling – I'd not only not had it, I'd had the opposite, where everyone had been despising me; now soldiers were saluting me, not pushing me around. I was taken up to the waiting room in the magnificent setting of the old palace that made up the Secretariat: wood-panelled rooms, with statutes of Indian gods and goddesses. The waiting room was very full; I felt guilty when I got called first.

The chief secretary was a very kind, elderly man, with tired eyes. He was about to retire, I'd heard. He peered over his spectacles at me and rubbed his forehead in dismay when I told him my story, covering his eyes as if in shame. To one side of his massive desk, with the obligatory rows of chairs in front, was a computer on which he got his emails, and then in front of that was a flat-screen TV, on which cricket was playing – the T20 from Hyderabad, Punjab Kings XI versus Sunrisers Hyderabad. He looked up at it from time to time as we spoke. I had mentioned only a female CID officer; he asked me for her name. Reluctantly, I told him. She had concocted a story around me accusing me of all sorts of bad things, I continued, and I had ended up in prison for a bit, and had been in Hyderabad for nearly three months without my passport. He got on the phone immediately to Mr P. S. Subramanyam, but he was not available. He called for tea for me.

'Are you happy with the predicted election results?' I asked as I sipped. (The results were out on my Friday, but exit polls were published on Monday.)

'I am just a bureaucrat,' he said, waving dismissively at the TV, now showing details of the elections. 'I don't care for politics.'

||||||||||||||||||||

First Mrs Mantra was in charge of my case, then Mr S. Rajan Gopala Reddy, now Mr Rajshekhar. I went into CID on Friday to meet him, as had been organised for me.

Mr Rajshekhar looked up from his laptop as I arrived in his office.

'Who told you to come and see me? Did you just decide yourself?' he asked. He was openly angry. He had a very severe demeanour. As he glared at me, I observed that his ear lobes were incredibly hairy, but that this thick black hair seemed to be trimmed so that 1 cm at the top and bottom of each ear lobe was clear of any protuberance.

Mr Rajshekhar said he hadn't received my papers from Mrs Mantra, and so the case was still with her until she formally transferred the documents. She hadn't come back from lunch, but when she did she would hand over the papers and then he would go through them. Meanwhile, I should wait in his office, and he motioned for me to sit on a plastic chair at the far edge of his space.

He asked me why Mantra was being removed from this case. 'Is there any personal animosity between you?'

'No,' I said. 'She made up bad allegations against me, in order to get large bribes.'

He shook his head, scolding me. 'You mustn't criticise police officers.' Turning back to his work, he added, 'It's what we do. We can make up any allegations we want about you, don't get angry at us for that; save your anger for the courts, not the police. It's up to you to prove our allegations are false in court if you must.'

Having thus reprimanded me, he turned to one of his junior officers and they talked in Telugu, ignoring me. For thirty minutes I sat there and wondered what the hell I was doing there, with that awful feeling of being worse than unimportant in someone's eyes. After another fifteen minutes, I asked, 'Should I leave?' Rajshekhar, annoyed at my interruption, said, 'No.' After another ten minutes they both got up, but Rajshekhar indicated that I should stay.

Election coverage was on his laptop screen. The election results were to be announced that day – nothing was announced until the whole country had voted. I'd been watching it during the day in my room before coming out. Something surprising hit me about it all. Before the election result, for the past few weeks, the newspapers and media programmes had been full of stories of political bribery and corruption. I'd read stories of how even the police were involved in corruption to get their chosen politicians elected.

However, now that the election result was out, no one was mentioning anything about corruption any more. That was my impression after seeing the coverage for a few hours, but it didn't change over the next days and weeks. So were the bribery and corruption not relevant to any of the results? If bribes made no difference, then presumably politicians wouldn't offer them. So bribes must have contributed something to the result. But how much? Could some of Modi's landslide victory, and Congress's landslide defeat, owe anything to bribery? Surely that was an important question? No one seemed to be asking it.

At 5.30 p.m., Rajshekhar returned, telling me Mantra hadn't yet arrived from lunch, so I should come back the next day, and if she came in they could transfer the documents and I could explain the case to him. 'But you must phone first, in case she hasn't come in,' he said.

I'd got Mantra removed, but Rajshekhar seemed, if anything, even less sympathetic. It was out of the frying pan and into the fire.

That evening, I had a long Skype with Sara. At least both of our internet connections were working reasonably well for a change, and we had an uninterrupted virtual time together. Seeing her immediately calmed me. I saw her smile, followed the contours of her hair, breathed in deeply so that I could almost smell her perfume, and felt comforted. We didn't say much, just silly things that we shared together, in our shared language. If only Mantra hadn't got in the way, we could have been together in Hyderabad now. Not really Mantra – it was love that had got in the way. Because of my love for her, I could not put her in any possibility of danger. So I had to keep her away, for now. And I had to be in Hyderabad, so I couldn't come to her either.

Sara did have some bad news that she had to tell me. Well, in one sense it was bad, but it could lead to good things.

Her father and mother had finally confronted her about her trips to Hyderabad and why she was always on the phone to me, and she had to confess that she was seeing me. Her mother had been sobbing all night, and her father had disowned her, she said. I was the wrong race, obviously the wrong caste, and, at twenty years her senior, very definitely the wrong age. Sara was not too worried, though; she thought it would all be resolved soon. 'But I need your help,' she said. She went through what I had to do next.

I was calm on Skype with her, but as soon as I heard that dreaded 'deflating' sound of the call ending, I felt down again. I went to the Taj Banjara where I chatted with Khem, the junior manager who held sway in the reception lobby. I asked him my question about political corruption and how much of an impact it could have made on the election result. He was reflective and agreed that, yes, outside the BJP office – the office of now Prime Minister Modi's party – in his part of town, party representatives had been handing out ₹100 notes to passers-by. I'd heard the same of people living around the hotel too. He explained it to me: 'It's a deal between us and the politicians. They can't do anything for us – nothing works. But at least they can give us some cash. And because we're all honest Indians, we take the cash and vote for them. It's the Indian way,' he said.

On Saturday, I'd phoned Rajshekhar as requested, and he told me curtly that 'the officer [i.e. Mantra] has not handed over the files yet', so he would phone me when she did.

He hadn't phoned by 2 p.m., so taking the initiative, I took an autorickshaw to the CID headquarters. I phoned Rajshekhar and he was really angry with me, rudely saying, 'I told you I would phone. Stop phoning me. I repeat, the officer has not handed over the files.' I waited until 6.30 p.m., not wanting to leave the only thin thread of hope that I had. But no one came, no one would let me know what was happening and no one would talk to me about my case. I felt totally humiliated.

Sunday and Monday I spent miserably in my room, trying to read, trying to do something, failing dismally. The humiliation, the loss of control over my life had left me without any energy. On Tuesday, I phoned Mr S. Rajan Gopala Reddy at 11 a.m. He told me that they'd been working all night on bifurcation – nothing had happened yet, but he would phone me 'in two hours'. I phoned him again at 3 p.m. He dropped the call. At 3.30 p.m. he did phone me, and said he would contact me in two hours, not to worry. I waited. Nothing. Only the humiliation of waiting and nothing happening.

Because of my actions, the case had been taken away from an officer and given to new officers who (a) had no hopes of taking bribes, (b) were aware that I'd made complaints about their colleague and (c) objected to this addition to their workload. What were they supposed to do, bless me?

For a couple of weeks I did nothing, but descended slowly into depression. I do not recall anything that happened during that time, except that I didn't get any calls from CID.

On Wednesday 28 May, I was in the Crosswords coffee shop,

sitting miserably nursing a cappuccino, when a young man came over to me, out of the blue, and said, 'Are you Professor James Tooley?' I blinked. Did I know him? He said he had read *The Beautiful Tree* and recognised me from my photo. He was excited about all I had achieved through the Educare Trust, he told me. 'From here in Hyderabad, you've started a global movement.'

He didn't find me very communicative, and left quickly. I sat there and reflected back on my work. Had I really achieved much? I had done nothing really, apart from land myself in this mess where I seemed forever trapped in India, victim to the police.

But, forced to think back over my work with the Educare Trust, I started to concede that, yes, there was quite a bit we'd achieved, and yes, there was quite a bit of impact. We'd had three or four areas of work, and each had been taken up by others.

First, the research we'd done had been particularly influential. We'd shown that the vast majority of children in the poor areas of Hyderabad were in low-cost private schools; only a minority attended government school. We'd tested children in mathematics, English and Urdu or Telugu, and found children in the low-cost private schools significantly outperforming those in the government schools, even after statistically controlling for family background and other variables. And we'd shown that all this was achieved in the low-cost private schools for a fraction of the cost of government schools. It was a huge achievement among the poor – something very much worth celebrating.

This research, coupled with similar work from other countries, had become very influential. Erstwhile British Secretary of State for International Development, the Rt Hon. Andrew Mitchell, had written:

> Professor Tooley's work on private education in developing countries ... had a significant impact on ... UK Government policy on education in developing countries, and in turn has helped improve the situation on the ground for large numbers of poor children and influenced UK and international thinking on how to make 'education for all' a reality.

The research inspired, among others, a huge voucher programme in Pakistan that enabled 'hundreds of thousands of poor girls to attend low-fee private schools', and the £300 million Girls Education Challenge Fund, which sought 'to stimulate non-state [i.e. private] providers to get up to a million girls into school in the hardest places'. My research, Andrew Mitchell had written, 'provided the evidence upon which we could situate our proposed policy; and it also opened up a space in public debate which meant that a policy approach recognising diversity of education supply in developing countries would be accepted'.

In Nigeria, the Lagos State Government and DFID Nigeria were also heavily influenced by the research. DFID created a £25 million 'Making Markets Work for the Poor' project, designed to further improve the workings of the low-cost private school market. I was patron of the Association of Formidable Education Development (AFED), the association of low-cost private schools in Lagos, with over 3,000 school members. Previously, the Lagos State Government set out to close all AFED schools. My research 'explicitly ... led them to a change of heart', as the president of AFED put it. A long process of engagement with the government led to the announcement in April 2013 that all AFED schoolchildren would be able to sit the state primary school exams, formerly forbidden to them and for the majority effectively ending their school careers. This reform allowed 600,000 children in AFED schools to be liberated to continue further education. From denial to condemnation to active support: several governments and agencies had undergone this process as a direct result of my research, which all started with the Educare Trust in Hyderabad.

A second area of work for Educare had been the school loan programme. Ask the school proprietors what is their greatest need and they will say capital. In poor areas of India, like much of the rest of the developing world, property rights are not well established, and so they can't use their buildings for mortgage collateral; in any case, many schools are in rented premises without that luxury. And the Old City of Hyderabad in particular, I understand, is blacklisted by most banks, so getting capital is virtually impossible. But school proprietors want capital to build extra classrooms to satisfy unmet demand, or to build computer labs desired by parents, or to construct separate toilets for boys and girls, beneficial to girls.

Through Educare Trust I raised funds and instituted a loan programme, whereby schools could borrow funds to create classrooms, labs and toilet blocks, repaying over two to three years, with an honour system among the proprietors rather like that used in microfinance, whereby each member agreed to honour any unpaid debts from any of the other members. It was amazingly successful. In its main features, I understand, the programme was taken up by the Indian School Finance Company, which was specially created by Bob Pattillo and Gray Matters Capital for this purpose, and taken to very large scale in Hyderabad and beyond, benefiting the lives of hundreds of thousands of poor children. It has disbursed $11 million to date, and increased loan capital to $140 million. One of the co-founders, Steve Hardgrave, went on to set up his own similar programme in Bangalore, extending across other states in India, while Pattillo is busy raising finance to replicate the model in other countries too. Similar ambitious loan programmes for low-cost schools have been created by Chris Crane, CEO of Edify Inc., and Irene Pritzker, with her Rising Schools programme in Ghana.

Couldn't I feel proud that all this impact on loans for needy schools had explicitly come out of the work I'd developed through Educare Trust? Slowly I began to prise memories of the Educare Trust away from prison and Mrs Mantra.

Third, we'd created a small-scale scholarship voucher programme that had been replicated in several places, including in

Delhi, and was perhaps even influential on a famous voucher study in Andhra Pradesh. And finally, I'd put together a model of a chain of low-cost private schools, based on our work in Hyderabad, linking it with innovative learning programmes in English especially. Stand-alone low-cost private schools were outperforming the government alternative. But on their own they couldn't afford much in the way of curriculum development, teacher training and so educational improvement. But imagine, I thought, what could be achieved if you could have a chain of a hundred or more of these schools, where the small margin from each school could be combined to create enough funds – or to inspire enough investors – to heavily invest in school improvement. Explicitly based on my work for Educare Trust, I'd written about the potential for creating chains of low-cost private schools in an essay that won gold prize in the International Finance Corporation/Financial Times private sector development competition in 2006. Shortly after I'd published this, one Jay Kimmelman came to visit me in Newcastle to discuss creating chains of low-cost private schools around the world. He went on to create, with his wife Shannon, Bridge International Academies, starting in Kenya, expanding to Uganda, Nigeria and then back to Andhra Pradesh – the largest chain of low-cost schools in the world, supported by, among others, Mark Zuckerberg and Bill Gates. And Sir Michael Barber created a dedicated investment fund, PALF (Pearson Affordable Learning Fund), which has the mission of investing in low-cost private education opportunities around the world. All this because of my work emanating from the Educare Trust.

What have I ever achieved?, I thought. Nothing apart from all of this. And would I rather have not done any of this work, and avoided the mess I was currently in? No – it had to have been worth it. Please, James, it had to be worth it.

I slowly pulled myself together. I had to get myself out of there, so that I could carry on this work. I could not let Mrs Mantra win.

The next day, Thursday 29 May, I felt lighter. I got up, showered, and dressed. At 11, 11.30 and 11.45 a.m., I phoned Mr Reddy, determined that it must be sorted out. He didn't pick up. I was sitting again in Crosswords coffee bar. Finally I got hold of him, and he told me he was in a meeting and would call me later; something I'd heard from him and his colleagues so many times, and which normally meant nothing.

It was hard keeping my mood upbeat, however much I tried to remind myself of what Educare had achieved. I threw the phone down on my table, annoyed, upset, depressed again. I sat staring into my coffee. But two minutes later, the unexpected happened: he phoned back. 'Come in to see Mr Rajshekhar, even if I'm not there, at three o'clock,' he said. I could not keep tears from my eyes. This was an extraordinarily emotional moment for me – finally there was to be movement, finally something was going to happen. I felt so happy, some hope back again. Of course, I tempered this with the thought of how Mr Rajshekhar responded to me last time – rebuking me angrily and saying he would call me. I knew he was not going to be easy to handle. But at least the waiting was over. Something, whether good or bad, would happen.

I informed Kavitha, my lawyer, and we met at 3 p.m. at the CID HQ. I felt overwhelmed with emotion; I hadn't been there for a couple of weeks, and I'd almost missed this place, so steeped in memories as it was.

We went up to the third floor, bumped into what now seemed like old CID friends on the way, who called out pleasantly, 'Isn't your case solved yet?'; one who had stayed the night in hospital with me warmly shook my hand.

Mr S. Rajan Gopala Reddy wasn't in his office, but we went down the corridor between the cubicles, past Mrs Mantra fast asleep at her desk. Mr Rajshekhar was there, looking grimly determined. He motioned for us to wait in another cabin, which we did, but for only twenty minutes – far less than we usually had to wait with Mantra. Then we were called in.

Rajshekhar was sitting at his desk, with a raised sloping platform on which were arranged various files on my case; all the documents that we had given Mantra were in boxes in the corner of his office. I hadn't seen this level of efficiency before in the CID. Quickly, he said, 'I need answers to several questions,' and he began to question Kavitha in Telugu, who occasionally involved me in the answers. Sensible things, questions about when I had resigned from the trust, when the foreign currency had been received. He looked very severe at first, and raised his voice several times, but I realised that this was a contrived manner – underneath he had a twinkling smile. He was straightforward and professional, all I had prayed for. He got out the calculator to check foreign currency amounts, wrote notes in the margins to cross-reference his findings with the evidence we provided, got a yellow marker to highlight things that he wanted to talk about.

Although they were talking in Telugu, I picked up enough of the conversation to realise that there seemed to be progress: '(Telugu words), passport, (Telugu words), court, (Telugu words), lodge no objection'.

What he had said to Kavitha was that we should put in a petition to get my passport back to the court the next day, Friday, and that he would make sure the public prosecutor lodged 'no objection'. 'It's a very simple case,' he turned to say to me. 'You should not be stuck here. But it is in the end up to the courts to decide what to do with you.'

I felt an immense relief. So it was absolutely the right thing to have done to involve Haridevan and Dr I. V. Subba Rao, and to get Mantra removed. If she had still been on the case, we knew that there would've been no movement. It was strange, reflecting back over the three months at CID HQ, with a peculiar fondness now that it seemed it was all going to be over. Like listening to Beethoven: painful but beautiful. I had learnt so much about myself during this period: I had learnt to like myself, I had learnt to give time for friends and for Sara, I had learnt to slow down and attach less importance to my work. I had learnt about pain and struggle and desperation and how to cope with it. All in this ugly building, this hot and stuffy and dirty building.

Suddenly, however, as I was outside with Kavitha, I realised there was a terrible urgency about the whole thing. Bifurcation of the state would happen on Monday. Mr Rajshekhar could be removed from his post and transferred to the new state that was being created. Someone else could have this case, someone like Mantra again! We had to move quickly. Then I remembered something even worse: my friendly judge could also be transferred, to be replaced by someone far less sympathetic.

I was tremendously hopeful, but there was such a small window in which to realise anything. Wonderful but frightening.

With things moving forward, I decided to risk flying again. There were things I had to do; Sara was waiting. It was the first weekend in June, three months since my arrest. I arrived at Sara's home town on Saturday evening, having taken two flights, really worried all the time about them not allowing me through with my second passport, without any Indian visa, but each time no one checked anything except my name and photograph.

I was feeling tense and depressed, frightened of meeting her father and mother, because I knew that I'd caused the family such pain. I felt worthless and tired; I'd been practising a few words of Hindi in the taxi, but no one seemed to hear them when I tried them out, and anyway they are not much to show for coming to India for so many years. I made my excuses and went to bed to sleep.

In the morning, Sunday, I got up refreshed, and came down to an empty house. Eventually Sara's mother appeared, and I made some tea. Feeling emboldened, I tried an opening gambit: 'I'm really sorry for causing problems to your family,' I said. I'd even learnt the word in Hindi: 'Mafkaro' – Sorry. But as I said these words, she began to cry bitterly, wiping her nose and eyes ostentatiously with her apron. I didn't know what to do. I stood and said nothing and eventually Sara came down and saved me.

The day was spent miserably. I went for a drive with Sara, then back to the house, to sit with her father, who seemed surprisingly friendly, warm, not like Sara had warned he was going to be at all. I told him details about my time in prison and being stuck in Hyderabad waiting for my passport to be returned. He said that I had been blessed with the experience, and I must publish it because the world needed to know, because India could not be like this in the twenty-first century.

The final of the T20 cricket was taking place – Punjab Kings XI versus Kolkata Knight Riders. We watched it together, the whole family sitting in the parents' bedroom. And I loved and I hated the cosiness of the Indian family. I yearned for my solitude, and wondered why the hell I had got into this mess in the first place, with my silly banal wishes always for the exotic. Now the most exotic place I could think of was Great Britain; on the plane I'd read one of Alexander McCall Smith's novels about a woman academic in Edinburgh and yearned for the simple, drearily familiar things that he described.

I slept fitfully, knowing that I had to do the needful with her father. Sara Expects. Over breakfast, Father, Mother and I sat together, and I hoped that Mother would leave the two of us together for our man's talk, because, as Sara said, it wasn't a good idea to involve Mother – she'd only start crying again and complicate matters. So although I tried to look as though I wanted a serious conversation, I wasn't sure I could begin it there in front of her; and anyway, what is the protocol for this kind of conversation? How much time do you have to leave for it? Is it rude to do it when you are just expecting to go out, as we were?

Suddenly, her father was on his own downstairs by the dining room table. I asked him if I could speak to him in private for a moment. He led me into the lounge and we sat close together on the sofa.

'I am sorry that I have caused you and your family such an upset,' I began.

He butted in straight away. 'It is not me, nor my family. It is the community here; they are close-minded, they cannot accept new or different things. But,' he continued, 'I can accept new things.'

He told me a story of the sparrow: 'The sparrow builds a nest and raises the youngsters, and then when they are ready, they leave the nest and all is well; they fly away happily,' he motioned with his arms to show the birds flying away. 'That's the way I've always wanted it to be. When my family was growing up, I wanted only everything good for my family – the best education, they should travel if they wanted to – I wanted everything right and good for them.'

'And they are the best,' I said. 'See how Sara is so famous now, getting invited to Germany and America; the world knows her and her work.' Then, gulping, I said in as convoluted a way as I possibly could, 'I am very fond of your daughter. I care for her deeply. Would you ever consider it possible for me to marry her?'

'Not here,' he said quickly. 'We can't do it here, but we can elsewhere. In a metropolitan city – Bombay, Kolkata or Delhi – where people are more open, we can do it those places.'

'And,' I said, 'I need never come to your home town again if you don't want me to.' He said that this was my home; I could come any time. I bowed down to touch his feet (having checked their position earlier for this activity). He tried to stop me, but I was feeling respectful towards him and continued.

We exchanged some more pleasantries, and then it was time for me to leave, back to Hyderabad. And now I was feeling incredibly happy. I loved India, loved this family, loved the idea of creating schools all over India with them. (We had earlier talked about my idea for fifty schools – no reason we can't create 1,000, Sara's father had said.)

And so I drove off with my future wife and a male chaperone taking me to the airport, waving goodbye to her father and mother – my future in-laws.

All will be well now, God willing. Now to get my passport back.

WHY CORRUPTION? DISCRETION AND THE RULE OF LAW

ONE OF MRS MANTRA'S finer qualities was her candour. In particular, she was quite open about demanding bribes from me, and didn't mind doing so in front of her junior colleagues or my lawyers. In the previous interlude we saw that this commendable quality was there in all of India's police – no one need bother with the expense of an intermediary agent when dealing with them; the police themselves won't be shy in letting you know what bribes are required. (In my case, Mrs Mantra had been upfront throughout, but added Jivan to the mix when she thought I was being a bit slow on the uptake.)

Why is there such a high level of corruption in the Indian police, and in India in general? It's something I thought about a great deal during my enforced captivity in India.

One possible line of inquiry came from the way Mrs Mantra always invoked God when reflecting on her dealings with me. 'God be my witness,' she would say when defending my imprisonment, accompanied by her signature Namaste touching of the heart, forehead and pointing to the heavens. Others have taken up this theme. On my flight on my way to make my proposal to Sara's parents, I picked up a copy of John Elliott's *Implosion: India's Tryst with Reality* at the airport bookshop. Elliott, a former *Financial Times* journalist based in New Delhi, explores the possibility that 'India's religious and cultural base' permits, even encourages, corruption. He points to something that had bothered me too – that in the *Mahabharata*, the classic Hindu spiritual text, Lord Raja 'breaks the rules of warfare – one could say cheats' to win a battle. If God can cheat to win a war, then it's not a big jump to think that corruption too can all be part of life's rich tapestry. Elliott quotes notable Hindu scholars to this effect. Here's one:

> No invocation to Lakshmi, the goddess of wealth, emphasises the importance of making money only by conventional legitimate ways. The goddess represents wealth and prosperity; she is worshipped for these, not for how that prosperity is arrived at ... In fact, for all the condemnation that corruption publicly provokes,

> Indians are ambivalent about the practice. They con-
> sider it bad when they have to bribe when they don't
> want to; they consider it good if a bribe gets them
> what they want.

As tempting as it might be to think of religion as an explanation, however, it doesn't really bear scrutiny. For India is not
alone in being corrupt, and other countries as or more corrupt than India have nothing to do with Hinduism. As was
noted, in Transparency International's 'Corruption Perceptions
Index' (2010), India is ranked eighty-seventh out of 178 countries. That's roughly comparable to (Islamic) Morocco and
(Christian) Liberia. Nigeria (mixed Islam and Christian) is
much more corrupt (ranked 134th). And Pakistan, ranked
143rd, is of course an Islamic state.

So it seemed unlikely to me that Hinduism alone could be
guilty as charged. What of Mrs Mantra's protestations to the
contrary? I supposed that they could be seen more as post-hoc
justifications for her actions, not as the *motivation* for the corruption in the first place. That would seem to be a useful way
of understanding religion's role in corruption – as a justifica-
tion but not a motivation.

If not religion, then what? Oddly, Mrs Mantra praised the
British influence in India. She may have just been 'playing to
the gallery', as Kavitha my lawyer had told me afterwards, saying what she thought I would like to hear, buttering me up so
that I would be more amenable to paying her a bribe. I really

don't know. Certainly it's more common to *blame* the British for all they did in India. Arvind Verma, the admirably candid author and Indian Police Service (IPS) officer we encountered in the previous interlude, who served as police superintendent in Bihar, thinks this is a profitable line to take. The Indian Police Service, he points out, emerged out of the Indian Police (IP) that the British created to build their Raj. Their police officers were given 'unlimited power' in order to 'suppress any dissent' directed against the British. Consequently, 'corruption became endemic and rampant': even the 'lowest functionaries' in the police force 'had powers to arrest and detain any person ... The imperative need was to develop a sense of fear of authority in the entire population and the police department served this need.'

Unfortunately, he says, this system remains virtually intact today. So perhaps it's not just the British who are to blame, it's also India, for being tardy in reform. The 1861 Police Act and the Indian Penal Code, among other defining statutes from British rule, 'have remained unchanged from the British period'. The Police still 'terrorize' the citizens, 'as if the Raj still continues'.

This seems a more promising line of inquiry. But what is it about the system that the British brought to India, which is still intact today, and that allows such corruption to emerge? Verma spells it out for us. It's to do with the *discretion* police officers have. He writes, for instance, of the 'autonomy' enjoyed by the Station House Officer, the '"gatekeeper" for registering criminal cases'. This person 'controls most of the criminal investigations and makes the decision to arrest suspects. These powers ...

have enabled the officers to indulge in extortion and many other forms of corruption.'

The discretion given to police officers to 'arrest anyone on mere suspicion', he says, 'enables them to extort money...' Moreover, Indian police departments are typically large: 'a superintendent will have jurisdiction over two hundred or more investigators'. This means that the superior officers are only able to exert control over the most prominent cases, 'leaving effective control over most of the cases to the investigating officers'.

This idea of the discretionary powers of the police is also taken up in *Corruption in India*, which says that 'From the constable to the topmost tiers, discretion is critical in accepting a complaint to registering an FIR [First Information Report], to investigating it properly, to prosecution. Discretion is also an issue in the case of bail, undertrials and prisons.'

The authors also agree that some of this discretion emerged in colonial times: 'A large set of processes, procedures, rules and laws have been created from pre-Independence days that prevent a bureaucrat to take any decision in isolation, however senior she may be. Note that some of these processes may have come about precisely to limit avenues of corruption and bribery.'

(It occurred to me that one major reason why the army was trusted in India but not the police – for instance, in supervising elections or quelling communal unrest – was precisely because soldiers had no discretion whatsoever; everyone simply had to obey orders up the chain of command.)

This issue of discretion brings us back squarely to our earlier discussion of the rule of law. Gandhi was proud to be creating the Magna Carta for Indians in South Africa, embracing them in the rule of law. But the very definition of the rule of law brings in the need to combat discretionary powers in the hands of officials – Wikipedia puts it like this (my emphases): 'The rule of law ... is the legal principle that law should govern a nation, as opposed to *arbitrary decisions by individual government officials*. It primarily refers to the influence and authority of law within society, particularly *as a constraint upon behaviour, including behaviour of government officials*.'

Indeed, the great classical liberal thinker and Nobel Prize winner Friedrich Hayek, writing in *The Constitution of Liberty*, suggested that combating discretionary power was a fundamental implication of the rule of law. The libertarian writer David Boaz, in *The Libertarian Mind*, put it like this: 'Those who administer the law should have minimal discretion, because discretionary power is the very evil that the rule of law is intended to prevent.'

The more I thought about it, while stuck in India, the more it seemed that this idea made the most sense. It was the discretion permitted to Mrs Mantra concerning the petty regulations for foreign currency that allowed her to come after me. There was certainly police discretion about how long I could be kept in police custody and in prison, and police discretion about how long the investigation would last, and so on. Similarly, I felt sure that discretion played a role in many of the unfortunate cases I encountered in prison – for instance, Arjun the cycle rickshaw puller, an undertrial who had been in prison for three years without even being charged. If there was less discretion given to police about the 'who, what and when' of prosecution, then police corruption could begin to wither on the vine.

It's not a particularly glamorous explanation for corruption – not as exotic as stories of religion or the legacy of the British Raj. But it seemed to have the ring of truth to me, the more I thought about and encountered new cases of police corruption each day I stayed in India.

But it's not quite a sufficient explanation. Discretion alone is likely to lead to corruption. But the Indian situation is exacerbated by a further problem – the huge extent of legislation and regulation that the police have discretion over. Again, in my case, the regulations on foreign currency are vast and largely incomprehensible; it's very difficult to know whether or not you are breaking some of these regulations, which seem to defy common sense in many places. For instance, what counts as foreign currency? If a trust, approved for foreign currency, brings some in under the strict approval regime, you'd think that the funds thus brought in and converted to rupees would no longer be counted as foreign currency. And you'd be right, for general purposes. But if that trust should pass any of those funds on to another trust, then suddenly it becomes foreign currency again – so a trust inadvertently receiving funds from another trust that had originally come in as foreign currency will be guilty of foreign currency violations, even if it had no inkling that the funds had originated overseas.

The Romans understood the link between the growth of

legislation and corruption. The great commentator Gaius Cornelius Tacitus wrote: 'And now bills were passed, not only for national objects but for individual cases, and laws were most numerous when the commonwealth was most corrupt.'

It's the same principle that James Madison pointed out in *The Federalist Papers*, that democracy itself is of little consequence if it results in huge amounts of legislation:

> It will be of little avail to the people that the laws are made by men of their own choice if the laws be so voluminous that they cannot be read, or so incoherent that they cannot be understood; if they ... undergo such incessant changes that no man who knows what the law is today, can guess what it will be tomorrow.

That's precisely what the mass of legislation and regulation com-monly termed the 'Licence Raj' (with a nod to blaming the British) consists of in India today. It is so voluminous that it cannot be read, and so incoherent that it cannot be understood. Presiding over this huge raft of legislation are the police, at their discretion to follow cases wherever they wish. This combination seems to be the problem leading to Indian police corruption.

I would be thinking much more about Gandhi as I entered the last month of my Indian internment. Gandhi had said, 'Loyalty to a state so corrupt is a sin, disloyalty a virtue.' The state he was talk-ing about was, of course, that imposed by the British. Presumably he would have to repeat the same sentiments about India today.

CHAPTER 8

THINGS
FALL APART

FOR THE FIRST WEEK of June, I waited for my court hearing to be called. Each day I sat at my desk, almost shivering with excitement... My case will get heard today! And there will be no objection from the public prosecutor, which will mean, at most, a day's deliberations by the judge – hoping that he is still the kindly, wise, handsome one that I've grown to respect, and that state bifurcation hasn't moved him – and then he'll order the return of my passport, and I will be free!

Each day I waited in hope, but each day nothing happened. I went to bed, disappointed, but woke up optimistic the next day. Like the people in prison always anticipating bail 'today', I too had become an optimist. All my life I'd seen myself as pessimistic, taking after my father. (When we were young, he used to make up rhymes. One of these was 'Never grumble when things look glum; always remember there's worse to come.') Now, I sat and wrote emails to friends and family saying I would be home either this week or next. I was ordering books from Amazon to Daisy Cottage and a subscription to *The Economist* so that I could have things to read when I got home. But my nightmares got worse again, now that I was back in court – nightmares of being trapped in closed rooms with evil monsters, trying to get out but failing.

I was waiting for court; everyone else was waiting for the rain. The monsoon was predicted to arrive in seventy-two hours. I loved predictions like that, showing, if not mastery of the elements, at least our understanding of them. I could also see how you could get used to the seasons in India and become fond of the changes just as I am of those in England. The brutal heat of the summer (44 degrees centigrade the day before) was not like the heat I knew from west Africa – not humid, not sapping all your energy. It was more like sitting in a hot oven – not that I'd done that very often. Breathing was totally unsatisfying; you couldn't seem to get enough oxygen in. But then this heat builds up to the arrival of the monsoon, which sweeps it all away, then takes you into an Indian summer in September and October, and then fades calmly into the winter, which is pleasantly warm (to us outsiders, although I do recall people reportedly dying of the cold in Hyderabad when it plummeted to 12 degrees centigrade).

Waiting for the rain, and waiting for my case.

Michael, the Nigerian I'd met in prison, phoned one day. He was in an impossible situation. He had been arrested as part of a group, but the key 'suspect' had absconded from Kolkata. So the court said that nothing could happen until he was found. Meanwhile, what was Michael supposed to do? He could not work, because he had no work permit. He was poor, so couldn't afford to support himself. After prison, I'd paid for him to go to Mumbai, so that he had at least somewhere to stay, with another Nigerian. But he had to return to court this week in Hyderabad, he told me, and had no money even for the bus fare. He had no other identification apart from his passport (which had been seized) and travelling by bus was difficult without identification. What was the poor guy supposed to do? Had the authorities thought that one through? If he didn't make court then he'd be in breach of his bail conditions and would face re-imprisonment. My heart went out to him, and I told him if he could borrow the bus fare I'd give him the money when he arrived. I felt helpless that I couldn't do any more.

Finally, on Friday 6 June, my case was called.

I dressed in my suit and tie for court. On the way in the autorickshaw that morning, I was full of faith and confidence.

When I arrived at court, however, the sense of the place overwhelmed me immediately and completely. Involuntarily, despite the optimism that had carried me along all week, I could feel people's pain and anguish and uncertainty all over again; it was all there soaked up in the walls. I could feel the pain of people through the ages.

The court had just opened after the month-long summer holidays of May, the hottest time of the year. I sat down in my usual place, selecting the hardest chair; I was in penance mood again.

The traditions of the court were still the same: the court clerk called out *sotto voce* the name, and then the court crier in his white costume, white hat and red sash barked it out harshly, his cries echoing down the corridors. It still made me afraid, this echoing cry of the terrifying mystery of the law.

As we sat waiting for the judge to arrive, the court crier decided to rearrange the furniture, moving the horseshoe of desks a couple of feet across the room. I saw that this was to allow the lawyers – the only important people present – to be better positioned under the fans, but it meant that we in the witness/defendant seats now had the backs of the lawyers' chairs crammed up against us. It was stiflingly hot, waiting for the monsoon. As the court crier moved the furniture, I noticed that the horseshoe was made up of a semi-circle and two rectangles. These are the kinds of mundane thoughts that occupy you as you wait for your turn in court.

With the judge installed, a huge procession of people were called, and proceeded to stand behind the wooden balustrade – twelve people altogether, four women among them. As their names were called, nine or ten lawyers got up and huddled around the mezzanine level before the judge.

But the court clerk simply called out a date, and the whole troop marched out again and their lawyers decamped to the horseshoe table. Perhaps the defendants had taken a whole day off work for that.

There was an optimistic older man who had come in to represent his son. They had been sitting by me, waiting for their case to be called. They were clearly not very well-off; I could imagine the discussion behind the scenes: 'Don't worry, you don't need an advocate, I can do it for you, how else can we afford it?' Their case was called. The older man stood confidently at the mezzanine level, ready to defend his son. 'Is he an advocate?' the judge asked of his clerk, who asked it of the man standing there. The fact that he was not wearing advocate's attire gave the game away. After only a little discussion, the judge curtly dismissed him, abruptly flicking his hand to show his distaste; the son's case was not heard. I saw the father's confidence drain away in front of me, replaced by pain and a sense of inferiority.

The judge was wearing glasses after his summer holidays. It happens to the best of us, I thought; age gets to us all in the end. His glasses had rather ornate edges, which glinted in the sunlight; they were quite colourful. He'd grown sideburns too, which I didn't recall from before the summer vacation. This is the kind of thing you notice, waiting for your turn in court.

And there was a new coat of paint, beige, actually almost orange, that had been applied to the courtroom too; yes, it was definitely smarter after the summer break. I could see where the painter had splashed the beige/orange paint all across the floor tiles. In the stairwells he had obliterated the red spit stains up to a level of about 4 feet, when they reappeared where he had run out of paint.

The pigeons were gone too from the corridors, their nesting season over. They'd come back when it was cooler. It was too hot for any mosquitoes – that was the one real blessing of the heat.

At around 12.30 p.m., my case was called. I really don't understand the Indian legal system. Kavitha was the well-paid Shuramarthy Law lawyer on my case; indeed, she was a junior partner. We hadn't got the top guy, although we were paying for some of his time. But then, this being India, she had to devolve the responsibility down further to an even more junior person. He was hopeless. Kavitha stood next to him while he mumbled away, and she looked embarrassed as if she wanted to intervene, but didn't say anything and he rambled on. It felt so Indian: superiors who are very capable of doing something declining to do so, because it's the job of their inferiors. Like the woman who sits at her table and asks her servant to pass her the salt, even though it's easily within her reach.

The public prosecutor stood up and ran rings around my new counsel. I did a double take. I thought he was going to give 'no objection'? That's what Rajshekhar had assured me. That's what my lawyers had said: that he fully understood the law now, and would not put any objections to my early release. But instead, he was telling the same old stories against me

– that the investigation was at a crucial stage, that I hadn't cooperated with the CID at all, that I would abscond, and so I couldn't possibly get my passport back yet. Worse, he then said that the investigating officer, Mrs Mantra, had been changed *at my insistence*, so they needed much more time, now that someone new was on the case. Getting Mantra removed had made things *worse* for me. I listened and felt sick.

I was called forward by the public prosecutor.

'How much bond can you provide?' he asked.

'I can provide whatever is required,' I said, directly to the judge, who silenced me straight away: 'You don't speak directly to me; your advocate is here, talk to me through him.'

I felt dismal afterwards. The judge seemed to suggest that he could give his verdict on Monday, the public prosecutor half-heartedly suggested Wednesday, *and my lawyers agreed* to Wednesday. They could easily have insisted on Monday! Didn't they realise that those two days would make so much difference to me? I felt like a toy in all of their hands; they were all playing with me, not realising that getting through each day was a challenge, the nights full of terrifying nightmares.

Miserably, I went back to my apartment. I had lost hope again. The apartment supervisor told me that the monsoon arrived that day in the state of Kerala – a part of India to the south west of where we were, on the coast of the Indian Ocean. So the monsoon wouldn't arrive this week after all; people were now saying it would arrive in Hyderabad next Friday. Just like my case, it too had been postponed.

||||||||||||||||||||

In the meantime I still had to go for my interrogations. On the appropriate Sunday I arrived at CID HQ at 10.30 a.m. At 11 a.m. I managed to get through to Rajshekhar on the phone. He was polite, but said he was not coming in. He then dropped the bombshell: he had been removed from my case because of state bifurcation. He'd been moved to the new state, and so I had to come in the following day and he would introduce me to my new police inspector. This felt catastrophic on so many levels.

I phoned Kavitha and she told me that the amount for the bond may be up to ₹5 lakhs (£5,000), so I needed to get that money ready. As if I had that sort of money sitting around. This was another nice little catch-22: foreigners were not allowed to bring in this kind of money, so how was I to get it for my bond? Ah, she said, she hadn't thought of that. As if it was a tiny amount of money. Perhaps it was, for them, given the extortionate amounts of money they were extracting from me and the university for my case. I felt annoyed at the lack of understanding from my lawyers.

The next day, Monday 9 June, I would meet my new police officer, the fourth on my case. Upstairs at breakfast, the kindly Nepali kitchen supervisor had said, 'The monsoon may arrive this evening.' It was very humid, and there were heavy gusts of wind. It might arrive earlier than anticipated.

I arrived at CID headquarters at 11 a.m. I phoned Rajshekhar and he said 'within one hour I'll be there'.

It was all change at the CID HQ. New guards were downstairs, sporting ostentatious, colourful headgear like you see on those patrolling the Pakistani/Indian border. The building had become CID HQ for the new state of Telangana. Mr P. S. Subramanyam had been moved, and the new in-charge clearly wanted to make an impression. There was a new security check at the entrance; before I could wander around freely without anyone disturbing me – I now had to go through one of those faux checks. The guards perfunctorily checked only one pocket in your bag – but perhaps the bomb or gun was in the other side? It was all appearance – nothing more.

And upstairs, it was all change too. It felt like the first day of school; there was something in the tone of people's voices, of sounding each other out: over-jolly, over-excited, but apprehensive too – pleased and displeased. Most people had cleared out their files, and a huge number of filing cabinets blocked the entrance to the stairwell and the lift. One person had not yet cleared out her desk, however: Mantra. I saw her arriving, shuffling along leaning backwards at 110 degrees to the horizontal, miserably demanding that someone shift her boxes for her, that she was a poor widow and how could she be expected to manage on her own?

I was left with that terrible feeling of defencelessness that I'd had ever since the first time I'd been there. I was a foreigner in the heart of this law-enforcement zone, which was actually the anti-law-enforcement zone. I knew there were rules that I couldn't comprehend. It had modes of operation and principles that were truly foreign to me. I felt very alone and vulnerable, putting on a brave face but knowing at any moment they could turn on me. And of course, I was totally at their disposal time-wise. Mr Rajshekhar had refused to see me for three weeks; now he had asked to see me two days running, but he could let me fester until he was ready. I felt worthless.

Mr Rajshekhar arrived at 12.30 p.m., rushing in with the new inspector, Mr Revanth, who would be taking over my case. I told Mr Rajshekhar that the public prosecutor didn't say 'no objection' in court as he had promised. 'That's not our job,' he said. 'We know you are innocent, but we can't say that in court. It's against the rule book. It's up to your lawyer to defend you; that's the way it works.'

He confirmed that my case was to be heard in court on Wednesday.

'Will I get my passport back?' I asked pitifully.

'Let's see. There are still important parts of the investigation to be done. We need to interview the Ministry of Home Affairs; we've only heard your side of the story.'

I protested that they had 10,500 pages of documents, which surely showed something more objective than that.

'No,' he said. 'Still your side of the story. Now we need to hear theirs, and it will take time.'

Mantra shuffled in to see us, and my heart sank. I bristled when she was close – didn't want her infecting the new guy with her stories. To try to lower the tension, I asked her which state she was joining, Telangana or the one keeping the name of

Andhra Pradesh? She said, 'I am not going to tell you anything. I tell you the truth but then you tell others and so everyone knows, but God is my witness...' She made that Namaste sign with her hands together, pointing to her heart, her forehead and the heavens as she shuffled away.

My new Mr Revanth was very junior, a young man, perhaps not even thirty, very tall and well dressed, but I felt nervous about being put under someone so inexperienced. He and Rajshekhar were searching for the notebook that Mantra had created for my signing-in purposes, but couldn't find it, and she refused to help. Mr Rajshekhar pointed out that the second Saturday and Sunday of each month, my interrogation days, were holidays for government servants, so it wasn't practical for me to have a formal interrogation on those days; I should just come in and sign the notebook in the control room downstairs. This had the advantage that my visits would involve signing only rather than interrogation, which was great; but the notebook eluded their search.

Mr Revanth handed me over to another policeman who took me downstairs to the control room, to show me where I would have to sign. This new man didn't speak any English. In the control room there was a discussion in Telugu, and another policeman said I should go back upstairs with him. I nearly refused, anxious not to get sucked into any more interactions with Mantra. Fortunately, I did as he said, and this policeman for some reason knew where Mantra's signing book was; he produced it with a flourish. Mr Rajshekhar said curtly that I should sign in for the previous day. After that, they dismissed me.

And then I was back to my miserable existence, moving between apartment and Crosswords and the Taj Banjara, hardly able to bear the heat any more. The loneliness and my sense of worthlessness was complete. I sat at my grubby desk peering through the grubby curtains. The severe heat was straining the power grid, so there were frequent power cuts; my computer battery was completely drained so I couldn't even pretend to do some work. The power cuts did not seem to be affecting the Imam preacher shouting out his message at the nearby mosque. I'd not heard such vigorous, nasty-sounding preaching from an Imam around there before. It was very loud and distracting, for days on end. It all added to my misery.

Wednesday 11 June came: red-letter day in court. It had to go my way.

At 10 a.m. that morning, Kavitha phoned to say that her senior partner had been taken ill and so she wouldn't be able to come to court with me. However, she would be leaving me in the very capable hands of another lawyer, Ms Ravleen Sahani, and of course the counsel (who had been so pathetic in court the previous week), whose name I found out was Narasha. Ms Sahani seemed pleasant enough, but was upfront with me that she knew nothing about my case.

I sat in court, on my usual hard chair. There was a part-hearing going on. I didn't understand why there were so many lawyers crowding around the top stage – one person giving evidence, the public prosecutor asking questions of him, the judge listening then doing that dictation of the key points to the (this time, unusually) woman court typist. While he was doing the dictation, of course, further points were raised, which he seemed to miss. And why were there seven or eight advocates standing in front of him? What were they there for? Again I was struck by the inefficiency and stupidity of this system. The professions have been created by men in order to keep men busy, and no one has ever thought to change anything, or no one can because the vested interests have become too entrenched.

At 11.15 a.m., I was called, 'JAMES NICHOLAS' bellowed out as if by an auctioneer putting me up for sale. When I was in prison, I was T. James Nicholas. Now even the T had been dropped.

Then it all started going wrong. I'm not exactly sure what happened next, because I heard two versions. One version was that the judge wanted more discussion with the parties – about the law, he wanted advice on the law? – but because the public prosecutor hadn't arrived yet, he put a 'let' (or 'stay' – what was the word?) on my case for ten minutes. The other version was that Ms Sahani, my lawyer's pleasant enough but ignorant substitute, asked for the stay, because we didn't have the legal documents with us. Ms Sahani told me the first version, while Narasha told me the second. He was probably the most honest one, so I guessed that it was us who caused the delay.

I waited in the corridor and listened to Ravleen Sahani talking to Kavitha on the phone, to see where they could get a copy of the Foreign Contribution (Regulation) Act (FCRA), under which my case fell. Apparently they could find it in the bookshop by the High Court. It all felt so dilettantish – surely they'd got a copy of this by now? Surely they knew the law under which the allegations against me fell by now? Once again it seemed my lawyers were letting me down. I texted Kavitha to this effect, telling her 'I feel abandoned', and she phoned immediately, telling me that the judge only wanted to know more details about the penalties under the Act. But surely we knew these already and could just tell him?

So, we were waiting for the public prosecutor to return and for a copy of the FCRA to arrive so that my guys could know what the legal position was. If the public prosecutor arrived first, then we were not prepared.

Narasha said, 'We need to know what the penalties are.'

'It's 5 per cent of the amount received without permission,' I told him.

'Yes,' he said. 'If it's 5 per cent, or 2 per cent, or 1 per cent or...'

'No, no,' I interrupted. 'It *is* 5 per cent.' Unlike everyone else there, I'd read the Act. I knew what the law said. I was totally dismayed by the way everything was so last-minute, even with this highly paid supposedly international New India law firm.

The public prosecutor arrived at 11.55 a.m. – there was no sign of our copy of the FCRA. At 12.15 p.m., someone arrived with a copy of the Act. I saw my legal counsel looking at this, clearly for the first time. My counsel then showed it to the public prosecutor, also apparently reading it for the first time. What kind of legal process was this, where I was the only person in court who had read what my case was about?

Finally, my case was called. But somehow my counsel, Narasha, had wandered off somewhere, and was nowhere to be seen. I stood in front of the judge and public prosecutor and Ms Sahani stood with me for a while, but then she too went off to find Narasha. Meanwhile, I was left standing on my own, and the public prosecutor turned to me, totally defenceless, and asked why hadn't I just paid the penalty to the Ministry of Home Affairs, as that's what should be done for this offence. I just had to pay ₹1 lakh 75,000 (£1,750) and I'd be free for ever.

In fact, I'd asked the same question of Kavitha two months ago, and she had told me that I wasn't able to do that. The public prosecutor said I was allowed, and then turned to the judge with his trump card: 'The fact that he has not paid shows he is not serious about obeying the law.' The judge seemed to concur. I was thus shown up in front of the judge to be not only a fool, but devious too. I mumbled something, unable to tell them the truth, because the truth was so incomprehensible.

My counsel, Narasha, meanwhile had returned, only to repeat the mistake he had made last Friday saying that my *sixty-day* investigation period had lapsed, so I should be freed. I had corrected him then, and I had to correct him in court again, to say that in fact it was now well over ninety days that had elapsed. The judge scowled at me again for saying anything in court. I should keep quiet and know my place, even if my counsel was making a hash of things.

After all that, the judge postponed my case for another full week. No one knew why he did that. Everyone was taken by surprise at his decision. When he was writing on my case papers, everyone assumed he was writing the order to return my passport, not a further delay. Even the public prosecutor had seemed persuaded that my case was trivial and should not be taking up court time. He was actually on my side by this time, and he had said that I could be released with a bond of only ₹2 lakhs (£2,000), and that I was not particularly required for the next stage of the investigation. With that endorsement, the judge should have given the order to release my passport.

I was convinced the judge delayed my case because he was fed up with my incompetent choice of lawyers and wanted to punish me. I got from the judge's body language a frustration with the whole process – why on earth has this case been brought to him at all? And so he was punishing everyone, including me.

Kavitha told me over the phone that there were three possible outcomes, and she wanted me to be realistic about my chances:

- Best case: In a week's time the judge gives an order for my passport to be returned. In this case, given delays with the bifurcation of the state, it could be back with me by the following Monday to Wednesday, 23 to 25 June.

- Worst case (A): The judge simply postpones again. He can do this without giving reason, and he can postpone for as long as he wants – one week, one month, you name it. After a second postponement, we can appeal to the High Court, but this is not recommended, as it is likely to put the judge's back up and lead to:
- Worst case (B): The judge rejects the petition. We can then appeal to the High Court. This process could take at least six weeks.

I had reached the end of my tether. Each of these 100 days and nights had taken its toll. I was now faced with the prospect of another week or two of this torture. And my legal team seemed to bear responsibility for that.

'Fuck off!' I shouted out as a motorbike came up behind me forcing me off the road. As I walked home from the Taj Banjara up Road No. 13, I started to feel completely detached from reality. I started shouting and swearing aloud at people in public. I started screaming and tearing at my clothes. I collapsed on to the roadside, crying uncontrollably.

Later, I came around in my bed, the kindly Nepalese kitchen supervisor stroking my hand. He told me that he had found me on Road No. 13 as he was arriving for his shift, but that I was going to be all right. I couldn't see how. I couldn't see how I was ever going to get out of there.

||||||||||||||||||

After I'd suffered that meltdown, the university became worried about my state of mind – I had phoned registrar John Hogan after the court went against me yet again, and was crying on the phone to him. They decided to send my colleague and friend, David Longfield, to visit me for a few days while I awaited my fate. I really didn't want anyone to see me in that state, and protested that I was fine on my own. But maybe I protested too much. Giving my full address and how to find me perhaps gave the game away, even as I emailed them that I didn't want any visitors.

On Tuesday 17 June, David arrived. I was worse behaved than I thought I could be in front of a colleague, swearing a lot, railing at the injustice of anything and everything, including the roads – how dare they treat ordinary people so badly? Did he know that there was not a single pedestrian crossing in the whole of the 11 kilometres of the six-lane airport road they'd ploughed through these poor communities? But people have to get across the road, so they take their lives in their hands, and poor people get killed. Because no one fucking cares for the common man here, no one cares.

But on Wednesday, David persuaded me to take him to the Charminar, the sixteenth-century triumphal arch in the Old City, the icon of Hyderabad, to get me out of myself a bit, to do something different. I was nervous of leaving my zone of little comfort but at least some familiarity – Roads No. 13 and No. 1, my daily perambulation to Crosswords and the Taj Banjara.

But it was not bad to be at the Charminar for a while. We left the ancient monument and walked down the back streets to the bookshop where William Dalrymple had had his epiphany that led to his brilliant *White Mughals*. We wandered in the back lanes some more and came across a bird market, the like of which I had never seen before. There were hundreds of little dingy shack-shops selling birds, some with half-dead puppies and emaciated cats sprawled out; there were (wild) rats roaming underneath some of the cages, a dozen or so roaming around in the drains a couple of feet away from the storekeeper and from us, feeding on the grain, totally ignored by the humans.

The birds ranged from budgerigars to exotic finches and weaver birds, lovebirds to parakeets; there were ducks too, in closely confined quarters, and one shop with a huge turkey in a cage the exact size of the turkey – there was no room for it to move – and geese in cages the exact size of each goose. Apart from perhaps the budgerigars, who were chirping away a bit, the birds all looked forlorn, resigned to their fate. I could imagine them struggling to get out of the cages in the past, but many just hung on to the sides now, no energy left to try any new means of escape. I told David about prison and the poor buggers left behind, some for years, without any hope.

And then there were the crows.

Why would anyone want crows as pets? Cages 4 feet by 5 feet by 9 inches were crammed with as many crows as you could fit inside; in one cage, they were pecking at the weakest member within. But the crows had a different role to play. An expensive Innova van drove down the lane, and three burka-clad Muslim women got out. They were clearly well-heeled – you could see, among other things, posh designer shoes peeking out from under their black gowns. They paid their dues to the shopkeeper, and a crow was selected from the cage, held tightly in the hand of the young man who waved it up and down over the woman's body like a security metal detector, held it in front for her to touch, then held one wing in the most awkward fashion and, as the lady made a silent prayer, flung it high into the air. Much to my surprise, the bird then flew off, apparently unharmed.

The crows had an escape route. Every other animal seemed hopeless. My spirits came crashing down, as my sense of powerlessness again came to the fore.

On Wednesday morning, the day of my court appearance, I woke up after a fitful, heavy night of sweating, feeling angry. Not oppressed or pitiful, but angry for the first time. How dare they keep me like this in this inhumane way? How dare they – knowing that I've done nothing wrong – how dare they inflict this pain on me?

Back in court after a week away, I saw that the judge had abandoned his new glasses. The court crier was friendly to me. He said he had heard my court order being dictated, but was not allowed to say what was in it. I saw someone giving him small money – perhaps ₹200 – surreptitiously by the door.

He was coughing quite a lot, coughing up phlegm, then walking across the corridor to shoot a jet of spit onto the stairs. Unlike others, he didn't even aim for the stair walls.

At around 1.45 p.m., I realised the judge was talking to the public prosecutor about my case. I heard the public prosecutor say, 'He's not needed here', and assumed that he was talking about my presence in court. Fortunately, my lawyer Kavitha arrived and stood with them, and the three of them started talking about my case. The judge didn't seem convinced that if I got my passport back I could be trusted to return to India for investigations. My heart started beating fast and my blood pressure went up, causing a splitting headache as I realised that the day might not bring good news after all.

They talked for ten minutes about my future. No one seemed to be pointing out the obvious: I'm not guilty. The trust I was involved with at best made some small errors, which carry a fixed penalty, which I've agreed I'll pay. I have a job at the university that I will lose if I don't get back soon. My father has become ill – I'd told my lawyers this – and I need to be with him. I've no way of supporting myself. I'm virtually in solitary confinement, under house arrest. No one seemed to be defending me along those lines.

Kavitha did give some technical arguments about how they could bring me back to India whenever I was needed, but I wasn't sure those appealed to the judge's sensibilities. And why the hell was he still asking these questions? Hadn't he made his mind up yet?

I felt like a small schoolboy with staff discussing my punishment.

I left David in court; I could not bear it any more. But it seemed likely that it wouldn't be good news at the end of the day. On the way home, the autorickshaw I was travelling in collided with another; neither driver paid much attention and just carried on as if nothing had happened. It made my headache worse.

At 5 p.m., Kavitha phoned. It was good news after all.

The judge said my passport could be returned with four conditions, and none of them on the face of it seemed onerous, given what I had feared he might say. I would need to provide:

1. A bond of ₹2 lakhs (£2,000).
2. A notarised statement saying I would return to Indian whenever asked by the court or CID.
3. A notarised proof of address and email.
4. A notarised authorisation for a special type of lawyer – called a Special Vakalat – to appear in court on my behalf, unless the judge specifically asked for me personally.

There were some complexities, but nothing much. It was Wednesday; I could get my passport back the next day or, at the latest, Friday!

Already, I felt I loved India again. Already, I was feeling sentimental about my time there. The walks up the road to Crosswords bookshop, to the Taj Krishna and Taj Banjara were now sepia-tinted; I forgot that I was depressed.

In the evening, Jivan, Mantra's conman, phoned. He was a broken man. Mantra was angry with him for screwing it all up, he said; he was in big trouble. She'd spent a lot of money getting him ready to con me, setting up the website, buying him a new suit, that kind of thing – now she was demanding it all back. Could I give him ₹1 lakhs (£1,000)? I didn't say to him, 'But I thought you were a multi-millionaire?' I didn't want to punish him or anyone else. I wanted everyone to be free of this.

CHAPTER 9

COMEUPPANCE

THURSDAY 19 JUNE I woke up and it all seemed too easy. Getting out of bed, I felt there was something missing ... and then realised what it was. Every morning for the past fifteen weeks it had been a strain to get up; every morning I'd wished the day away and wondered how I would struggle through it. That day, however, it was easy. David was there with me, and I knew that very soon – at the latest, tomorrow! – it would all be over.

Upstairs we had breakfast on the veranda. The rains had come – it was all marvellously fecund; the shrubs and small trees in their pots were responding to the weather, and birds were everywhere too. A famous cricketer was staying at the serviced apartments. David had looked him up; he was a well-known Indian and English county cricketer and had scored

308 'not out' once in a county game. He was there in Hyderabad, running a summer cricket camp for youngsters.

We sat with him for breakfast. He told us how he had played at Lords when India beat England in 2002. Had he enjoyed that game? I asked. No. David Sheppard (the umpire) had given him 'out' when he wasn't. Sheppard had said he was 'caught behind', but he knew the ball had brushed his pads, not his bat. He still remembered it, remembered the bad luck. 'But it's OK,' he said. 'These things happen in sport, as in life.'

Until then, I'd never really understood how people could tolerate umpires' or referees' mistakes, which was one of the reasons why I was not that keen on sports. He made me understand: 'It's all part of the game,' he said. 'We know human error creeps in, and so accept it, indeed we teach it, it's a very important part of learning sportsmanship. Above all, it's good training for life. Life is like that, wrong decisions, wrong things happen to you, and you have to deal with them. That's what we teach youngsters in cricket.'

That's what my life had been like for the past four months. I'd been given 'out' by the umpire when I shouldn't have been. It was the wrong decision, and bad things had come my way. I just had to deal with it and get on with my life.

'In life,' the cricketer told me, 'what goes around, comes around.' This was karma, he said. 'We each have our destiny to fulfil. And bad decisions by the umpire, we teach the children, are all part of our destiny, by which we grow in life.'

I'd heard these phrases so many times during these past four months – hadn't Karan, the Prison Deputy Superintendent, told me to accept my destiny? Hadn't Mantra used that same phrase too, when she was talking about her duty and the three crore Hindu gods? And my friends, and Sara, had explicitly said so many times, 'what goes around, comes around'. It was not just Hindus either – Muslim friends too had said it. And, over breakfast, David added the Christian version: 'For whatsoever a man soweth, that shall he also reap,' from St Paul's letter to the Galatians.

My friends had used it to reassure me about what would happen to Mantra afterwards. What goes around, comes around, and she would receive her just reward for what she had done to me. For Hindus it's not clear whether this 'coming around' will happen in this life or another life, but whenever, their comeuppance will arrive.

But in the past few weeks, as I'd become worn down with frustration and despair, and as my grip on reality seemed to loosen as a result, I'd started to think about it in a different way. By implication this meant that what *I'd* been suffering was also because what had 'gone around' had 'come around' for me, too. No one had ever spelled this out to me. Was it for fear of offending me, or was it a failure to think it through logically? 'What goes around, comes around' must mean that I'd been guilty of terrible things in my life, and this was my due, my cosmic punishment. An inspector has called, investigating one crime that I didn't commit. But is that to say I'm not guilty of other things?

When Jesus was asked about the woman caught in adultery, he didn't agree with his opponents that, yes, she had done wrong, so she should be punished, and only after that go on to address whatever sins the accusers had committed, and to punish them for those. Instead, he saw all sin as one. He said, 'He who is without sin, cast the first stone.' To him, it wasn't the particular crime that she was alleged to have committed that was important, it was the fact that we've all committed crimes. Increasingly, over the past few weeks, this realisation had crept up on me: it didn't matter that I was innocent of the allegations levelled against me; in cosmic reality I was being punished for things of which I was guilty. And they were plenty.

There can be sins of commission, and sins of omission.

My sins of commission were clear. I'd been the cause of so much hurt to several women I'd been involved with. I had got very involved with these women, but then hurt them deeply as I pushed them away when they wanted to settle down with me. I feel terrible about the pain I put each one of them through. I cannot believe I mistreated them in this way, denying them what they wanted from me. I deserve to be punished, I deserve my comeuppance; what has gone around has justly come around.

Sins of omission? Like everyone, I'm guilty of that all of the time. What do we do when we hear there are 250,000 undertrials in India alone – innocent people, mostly poor, stuck in prison because of an unjust system? We turn the page. Gandhi gave his whole life to fighting injustices like this. Jesus said, 'What you did for the least of my brethren you did for me.'

And what do we do? Nothing. I did nothing. I was guilty. My comeuppance was due.

What goes around, comes around. My mind had been wandering as David and the handsome cricketer talked on the lush veranda. We'd finished breakfast. It was time to go to court.

Today, it could all be over!

But then my lawyer Kavitha phoned and said, unfortunately, the court-approved notaries were on strike. You couldn't make this up. I needed to get my documents notarised by the court-approved notaries, and they were not there to do it for me on the one day I needed them. It was to do with bifurcation of the state, she said; they had some grievance, probably about out-of-state people taking their jobs. So there was no point in going to court that day. Perhaps they'd finish their strike by Friday, so we could do what was required then; if not, then on Monday.

Feeling a little down, I told David the news, but he said we should definitely get something done right away. Somewhat reluctantly, Kavitha agreed that we could meet her assistant, Ms Ravleen Sahani, and our counsel, Narasha, and at least get the bond paid into the court bank account, as that wouldn't require notaries.

At court, after depositing the £2,000 cash, Ms Sahani said to me, 'You'll get the money back when you are scot-free.' That's a phrase one doesn't hear very often, like 'what-not', 'what are you intimating?', 'are you bamboozling me?' and other phrases used commonly in India but that have died down elsewhere in the English-speaking world.

Narasha was surprised to hear about the notary strike, and clearly notaries were active in the grounds of the court. At our request, he phoned Kavitha; they talked for a while in Telugu, and then he told us the notaries' strike had ended. But, in any case, we could deposit documents like the ones the judge had ordered me to deposit in court only on Monday, Wednesday or Friday, so we would have to come back in any case on Friday. This meant we had nothing much to do on Thursday from midday, so we mooched around a bit, which wasn't good for my mood.

Friday 20 June brought a horrible symmetry. Exactly fifteen weeks before, Mrs Mantra had been trying to delay my appearance in court until that magical 4 p.m. Friday slot – the witching hour, after which nothing could be done. In her case she had sent me to hospital, and that guaranteed I'd be admitted to prison, even if a day or two later. In my lawyers' case, it turned out that they too were waiting for the same 4 p.m. slot on a Friday afternoon, for a different reason.

We were ready to submit our documents. I had my ticket booked for tonight to fly back with David on Emirates via Dubai to Newcastle. Freedom was so close. At 9.30 a.m., David and I set off for court. I had phoned Narasha half an hour before and told him we would be in court at 10 a.m. He agreed to be there.

At 9.50 a.m., Kavitha phoned me saying, 'Oh, you're already on your way to court' – she could hear the noise of the autorickshaw – 'unfortunately the clerk who you have to deposit the documents with at court is on leave today, so you'll have to wait until Monday.'

I asked the autorickshaw to stop and turn back. David, however, suggested we continue. We might as well get as many of the documents ready as possible, so that they could be deposited easily on Monday, he said.

We called Narasha at 10 a.m. to say we'd arrived, but he said he was not there and was not coming. Kavitha phoned us, rather crossly, and asked why we had come to court, given that she had told us not to bother. David persuaded her that we wanted to get us much as possible done before Monday. David was persuasive; reluctantly, she agreed that Narasha would come in to assist.

We waited downstairs in the court lobby area. I saw an African also waiting, waiting for his lawyer like everyone was doing, most for hours, like us, because lawyers were the important ones, swanning about in their academic gowns, and we were the unimportant ones, forced to wait in this massive, hot hall, with only one high fan by the entrance, in rows of uncomfortable chairs, in a filthy environment.

The African waved to me, and I realised it was Johnson, the South African whom I had been sleeping next to in prison! We sat together and chatted about prison time, how it was much better inside than we had thought it would be because of the prisoners' warmth, friendship and support, but that the conditions were far worse than we'd expected. Being outside of prison, we agreed, had been pretty grim. He had only been out for three weeks. He was waiting to meet with his lawyer, who had said that they could end his case if he paid a bribe of ₹3 to ₹4 lakhs (£3,000 to £4,000). Johnson was hopeful he could negotiate this down with the public prosecutor to ₹1.5 lakhs. In the end, he waited all day until 5 p.m. to see his lawyer. I sat on and off with him for companionable support, although we soon exhausted topics for conversation.

As we sat there, the prison buses arrived and disgorged their prisoners, escorted by the prison guards, handcuffed to each other, chains trailing in the dust.

Narasha, our counsel, arrived at 11.15 a.m. He was not in his court gown and had brought draft documents, though not on the required court stamp paper and which, in any case, were full of mistakes. We made corrections and he told us he would bring back the corrected versions on Monday. David put his foot down. 'We want the documents ready today,' he said. Because if we left it until Monday, we knew, this being India, that it wouldn't be done until Tuesday or later, which would delay my release yet again.

Meanwhile, I decided to go upstairs to court, to see where the documents would need to be deposited, so that I'd be ready for action on Monday. There, the court crier congratulated me on my court order. He asked why we hadn't put in our documents yet. I told him that I'd heard the clerk was not available that day. He pointed to the man standing by his side who was the appointed clerk and who was definitely there to receive them.

'But you are supposed to be absent today,' I said.

'Not at all,' he said. 'I'm waiting for your documents.'

By this time it was 12 noon. David phoned Kavitha and told her what I'd discovered, that the court clerk was there after all and very ready to receive my documents. She didn't apologise or even acknowledge any mistake. Instead, she got cross with me. She found it incomprehensible that anyone should not obey her and go home rather than cause trouble at court, her being a lawyer and me a humble client. Narasha, meanwhile, said he was going to the toilet and disappeared.

David told Kavitha that the documents must be done that day and could even be submitted, because I'd confirmed with the clerk that he would receive documents even in the afternoon. Kavitha said that Narasha couldn't do it, because he'd now got other engagements. David insisted that we do them, saying that we could go with Narasha to his office and get it done together.

Kavitha finally agreed with David that Narasha could help, and gave us an appointment for 4 p.m. at his office. I'd really gone native; I was so grateful: 4 p.m. *today*! How wonderful was that? I was so used to appointments by everyone – the CID, the court, the lawyers – being given days away, and seldom being kept. David, still on English timescales, said, 'No. We've been waiting since 10 a.m., so let's do it now.' He calmly, coolly insisted, and eventually Kavitha agreed.

Around 12.30, as I was absorbing the fact that my lawyers had been lying to me, and that I wouldn't be free within the next few days, and it was all their fault, there was a commotion on the stairs. With much yelling and screaming, a young

Indian man with frizzy hair and a wild, unkempt appearance came bolting down the stairs three at a time, hotly pursued by others. He barged through the entrance door but was readily floored, then beaten by the armed guards there. He could not really have thought he would get away – had he got through the doors, he would have been shot in the back as he ran off. My guess was that he simply flipped in court, having been told something by his arrogant lawyers, and couldn't handle it any more. There but for the Grace of God go I, I thought. I'd flipped a couple of times in and out of court and had very nearly done exactly the same thing. I could not stop my tears then, for him, for me, for Johnson, for all the prisoners trooping in, for the hundreds of people waiting there for their lawyers, for this whole evil, slow, monolithic, corrupt system.

Between 1 p.m. and 2 p.m., David phoned Narasha several times, but he didn't answer.

I took David to my 'cave', the shop where I'd first bought my cold drink at lunch time, where I'd found they were friendly, and where I'd gone every day that I'd been to court since. I could hide there; people were courteous to me, but never desired to talk, busy with their own things; I could sit in a chair, be alert to dangers in front of me, my back to the wall, feeling safe, and it was relatively cool sitting beneath the fan, too. So I sat there, and my thumping heart and tears subsided. David was with me.

'How do you keep so calm?' I asked.

'I just trust God,' he said. David finished his soft drink and went back to the court to wait for Narasha. I stayed a bit longer.

At 2.41 p.m., David phoned Kavitha. There was still no sign of Narasha.

At 3.40 p.m., Narasha arrived with the documents, which he got me to sign and then we got them notarised.

We were finally ready by 4 p.m. Narasha looked at his watch and said, 'Sorry, we'll have to submit them on Monday; the court stops receiving documents now.' I dashed upstairs to the court clerk, to see that this was indeed correct.

For whatever reason, Kavitha had not wanted to be present that day – perhaps she had more important business elsewhere. Our guess was that she had known she couldn't be there for a while, and had deliberately lied to us – first about the striking notaries and then about the clerk being absent – in order to conceal from us the fact that this further delay in getting my passport back was caused by my lawyers rather than the court or CID.

The words of Mr Haridevan, the wealthy businessman from the Taj Krishna, came back to haunt me. Don't trust your lawyers, they are the worst. He had said, '... they'll bleed you dry, take all the time in the world and extort maximum money from you'. New India had let me down, as much as Old India.

I was exhausted at the end of this awful day. My expensive, Westernised lawyer, Kavitha, had lied to me in order to cover up the fact that she couldn't be in court when my release could have been organised. The terrible thing was that she was prepared to lie to me, totally unconcerned about my welfare, and that she probably did it all the time, because mostly people wouldn't check up on their lawyers. Had I been on my own, I would have meekly gone back home at 10 a.m., probably drunk myself stupid because I was so desperately frustrated and could do nothing. It was only with David there that we continued to court and so found out her dissembling.

David and I had had a game over breakfast that morning: I said that for every court appearance something had gone wrong, but each time I couldn't have predicted what would go wrong or differently from expected. So, what could go wrong that day? We couldn't really think of anything; both of us believed I would have my passport back by 5 p.m. David had changed his flight and was leaving that night, so convinced were we that all would go to plan. We could not have predicted Kavitha lying to us. On Monday, what could go wrong? Come on, be clever, be imaginative!

||||||||||||||||||

As soon as David left for England on Friday evening, my spirits sank. I'd been stronger when he was there with me, but now I was weak again. I slept only fitfully all weekend. I was thinking about how terrible it was that lawyers could be so arrogant as to lie to you. But most of all, I was thinking about my comeuppance.

What goes around comes around, and it had come around to me. As my hold on my reality loosened further, I felt I had to resign myself, indeed consign myself, to the cosmic order and its punishment. By Sunday night I felt that I had given myself over totally to this spiritual will, acquiescing to whatever it would bring. I didn't care what happened the next day – I really did not care. Life continued and life was what it was, whether I went or stayed.

All weekend I dwelled on the reality that I was enduring a cosmic punishment for sins of commission and sins of omission. I thought how often I'd said to people I'd met, 'I'm 100 per cent innocent, yet I was arrested.' People seemed sympathetic. But of course it was only true in the rather pedantic, Anglo-Saxon sense, so far as the particular crime that I was alleged to have committed was concerned. But why stick to that sense? In a more holistic view, a cosmic view, I was guilty of many things.

'For the women I have hurt,' I thought, 'I am deeply sorry, now and always. Perhaps the level of punishment meted out to me thus far may not be enough to appease you. I will take whatever is needed.'

And for my sins of omission, how dare I neglect the poor, the needy, as if I'm entitled to my privileges, without so much as a backward glance to those stuck without them? I deserved whatever punishment the cosmic order wanted to mete out.

By the morning of Monday 23 June, I knew that I was on trial for my life's sins. And I was open to any possibility coming to pass.

I'd been in court since 10.30 a.m. My lawyers had turned up at midday. Kavitha, who confirmed without any shame that she had returned from more lucrative business in another Indian city, told me that even if things went my way that day, then it would be a week before the court order came through and my passport was returned. I looked shocked. 'I told you already,' she said. It was, of course, impossible for her to be wrong. You LIAR! I breathed, but did not say it. On the surface I remained calm. Because we are *all* liars, *all* guilty in the cosmic balance.

At that moment, I saw everything more clearly in its cosmic proportions. I remembered the discussion with Mantra and her son at Telugu New Year about string theory, the scientific attempt to reconcile quantum mechanics and relativity theory. The gods live in eleven-dimensional space, all three crore of them – that's what she had implied, or at least what I'd taken from the conversation.

And then it all fitted together with the book I'd read at Crosswords, *Flatland*. If one inhabited a two-dimensional world, then a three-dimensional object coming into your space would seem like any other familiar thing – it would have to, because you could only see it in two dimensions! So a wine glass put on a table will look like a circle to those stuck in two-dimensional space underneath it. But it's not a circle, it's a wondrous, curvaceous object with functions so strangely different from anything that anyone in two-dimensional space could ever imagine.

So it must be for us, I thought, as I sat there in the court waiting hall downstairs, waiting for my lawyers to arrive. Suddenly I saw everything in its full eleven-dimensional potential. What would an eleven-dimensional being look like in our three-dimensional world? Well, of course, they would look like something unremarkable, something familiar, for we can only see familiar things. They could look, well, like a person! Like Mantra, a cosmic being of multiple dimensions intersecting with our world in human form in order to dispense cosmic justice.

Now I saw Mantra in a different light. She was not some evil earth-bound ogre. She was the noble dispenser of cosmic justice. I saw her as Kali, the Hindu black goddess, lady of death, dark and violent. The consort of Lord Shiva, I saw her standing over her Lord, bloody dagger in hand as she killed him once her sexual appetite had been satisfied. In three-dimensional space, she was Mantra, but in the true reality that, in my disturbed state, I could now comprehend, she was Kali, meting out God's will. With her Namaste gesture to the heavens via her heart and forehead, she had been hinting to me all along of her cosmic role.

I'd never known this waiting hall so noisy. There were many women there, gangs of them, waddling along in their saris, bare, fat tummies out, dragging their feet, shuffling along, leaning slightly backwards, as Mantra/Kali does, talking so loudly they had raised the noise levels all around with machine-gun, rapid-fire verbal assaults. Now I saw beyond their three dimensions. Others were also three-dimensional manifestations of eleven-dimensional beings, doing things that were incomprehensible from an earthly perspective, but fully comprehensible when understood in the context of the cosmos.

I was in an endless, timeless warp. But it didn't matter. Nothing mattered.

Then it occurred to me that if this was part of my cosmic punishment, my comeuppance, then could I not feel my guilt dripping away? My comeuppance, my 'appearance before a judge', had led to this four months of just retribution. But having served my time, should I not be able to let go of some of my guilt?

At 11 a.m. in the court, the judge suddenly stood up, disturbed by something. The crier called out '*Silence!*', we all Namaste-ed or (in my case) bowed, and off the judge went. Perhaps this was further cosmic justice. He was normally in all morning until lunch time.

At 2.30 p.m. I was sitting in the court again, under Gandhi's portrait. I was finishing Guha's biography, *Gandhi Before India*. Throughout the whole time I'd been stuck in India, I'd been reading about Gandhi. Before it all started, I had detested the man; I'd always seen him as someone whose ideas I was drawn to, but whom I couldn't like as a person. It was his fastidiousness, the way he seemed to love ideals more than people. That day in court, I finally gave up resisting his power over me. Gandhi inspires me, I thought. Without those characteristics I didn't like about him as a person, he could not have achieved what he was able to achieve. He had to separate himself from the world, from his family, in order to serve them. And what a spirit drove this man! His tenacity, his will, his desire to fight injustice and pursue right wherever it took him, even to jail, even unto death... And suddenly I wanted to be like him too. Like him, I would continue my work wherever it took me. I had need of nothing, only to give love and to fight educational injustice. This would be my life's work, and nothing that had happened in India could change that. At that moment, I realised I had learnt to love Gandhi.

I was texting David, who was now back in England. At this point, I texted him:

> Don't pray for me. Pray for Michael, and others like him, foreigners without any chance of influencing their cases, stuck here for ever. Pray for Arjun, and others like him, the 250,000 undertrials stuck in Indian prisons with no chance of getting out. Pray for all them, stop praying for me.

Then later, more urgently, I texted: 'Stop praying for me. Pray for all the prisoners who we know are innocent. Pray for those who are not, for they need our help too. I want no more prayers.'

In court, at 3 p.m., Narasha was asleep. There were nine lawyers sitting around the horseshoe table waiting for the judge to arrive, most dozing in the heat. Kavitha was looking through her Facebook on her iPad. The lawyer who would be my personal representative in court, my special Vakalat, was also asleep, snoring gently.

At 3.06 p.m., the judge returned. There were several people waiting for their cases to be heard. He was very egalitarian, and saw all the others before me. One case featured two Muslim ladies, mother and daughter I guessed, the daughter aged about thirty-five, very handsome, clearly intelligent. Covering her hair with her shawl, she craned her neck trying to listen to the witness, a scruffy man in the chair at one end. I wondered how he was related to her – her husband perhaps, or her lover? But my lawyers were sitting directly in front of her, in her line of hearing, and they were chatting away, contemptuous of any court proceedings, totally oblivious to the fact that anyone might want to listen to the evidence being heard. The judge went through all of these cases before coming to mine at around 4 p.m.

Just as my case was called by the court crier, my counsel Narasha had wandered off again. This time he was found quickly, and the four of us stood there in front of the judge, and for the first time he spoke directly to me, in a soft, kind voice:

'Have you read and understood the conditions?' he asked, gently.

'Yes I have, sir,' I said, wanting to say the right words in a special way, not knowing if I had succeeded.

He nodded, sagely. He was given the case documents that we had prepared. He signed in the corner of each of the sixty pages.

We walked out of the court, me bowing to him, mouthing 'thank you, thank you', touching my heart and my forehead. Now to get my passport back. I assumed this wouldn't be straightforward, but Kavitha said, as if everything was normally so efficient and apparently retracting what she had said only earlier about it taking another week, 'Let's go over here and get your passport.' And across the corridor in a little cubby hole, it was ready, dear Reader – they'd got it ready for me. Before it was given to me, I had to sign that I'd received the original copy of my passport. But how did I know it was the correct one? 'Yours is the only British passport,' I was told.

At 4.16, I felt totally stunned, in shock, neither happy nor sad. I walked out of the courtroom, perhaps for the last time, and got an autorickshaw straight back to Banjara Hills Road No. 13. I had prepared most things, but wanted to say goodbye to so many people: Mohammed in the old city, to the Taj Banjara to see Khem and John, and Mr Haridevan at the Taj Krishna – so much to do, so many people to wish farewell to. Wisely, on the phone Sara said, 'Don't push yourself now. Just go to the airport; you can say goodbye by email, see them another time to thank them.'

My car had arrived, and I set off for the airport. I was terrified that something would change, that Mantra would have found some new way of stopping me. Looking out of the taxi window from the airport flyover as India continued on its way just below us, I asked myself: Do I love India? Will I come back? Of course it was easier to love it now. I watched as we passed through the districts where I have been involved in schools. I was so sorry I couldn't get down to see my friends below. I hoped they'd understand that I had to get to the airport early. Because there was still one problem to overcome.

At the airport I fought with the Emirates staff, haggling over how much baggage I was allowed, getting a bad headache as I raised my voice against them. I was disappointed that the university hadn't thought to pay business class for me. I knew then that, although it would be important for me to return, everyone else would be busy with their own things, and I knew I mustn't be disappointed with how insignificant I was going to be back in England.

Then the difficult bit, the final problem to overcome. In my returned passport, my visa said that I should have registered with the Commissioner of Police within fourteen days of arrival. Of course I had been in prison, then the court had held my passport, so hadn't done this. A catch-22. I'd been worrying about it non-stop for the past five days.

What could I do? Of course I could have gone to the police and tried to get my passport stamped, but I knew what would have happened – it would have led to many further delays or even arrest for disobeying the law, and certainly a demand for bribes. So I thought it best – and Sara had agreed – to just take the risk at immigration. Have some small cash ready, someone had said, in case you need to bribe the immigration officer. I knew that I wouldn't be able to do that, even though I had some cash at the ready in my trouser pocket.

In the queue, the person next to me said, 'You look so tired.' I felt so tired, so drained. And now this. How was it going to go?

The officer called me for my turn. India has become very advanced – you don't have to fill in an exit form any more.

'When did you arrive?' he asked.

My heart sank. 'March,' I said.

'March?' he exclaimed. 'It's nearly July. What have you been doing all this time?'

I told him about giving advice on educational matters to education companies in India, and to federations of schools. He listened. 'Which university are you with here?' he asked.

I explained I was not with any university in India, but that 'I am from a top British university, Newcastle, part of the Russell Group of elite, research-based universities.'

He was not looking persuaded, so I talked quickly about NISA – the National Independent Schools Alliance – for which I'm chief mentor, and all the good work we were doing in low-cost schools, schools for the poor, for the downtrodden, helping improve educational opportunities for the less blessed in society.

He interrupted me again. 'It says here you arrived in February; you said March.'

'I thought you meant Hyderabad. I came to Hyderabad in March, but India, yes, late February.'

He flicked through my passport, checked my face again.

'It sounds like good work you are doing. Do you like India?' he asked.

'I love India very much, sir,' I said.

'Then you'll come back and continue your work?'

'I will very much, sir.'

'Good.' (Stamp.) 'See you again soon!'

And I was through.

I was in shock. I was not feeling happy, not feeling sad. I felt agitated. How contrary I was – finally free, but feeling agitated, by my headache, by the way my feet were killing me, by my exhaustion. I was free, but what about all the other poor souls left behind? I boarded the aircraft. I sat in my economy-class aisle seat. I was tense until the moment we took off; only then did I feel that nothing could stop me from leaving. But I didn't feel any emotion until I was back in Daisy Cottage and the soft breeze was blowing open the curtains and I could hear the swallows and the house martins twittering away in the blue skies above, catching food for their young. And then I broke down and cried.

EPILOGUE

A YEAR AFTER I got away, my case was still ongoing. Trying to pay the penalty to the Ministry of Home Affairs brought similar Kafkaesque encounters as experienced throughout my case. My lawyers wrote the required letter to the Ministry of Home Affairs requesting that I be allowed to pay the penalty for compounding the offence. The ministry simply ignored that and subsequent follow-up letters, for a whole year. My lawyers then issued a writ in the High Court against the Ministry of Home Affairs and the police of Hyderabad, to get them to do *something*. The High Court came down on my side and eventually officials at the Ministry of Home Affairs agreed to review my papers, all 11,000 of them.

The case started back in 2005 because my team leader at Educare Trust refused to pay a bribe to officials at the Ministry of Home Affairs in Delhi to get foreign currency approved. Eleven years later, different officials, but apparently made of the same stuff, told my lawyers that my case would continue for as long as they wanted unless I paid ₹8 lakhs (£8,000) to them. What should I do? The case hanging over me makes me nervous about going to India, where so much of my work and life remains. Dear Reader, what would *you* do?

Since I've been home in England, it has not been easy. Part of it is that my deep empathy hasn't gone away, and I'm feeling the pain of people all around me. Notably, I've found people who have had similar experiences – including poor Nick Dunn, a young man from the same county of Northumberland where I live, who has also fallen afoul of police corruption, extortion and wrongful imprisonment in India. His case has made me realise how lucky I was – and how important the high-level contacts were to getting my passport returned. Nick Dunn was in prison for *six months* awaiting trial, was released and is now imprisoned again. The British authorities are refusing to get involved, as India is following due process – ha ha. I'm in close touch with his extraordinarily dedicated and articulate sister, Lisa, a sister in a million, who is constantly working to try to get Nick freed. I'm powerless to do anything about Nick's case, however, as it turns out my high-level contacts were very state-specific; his case is in the neighbouring state of Tamil Nadu, where they have no remit.

It's not been easy being back at the university. The registrar John Hogan and his team have been wonderful, as expected. But even during only four months away, I lost two large grants worth over a million dollars, partly because I simply wasn't able to follow up while stuck in Hyderabad. Losing grants meant I lost key members of my team, built up over the years, as most were on short-term grant-specific contracts. The university insurers also forbade me returning to India while my case was ongoing, and they're reluctant to let me go to other countries I normally visit – I'm a little nervous too. So I've lost my identity; I'm no longer the Indiana Jones of education policy.

But worst of all, putting all the above into dismal perspective, I've lost Sara. I couldn't go to India, and I don't think Sara's family really believed it was because the university had told me not to. We'd planned to get married a few months after I returned, but without being able to get to India, we'd postponed. Sara lost faith in me, my proposal too modest to carry me through my enforced absence. I hear Sara is now with someone else. Of course, I'm heartbroken.

Now multiply that misery 250,000 times for each and every undertrial in Indian prisons today. Multiply it more, much more, because I got off lightly; many, like poor Arjun, the victim of police extortion in the first place, remain stuck in prison with no hope at all because they are too poor to get to court. Multiply the misery even more, because most are likely to be innocent. That's the misery that India's affront to the rule of law is causing today.

Can I do something about it? I've written this memoir as a first step along that path.

NOTE ON NAMES

Many of the names and identifying details have been changed to protect the privacy or safety of individuals.

REFERENCES

Boaz, David (2015), *The Libertarian Mind: A manifesto for freedom*, Simon & Schuster, New York

CMS Transparency (2010), *India Corruption Study, 2010*, CMS, New Delhi

CMS Transparency (2012), *CMS-India Corruption Study: 2012 Expanding Slums... Growing Corruption*, CMS, New Delhi

Debroy, Bibek and Bhandari, Laveesh (2012), *Corruption in India: The DNA and the RNA*, paperback edition, Konark Publishers, New Delhi

Elliott, John (2014), *Implosion: India's Tryst with Reality*, HarperCollins India, New Delhi

Gandhi, Mohandas (1914), 'A Farewell Letter', *Indian Opinion* (29 July 1914), Pretoria, https://www.bl.uk/collection-items/mohandas-mahatma-gandhis-a-farewell-letter-in-the-newspaper-indian-opinion#sthash.sdlMNPC3.dpuf

Hayek, F. (1960), *The Constitution of Liberty*, University of Chicago Press, Chicago

The Hindu (2014), Two-thirds of prison inmates in India are undertrials, 30 October, http://www.thehindu.com/news/national/twothirds-of-prison-inmates-in-india-are-undertrials/article6545617.ece (accessed 23 February 2015)

Lamani, Ravikanth, B. and Venumadhava, G.S. (2013), Police Corruption in India, *International Journal of Criminology and Sociological Theory*, 6.4, 228–34

Liberty (no date), Extended pre-charge detention, https://www.liberty-human-rights.org.uk/human-rights/countering-terrorism/extended-pre-charge-detention (accessed 23 February 2015)

Madison, James (1788), *The Federalist No. 62*, The Senate, *Independent Journal*, Wednesday 27 February 1788

Nambiar, Bindu, M. (2013), A study of undertrial prisoners in India, *Paripex: Indian Journal of Research*, 2.9, 126–7

Supreme Court of India (1996), 'Common Cause' A ... vs Union of India and Ors, 1 May 1996 (1996 AIR 1619, 1996 SCC (4) 33). Author: B. Jeevan Reddy. Bench: Jeevan Reddy, B.P. (J) https://indiankanoon.org/doc/728407/?type=print

Tiwari, Garima (2013), Undertrials: Sentenced without conviction, posted on A Contratio, Reflections and Commentary on Global Justice Issues, 31 July 2013, https://acontrarioicl.com/2013/07/31/undertrials-sentenced-without-conviction/ (accessed 19 February 2015)

Transparency International India (2005), *India Corruption Study, 2005,* Centre for Media Studies, New Delhi

Transparency International India (2008), *India Corruption Study, 2008,* Centre for Media Studies, New Delhi

Verma, Arvind (1999), Cultural Roots of Police Corruption in India, *Policing,* 22.3, 264–79 (NCJ number 179045)

ACKNOWLEDGEMENTS

I am deeply grateful to Roy Carlisle, who suggested the idea of a memoir when I had just returned from India and cajoled and encouraged me throughout the writing process. James Bartholomew, Barrie and Ann Craven and David Longfield were loyal and caring friends throughout the experience, and also read the manuscript in full or in part and suggested improvements. Others I want to thank for their support include Ayham Ayche, Michael Barber, John Blundell, Andrew Coulson, Chris Crane, Gurcharan Das, Martin Durkin, Reinhard Fichtl, Chester Finn, Jack Grimshaw, Steve Heyneman, John Hogan, Terence Kealey, Lord Lingfield, Irene Pritzker, I. V. Subba Rao, Udo Schultz, Ralph Tabberer, Evina Tzani and my four siblings and their spouses. I am grateful to all those at Biteback who have been patient and understanding throughout this publishing process, especially my editor Olivia Beattie and editorial assistant Laurie De Decker.